The End of Laissez-Faire

The Economic Consequences of the Peace

John Maynard Keynes

Must Have Books
503 Deerfield Place
Victoria, BC
V9B 6G5
Canada

ISBN: 9781773237923

Copyright 2021 – Must Have Books

The End of Laissez-Faire

Note
This essay, which was published as a pamphlet by the Hogarth Press in July 1926, was based on the Sidney Ball Lecture given by Keynes at Oxford in November 1924 and on a lecture given by him at the University of Berlin in June 1926.

I

The disposition towards public affairs, which we conveniently sum up as individualism and *laissez-faire,* drew its sustenance from many different rivulets of thought and springs of feeling. For more than a hundred years our philosophers ruled us because, by a miracle, they nearly all agreed or seem to agree on this one thing. We do not dance even yet to a new tune. But a change is in the air. We hear but indistinctly what were once the clearest and most distinguishable voices which have ever instructed political mankind. The orchestra of diverse instruments, the chorus of articulate sound, is receding at last into the distance.

At the end of the seventeenth century the divine right of monarchs gave place to natural liberty and to the compact, and the divine right of the church to the principle of toleration, and to the view that a church is 'a voluntary society of men', coming together, in a way which is 'absolutely free and spontaneous' (Locke, A Letter Concerning Toleration). Fifty years later the divine origin and absolute voice of duty gave place to the calculations of utility. In the hands of Locke and Hume these doctrines founded Individualism. The compact presumed rights in the individual; the new ethics, being no more than a scientific study of the consequences of rational self-love, placed the individual at the centre. 'The sole trouble Virtue demands', said Hume, 'is that of just Calculation, and a steady preference of the greater Happiness.' (An Enquiry Concerning the Principles of Morals, section LX).

These ideas accorded with the practical notions of conservatives and of lawyers. They furnished a satisfactory intellectual foundation to the rights of property and to the liberty of the individual in possession to do what he liked with himself and with his own. This was one of the contributions of the eighteenth century to the air we still

3

breathe.

The purpose of promoting the individual was to depose the monarch and the church; the effect - through the new ethical significance attributed to contract - was to buttress property and prescriptions. But it was not long before the claims of society raised themselves anew against the individual. Paley and Bentham accepted utilitarian hedonism from the hands of Hume and his predecessors, but enlarged it into social utility.

> ('I omit' says Archdeacon Paley, 'much usual declamation upon the dignity and capacity of our nature, the superiority of the soul to the body, of the rational to the animal part of our constitution; upon the worthiness, refinement, and delicacy of some satisfactions, and the meanness, grossness, and sensuality of others: because I hold that pleasures differ in nothing but in continuance and intensity' - Principles of Moral and Political Philosophy, Book 1, chap. 6).

Rousseau took the Social Contract from Locke and drew out of it the General Will. In each case the transition was made by virtue of the new emphasis laid on equality. 'Locke applies his Social Contract to modify the natural equality of mankind, so far as that phrase implies equality of property or even of privilege, in consideration of general security. In Rousseau's version equality is not only the starting-point but the goal.' (Leslie Stephen, English Thought in the Eighteenth Century, II, 192).

Paley and Bentham reached the same destination, but by different routes. Paley avoided an egoistic conclusion to his hedonism by a God from the machine. 'Virtue', he says, 'is the doing good to mankind, in obedience to the will of God, and for the sake of everlasting happiness' - in this way bringing I and others to a parity. Bentham reached the same result by pure reason. There is no rational ground, he argued, for preferring the happiness of one individual, even oneself, to that of any other. Hence the greatest happiness of the greatest number is the sole rational object of conduct - taking utility from Hume, but forgetting that sage man's corollary: 'Tis not contrary to reason to prefer the destruction of the whole world to the scratching of my finger.' 'Tis not contrary to reason for me to choose my total ruin to prevent the least uneasiness of an Indian, or person totally unknown to me ... Reason is and ought only to be the slave of the passions, and can never pretend to any other office than to serve and obey them.'

Rousseau derived equality from the state of nature, Paley from the will of God, Bentham from a mathematical law of indifference. Equality and altruism had thus entered political philosophy, and from Rousseau and Bentham sprang both democracy and utilitarian socialism.

This is the second current - sprang from long-dead controversies, and carried on its way by long-exploded sophistries - which still permeates our atmosphere of thought but it did not drive out the former current. It mixed with it. The early nineteenth century performed the miraculous union. It harmonised the conservative individualism of Locke, Hume, Johnson, and Burke with the socialism and democratic egalitarianism of Rousseau, Paley, Bentham, and Godwin.

> (Godwin carried *laissez-faire* so far that he thought all government an evil, in which Bentham almost agreed with him. The doctrine of equality becomes with him one of extreme individualism, verging on anarchy. 'The universal exercise of private judgement' he says, 'is a doctrine so unspeakably beautiful that the true politician will certainly feel infinite reluctance in admitting the idea of interfering with it' - see Leslie Stephen, op. cit. II, 277).

Nevertheless, that age would have been hard put to it to achieve this harmony of opposites if it had not been for the *economists*, who sprang into prominence just at the right moment. The idea of a divine harmony between private advantage and the public good is already apparent in Paley. But it was the economists who gave the notion a good scientific basis. Suppose that by the working of natural laws individuals pursuing their own interests with enlightenment in condition of freedom always tend to promote the general interest at the same time! Our philosophical difficulties are resolved-at least for the practical man, who can then concentrate his efforts on securing the necessary conditions of freedom. To the philosophical doctrine that the government has no right to interfere, and the divine that it has no need to interfere, there is added a scientific proof that its interference is inexpedient. This is the third current of thought, just discoverable in Adam Smith, who was ready in the main to allow the public good to rest on 'the natural effort of every individual to better his own condition', but not fully and self-consciously developed until the nineteenth century begins. The principle of *laissez-faire* had arrived to harmonise individualism and socialism, and to make at one Hume's egoism with the greatest good of the greatest number. The political philosopher could retire in favour of the business man - for the latter could attain the philosopher's *summum bonum* by just pursuing his own private profit.

Yet some other ingredients were needed to complete the pudding. First the corruption and incompetence of eighteenth-century government, many legacies of which survived into the nineteenth. The individualism of the political philosophers pointed to *laissez-faire*. The divine or scientific harmony (as the case might be) between private interest and public advantage pointed to *laissez-faire*. But above all, the ineptitude of public administrators strongly prejudiced the practical man in favour of *laissez-faire* - a sentiment which has by no means disappeared. Almost everything which the State did in the eighteenth century in excess of its minimum functions was, or seemed, injurious or unsuccessful.

On the other hand, material progress between 1750 and 1850 came from individual initiative, and owed almost nothing to the directive influence of organised society as a whole. Thus practical experience reinforced a priori reasonings. The philosophers and the economists told us that for sundry deep reasons unfettered private enterprise would promote the greatest good of the whole. What could suit the business man better? And could a practical observer, looking about him, deny that the blessings of improvement which distinguished the age he lived in were traceable to the activities of individuals 'on the make'?

Thus the ground was fertile for a doctrine that, whether on divine, natural, or scientific grounds, state action should be narrowly confined and economic life left, unregulated so far as may be, to the skill and good sense of individual citizens actuated by the admirable motive of trying to get on in the world.

By the time that the influence of Paley and his like was waning, the innovations of Darwin were shaking the foundations of belief. Nothing could seem more opposed than the old doctrine and the new - the doctrine which looked on the world as the work of the divine watchmaker and the doctrine which seemed to draw all things out of Chance, Chaos, and Old Time. But at this one point the new ideas bolstered up the old. The economists were teaching that wealth, commerce, and machinery were the children of free competition - that free competition built London. But the Darwinians could go one better than that - free competition had built man. The human eye was no longer the demonstration of design, miraculously contriving all things for the best; it was the supreme achievement of chance, operating under conditions of free competition and *laissez-faire*. The principle of the survival of the fittest could be regarded as a vast generalisation of the Ricardian economics. Socialist interferences became, in the light of this grander synthesis, not merely inexpedient, but impious, as calculated to retard the onward movement of the mighty process by which we ourselves had risen like Aphrodite out of the primeval slime of ocean.

Therefore I trace the peculiar unity of the everyday political philosophy of the nineteenth century to the success with which it harmonised diversified and warring schools and united all good things to a single end. Hume and Paley, Burke and Rousseau, Godwin and Malthus, Cobbett and Huskisson, Bentham and Coleridge, Darwin and the Bishop of Oxford, were all, it was discovered, preaching practically the same thing - individualism and *laissez-faire*. This was the Church of England and those her apostles, whilst the company of the economists were there to prove that the least deviation into impiety involved financial ruin.

These reasons and this atmosphere are the explanations, we know it or not - and most of us in these degenerate days are largely ignorant in the matter - why we feel such a strong bias in favour of *laissez-faire,* and why state action to regulate the value of money, or the course of investment, or the population, provokes such passionate suspicions in many upright breasts. We have not read these authors; we should consider their arguments preposterous if they were to fall into our hands. Nevertheless we should not, I fancy, think as we do, if Hobbes, Locke, Hume, Rousseau, Paley, Adam Smith, Bentham, and Miss Martineau had not thought and written as they did. A study of the history of opinion is a necessary preliminary to the emancipation of the mind. I do not know which makes a man more conservative - to know nothing but the present, or nothing but the past.

II

I have said that it was the economists who furnished the scientific by which the practical man could solve the contradiction between egoism and socialism which emerged out of the philosophising of the eighteenth century and the decay of revealed religion. But having said this for shortness' sake, I hasten to qualify it. This is what the economists are supposed to have said. No such doctrine is really to be found in the writings of the greatest authorities. It is what the popularisers and the vulgarisers said. It is what the Utilitarians, who admitted Hume's egoism and Bentham's egalitarianism at the same time, were driven to believe in, if they were to effect a synthesis.

(One can sympathise with the view of Coleridge, as summarised by Leslie Stephen, that 'the Utilitarians destroyed every element of cohesion, made Society a struggle of selfish interests, and struck at the very roots of all order, patriotism, poetry, and religion').

The language of the economists lent itself to the *laissez-faire* interpretation. But the popularity of the doctrine must be laid at the door of the political philosophers of the day, whom it happened to suit, rather than of the political economists.

The maxim *laissez-nous faire* is traditionally attributed to the merchant Legendre addressing Colbert some time towards the end of the seventeenth century.

('Que faut-il faire pour vous aider?' asked Colbert. 'Nous laisser faire' answered Legendre).

But there is no doubt the first writer to use the phrase, and to use it in clear association with the doctrine, is the Marquis d'Argenson about 1751.

(For the history of the phrase, see Oncken, 'Die Maxime Laissez faire et laissez-passer' from whom most of the following quotations are taken. The claims of the Marquis d'Argenson were overlooked until Oncken put them forward, partly because the relevant passages published during his lifetime were anonymous - *Journal Oeconomique*, 1751 - and partly because his works were not published in full - though probably passed privately from hand to hand during his lifetime - until 1858 - *Mémoires et Journal inédit* du Marquis d'Argenson)

The Marquis was the first man to wax passionate on the economic advantages of governments leaving trade alone. To govern better, he said, one must govern less. ('Pour gouverner mieux, il faudrait gouverner moins.')

The true cause of the decline of our manufactures, he declared, is the protection we have given to them. ('On ne peut dire autant de nos fabriques: la vraie cause de leur déclin, c'est la protection outrée qu'on leur accorde.')

'Laissez faire, telle devrait être la devise de toute puissance publique, depuis que le monde est civilisé.' 'Détestable principe que celui de ne vouloir grandeur que par l'abaissement de nos voisins! Il n'y a que la méchanceté et la malignité du coeur de satisfaites dans ce principe, et l'intérêt y est opposé. Laissez faire, morbleu! Laissez faire!!'

Here we have the economic doctrine of *laissez-faire,* with its most fervent expression in free trade, fully clothed. The phrases and the idea must have passed current in Paris from that time on. But they were slow to establish themselves in literature; and the tradition associating with them the physiocrats, and particularly de Gournay and Quesnay, finds little support in the writings of this school, though they were, of course, proponents of the essential harmony of social and individual interests. The phrase *laissez-faire* is not to be found in the works of Adam Smith, of Ricardo, or of Malthus. Even the idea is not present in a dogmatic form in any of these authors. Adam Smith, of course, was a Free Trader and an opponent of many eighteenth-century restrictions on trade. But his attitude towards the Navigation Acts and the usury laws shows that he was not dogmatic. Even his famous passage about 'the invisible hand' reflects the philosophy which we associate with Paley rather than the economic dogma of *laissez-faire*. As Sidgwick and Cliff Leslie have pointed out, Adam Smith's advocacy of the 'obvious and simple system of natural liberty' is derived from his theistic and optimistic view of the order of the world as set forth in his *Theory of Moral Sentiments*, rather than any proposition of political economy proper. (Sidgwick, *Principles of Political Economy*, p. 20).

The phrase laissez-faire was, I think, first brought into popular usage in England by a well-known passage of Dr Franklin's. (Bentham uses the expression 'laissez-nous faire' - Works, p. 440). It is not, indeed, until we come to the later works of Bentham - who was not an economist at all - that we discover the rule of laissez-faire, in the shape in which our grandfathers knew it, adapted into the service of the Utilitarian philosophy. For example in *A Manual of Political Economy*, (written in 1793, a chapter published in the Bibliothèque Britannique in 1798, and the whole first printed in Bowring's edition of this Works - 1843) he writes: 'The general rule is that nothing ought to be done or attempted by government; the motto or watchword of government, on these occasions, ought to be - *Be quiet* ... The request which agriculture, manufacturers, and commerce present to governments is as modest and reasonable as that which Diogenes made to Alexander: Stand out of my sunshine.'

From this time on it was the political campaign for free trade, the influence of the so-called Manchester School and of the Benthamite Utilitarians, the utterances of secondary economic authorities and the education stories of Miss Martineau and Mrs Marcet, that fixed *laissez-faire* in the popular mind as the practical conclusion of orthodox political economy - with this great difference, that the Malthusian view of population having been accepted in the meantime by this same school of thought, the optimistic *laissez-faire* of the last half of the eighteenth century gives place to the pessimistic *laissez-faire* of the last half of the nineteenth century.

> (Cf. Sidgwick, op. cit. p. 22: 'Even those economists, who adhered in the main to Adam Smith's limitations of the sphere of government, enforced these limitations sadly rather than triumphantly; not as admirers of the social order at present resulting from"'natural liberty", but as convinced that it is at least preferable to any artificial order that government might be able to substitute for it.')

In Mrs Marcet's *Conversations on Political Economy* (1817), Caroline stands out as long as she can in favour of controlling the expenditure of the rich. But by page 418 she has to admit defeat:

> CAROLINE. The more I learn upon this subject, the more I feel convinced that the interests of nations, as well as those of individuals, so far from being opposed to each other, are in the most perfect unison.
> MRS B. Liberal and enlarged views will always lead to similar conclusions, and teach us to cherish sentiments of universal benevolence towards each other; hence the superiority of science over mere practical knowledge.

By 1850 the *Easy Lessons for the Use of Young People,* by Archbishop Whately, which the Society for Promoting Christian Knowledge was distributing wholesale, do not admit even of those doubts which Mrs B. allowed Caroline occasionally to entertain. 'More harm than good is likely to be done' the little book concludes, 'by almost any interference of Government with men's money transactions, whether letting and leasing, or buying and selling of any kind.' *True* liberty is 'that every man should be left free to dispose of his own property, his own time, and strength, and skill, in whatever way he himself may think fit, provided he does no wrong to his neighbours'.

In short, the dogma had got hold of the educational machine; it had become a copybook maxim. The political philosophy, which the seventeenth and eighteenth centuries had forged in order to throw down kings and prelates, had been made milk for babes, and had literally entered the nursery.

Finally, in the works of Bastiat we reach the most extravagant and rhapsodical expression of the political economist's religion.

In his *Harmonies Économiques,*

> I undertake [he says] to demonstrate the Harmony of those laws of Providence which govern human society. What makes these laws harmonious and not discordant is, that all principles, all motives, all springs of action, all interests, co-operate towards a grand final result ... And that result is, the indefinite approximation of all classes towards a level, which is always rising; in other words, the equalisation of individuals in the general amelioration.

And when, like other priests, he drafts his *Credo,* it runs as follows:

> I believe that He who has arranged the material universe has not withheld His regard from the arrangements of the social world. I believe that He has combined and caused to move in harmony free agents as well as inert molecules ... I believe that the invincible social tendency is a constant approximation of men towards a common moral, intellectual, and physical level, with at the same time, a progressive and indefinite elevation of that level. I believe that all that is necessary to the gradual and peaceful development of humanity is that its tendencies should not be disturbed, nor have the liberty of their movements destroyed.

From the time of John Stuart Mill, economists of authority have been in strong reaction against all such ideas. 'Scarcely a single English economist of repute', as Professor Cannan has expressed it, 'will join in a frontal attack upon Socialism in general,' though, as he also adds, 'nearly every economist, whether of repute or not, is always ready to pick holes in most socialistic proposals'. (*Theories of Production and Distribution*, p. 494). Economists no longer have any link with the theological or political philosophies out of which the dogma of social harmony was born, and their scientific analysis leads them to no such conclusions.

Cairnes, in the introductory lecture on 'Political Economy and *Laissez-faire*', which he delivered at University College, London, in 1870, was perhaps the first orthodox economist to deliver a frontal attack upon *laissez-faire* in general. 'The maxim of *laissez-faire*', he declared, 'has no scientific basis whatever, but is at best a mere handy rule of practice.'

> (Cairnes well described the' prevailing notion' in the following passage from the same lecture: 'The prevailing notion is that P.E. [note: Political Economy] undertakes to show that wealth may be most rapidly accumulated and most fairly distributed; that is to say, that human well-

being may be most effectually promoted by the simple process of leaving people to themselves; leaving individuals, that is to say, to follow the promptings of self-interest, unrestrained either by State or by the public opinion, so long as they abstain from force and fraud. This is the doctrine commonly known as laissez-faire; and accordingly political economy is, I think, very generally regarded as a sort of scientific rendering of this maxim - a vindication of freedom of individual enterprise and of contract as the one and sufficient solution of all industrial problems.')

This, for fifty years past, has been the view of all leading economists. Some of the most important work of Alfred Marshall - to take one instance - was directed to the elucidation of the leading cases in which private interest and social interest are not harmonious. Nevertheless, the guarded and undogmatic attitude of the best economists has not prevailed against the general opinion that an individualistic *laissez-faire* is both what they ought to teach and what in fact they do teach.

III

Economists, like other scientists, have chosen the hypothesis from which they set out, and which they offer to beginners because it is the simplest, and not because it is the nearest to the facts. Partly for this reason, but partly, I admit, because they have been biased by the traditions of the subject, they have begun by assuming a state of affairs where the ideal distribution of productive resources can be brought about through individuals acting independently by the method of trial and error in such a way that those individuals who move in the right direction will destroy by competition those who move in the wrong direction. This implies that there must be no mercy or protection for those who embark their capital or their labour in the wrong direction. It is a method of bringing the most successful profit-makers to the top by a ruthless struggle for survival, which selects the most efficient by the bankruptcy of the less efficient. It does not count the cost of the struggle, but looks only to the benefits of the final result which are assumed to be permanent. The object of life being to crop the leaves off the branches up to the greatest possible height, the likeliest way of achieving this end is to leave the giraffes with the longest necks to starve out those whose necks are shorter.

Corresponding to this method of attaining the ideal distribution of the instruments of production between different purposes, there is a similar assumption as to how to attain the distribution of what is available for consumption. In the first place, each individual will discover what amongst the possible objects of consumption he wants most by the method of trial and error 'at the margin', and in this way not only will each consumer come to distribute his consumption most advantageously, but each object of consumption will find its way into the mouth of the consumer whose relish for it is greatest compared with that of the others, because that consumer will outbid the rest. Thus, if only we leave the giraffes to themselves, (1) the maximum quantity of leaves will be cropped because the giraffes with the longest necks will, by dint of starving out the others, get nearest to the trees; (2) each giraffe will make for the leaves which he finds most succulent amongst those in reach; and (3) the giraffes whose relish for a given leaf is greatest will crane most to reach it. In this way more and juicier leaves will be swallowed, and each individual leaf will reach the throat which thinks it deserves most effort.

This assumption, however, of conditions where unhindered natural selection leads to progress, is only one of the two provisional assumptions which, taken as literal truth, have become the twin buttresses of *laissez-faire*. The other one is the efficacy, and indeed the necessity, of the opportunity for unlimited private money-making as an incentive to maximum effort. Profit accrues, under laissez-faire, to the individual who, whether by skill or good fortune, is found with his productive resources in the right place at the right time. A system which allows the skilful or fortunate individual to reap the whole fruits of this conjuncture evidently offers an immense incentive to the practice of the art of being in the right place at the right time. Thus one of the most powerful of human motives, namely the love of money, is harnessed to the task of distributing economic resources in the way best calculated to increase wealth. The parallelism between economic *laissez-faire* and Darwinianism, already briefly noted, is now seen, as Herbert Spencer was foremost to recognise, to be very close indeed. Darwin invoked sexual love, acting through sexual selection, as an adjutant to natural selection by competition, to direct evolution along lines which should be desirable as well as effective, so the individualist invokes the love of money, acting through the pursuit of profit, as an adjutant to natural selection, to bring about the

13

production on the greatest possible scale of what is most strongly desired as measured by exchange value.

The beauty and the simplicity of such a theory are so great that it is easy to forget that it follows not from the actual facts, but from an incomplete hypothesis introduced for the sake of simplicity. Apart from other objections to be mentioned later, the conclusion that individuals acting independently for their own advantage will produce the greatest aggregate of wealth, depends on a variety of unreal assumptions to the effect that the processes of production and consumption are in no way organic, that there exists a sufficient foreknowledge of conditions and requirements, and that there are adequate opportunities of obtaining this foreknowledge. For economists generally reserve for a later stage of their argument the complications which arise - (1) when the efficient units of production are large relatively to the units of consumption, (2) when overhead costs or joint costs are present, (3) when internal economies tend to the aggregation of production, (4) when the time required for adjustments is long, (5) when ignorance prevails over knowledge and (6) when monopolies and combinations interfere with equality in bargaining - they reserve, that is to say, for a later stage their analysis of the actual facts. Moreover, many of those who recognise that the simplified hypothesis does not accurately correspond to fact conclude nevertheless that it does 'represent what is 'natural' and therefore ideal.

They regard the simplified hypothesis as health, and the further complications as disease.

Yet besides this question of fact there are other considerations, familiar enough, which rightly bring into the calculation the cost and character of the competitive struggle itself, and the tendency for wealth to be distributed where it is not appreciated most. If we have the welfare of the giraffes at heart, we must not overlook the sufferings of the shorter necks who are starved out, or the sweet leaves which fall to the ground and are trampled underfoot in the struggle, or the overfeeding of the long-necked ones, or the evil look of anxiety or struggling greediness which overcasts the mild faces of the herd.

But the principles of *laissez-faire* have had other allies besides economic textbooks. It must be admitted that they have been confirmed in the minds of sound thinkers and the reasonable public by the poor quality of the opponent proposals - protectionism on one hand, and Marxian socialism on the other. Yet these doctrines are both characterised, not only or chiefly by their infringing the general presumption in favour of *laissez-faire,* but by mere logical fallacy. Both are examples of poor thinking, of inability to analyse a

14

process and follow it out to its conclusion. The arguments against them, though reinforced by the principle of *laissez-faire,* do not strictly require it. Of the two, protectionism is at least plausible, and the forces making for its popularity are nothing to wonder at. But Marxian socialism must always remain a portent to the historians of opinion - how a doctrine so illogical and so dull can have exercised so powerful and enduring an influence over the minds of men and, through them, the events of history. At any rate, the obvious scientific deficiencies of these two schools greatly contributed to the prestige and authority of nineteenth-century *laissez-faire.*

Nor has the most notable divergence into centralised social action on a great scale - the conduct of the late war - encouraged reformers or dispelled old-fashioned prejudices. There is much to be said, it is true, on both sides. War experience in the organisation of socialised production has left some near observers optimistically anxious to repeat it in peace conditions. War socialism unquestionably achieved a production of wealth on a scale far greater than we ever knew in peace, for though the goods and services delivered were destined for immediate and fruitless extinction, none the less they were wealth. Nevertheless, the dissipation of effort was also prodigious, and the atmosphere of waste and not counting the cost was disgusting to any thrifty or provident spirit.

Finally, individualism and *laissez-faire* could not, in spite of their deep roots in the political and moral philosophies of the late eighteenth and early nineteenth centuries, have secured their lasting hold over the conduct of public affairs, if it had not been for their conformity with the needs and wishes of the business world of the day. They gave full scope to our erstwhile heroes, the great business men. 'At least one-half of the best ability in the Western world,' Marshall used to say, 'is engaged in business.' A great part of 'the higher imagination' of the age was thus employed. It was on the activities of these men that our hopes of progress were centred.

> Men of this class (Marshall wrote in *The Social Possibilities of Economic Chivalry,* Economic Journal, XVII, 1907 - 9) live in constantly shifting visions, fashioned in their own brains, of various routes to their desired end; of the difficulties which Nature will oppose to them on each route, and of the contrivances by which they hope to get the better of her opposition. This imagination gains little credit with the people, because it is not allowed to run riot; its strength is disciplined by a stronger will; and its highest glory is to have attained great ends by means so simple that no one will know, and none but

15

experts will even guess, how a dozen other expedients, each suggesting as much brilliancy to the hasty observer, were set aside in favour of it. The imagination of such a man is employed, like that of the master chess-player, in forecasting the obstacles which may be opposed to the successful issue of his far-reaching projects, and constantly rejecting brilliant suggestions because he has pictured to himself the counter-strokes to them. His strong nervous force is at the opposite extreme of human nature from that nervous irresponsibility which conceives hasty Utopian schemes, and which is rather to be compared to the bold facility of a weak player, who will speedily solve the most difficult chess problem by taking on himself to move the black men as well as the white.

This is a fine picture of the great captain of industry, the master-individualist, who serves us in serving himself, just, as any other artist does. Yet this one, in his turn, is becoming a tarnished idol. We grow more doubtful whether it is he who will lead us into paradise by the hand.

These many elements have contributed to the current intellectual bias, the mental make-up, the orthodoxy of the day. The compelling force of many of the original reasons has disappeared but, as usual, the vitality of the conclusions outlasts them. To suggest social action for the public good to the City of London is like discussing the *Origin of Species* with a bishop sixty years ago. The first reaction is not intellectual, but moral. An orthodoxy is in question, and the more persuasive the arguments the graver the offence. Nevertheless, venturing into the den of the lethargic monster, at any rate I have traced his claims and pedigree so as to show that he has ruled over us rather by hereditary right than by personal merit.

IV

Let us clear from the ground the metaphysical or general principles upon which, from time to time, *laissez-faire* has been founded. It is *not* true that individuals possess a prescriptive 'natural liberty' in their economic activities. There is *no* 'compact' conferring perpetual rights on those who Have or on those who Acquire. The world

16

is *not* so governed from above that private and social interest always coincide. It is not so managed here below that in practice they coincide. It is not a correct deduction from the principles of economics that enlightened self-interest always operates in the public interest. Nor is it true that self-interest generally *is* enlightened; more often individuals acting separately to promote their own ends are too ignorant or too weak to attain even these. Experience does *not* show that individuals, when they make up a social unit, are always less clear-sighted than when they act separately.

We cannot therefore settle on abstract grounds, but must handle on its merits in detail what Burke termed 'one of the finest problems in legislation, namely, to determine what the State ought to take upon itself to direct by the public wisdom, and what it ought to leave, with as little interference as possible, to individual exertion.' (Quoted by McCulloch in his *Principles of Political Economy*). We have to discriminate between what Bentham, in his forgotten but useful nomenclature, used to term *Agenda* and *Non-Agenda,* and to do this without Bentham's prior presumption that interference is, at the same time, 'generally needless' and 'generally pernicious.' (Bentham's *Manual of Political Economy*, published posthumously, in Bowring's edition - 1843). Perhaps the chief task of economists at this hour is to distinguish afresh the *Agenda* of government from the *Non-Agenda;* and the companion task of politics is to devise forms of government within a democracy which shall be capable of accomplishing the *Agenda*. I will illustrate what I have in mind by two examples.

(1) I believe that in many cases the ideal size for the unit of control and organisation lies somewhere between the individual and the modern State. I suggest, therefore, that progress lies in the growth and the recognition of semi-autonomous bodies within the State - bodies whose criterion of action within their own field is solely the public good as they understand it, and from whose deliberations motives of private advantage are excluded, though some place it may still be necessary to leave, until the ambit of men's altruism grows wider, to the separate advantage of particular groups, classes, or faculties - bodies which in the ordinary course of affairs are mainly autonomous within their prescribed limitations, but are subject in the last resort to the sovereignty of the democracy expressed through Parliament.

I propose a return, it may be said, towards medieval conceptions of separate autonomies. But, in England at any rate, corporations are a mode of government which has never ceased to be important and is sympathetic to our institutions. It is easy to give examples, from what already exists, of separate autonomies which have attained or are

17

approaching the mode I designate - the universities, the Bank of England, the Port of London Authority, even perhaps the railway companies. In Germany there are doubtless analogous instances.

But more interesting than these is the trend of joint stock institutions, when they have reached a certain age and size, to approximate to the status of public corporations rather than that of individualistic private enterprise. One of the most interesting and unnoticed developments of recent decades has been the tendency of big enterprise to socialise itself. A point arrives in the growth of a big institution - particularly a big railway or big public utility enterprise, but also a big bank or a big insurance company - at which the owners of the capital, i.e. its shareholders, are almost entirely dissociated from the management, with the result that the direct personal interest of the latter in the making of great profit becomes quite secondary. When this stage is reached, the general stability and reputation of the institution are the more considered by the management than the maximum of profit for the shareholders. The shareholders must be satisfied by conventionally adequate dividends; but once this is secured, the direct interest of the management often consists in avoiding criticism from the public and from the customers of the concern. This is particularly the case if their great size or semi-monopolistic position renders them conspicuous in the public eye and vulnerable to public attack. The extreme instance, perhaps, of this tendency in the case of an institution, theoretically the unrestricted property of private persons, is the Bank of England. It is almost true to say that there is no class of persons in the kingdom of whom the Governor of the Bank of England thinks less when he decides on his policy than of his shareholders. Their rights, in excess of their conventional dividend, have already sunk to the neighbourhood of zero. But the same thing is partly true of many other big institutions. They are, as time goes on, socialising themselves.

Not that this is unmixed gain. The same causes promote conservatism and a waning of enterprise. In fact, we already have in these cases many of the faults as well as the advantages of State Socialism. Nevertheless, we see here, I think, a natural line of evolution. The battle of Socialism against unlimited private profit is being won in detail hour by hour. In these particular fields - it remains acute elsewhere - this is no longer the pressing problem. There is, for instance, no so-called important political question so really unimportant, so irrelevant to the reorganisation of the economic life of Great Britain, as the nationalisation of the railways.

It is true that many big undertakings, particularly public utility enterprises and other business requiring a large fixed capital, still need to be semi-socialised. But we must keep our minds flexible regarding the forms of this semi-socialism. We must take full advantage of the natural tendencies of the day, and we must probably prefer semi-autonomous corporations to organs of the central government for which ministers of State are directly responsible.

I criticise doctrinaire State Socialism, not because it seeks to engage men's altruistic impulses in the service of society, or because it departs from *laissez-faire,* or because it takes away from man's natural liberty to make a million, or because it has courage for bold experiments. All these things I applaude. I criticise it because it misses the significance of what is actually happening; because it is, in fact, little better than a dusty survival of a plan to meet the problems of fifty years ago, based on a misunderstanding of what someone said a hundred years ago. Nineteenth-century State Socialism sprang from Bentham, free competition, etc., and is in some respects a clearer, in some respects a more muddled version of just the same philosophy as underlies nineteenth-century individualism. Both equally laid all their stress on freedom, the one negatively to avoid limitations on existing freedom, the other positively to destroy natural or acquired monopolies. They are different reactions to the same intellectual atmosphere.

I come next to a criterion of *Agenda* which is particularly relevant to what it is urgent and desirable to do in the near future. We must aim at separating those services which are *technically social* from those which are *technically individual.* The most important Agenda of the State relate not to those activities which private individuals are already fulfilling, but to those functions which fall outside the sphere of the individual, to those decisions which are made by *no one* if the State does not make them. The important thing for government is not to do things which individuals are doing already, and to do them a little better or a little worse; but to do those things which at present are not done at all.

It is not within the scope of my purpose on this occasion to develop practical policies. I limit myself, therefore, to naming some instances of what I mean from amongst those problems about which I happen to have thought most.

Many of the greatest economic evils of our time are the fruits of risk, uncertainty, and ignorance. It is because particular individuals, fortunate in situation or in abilities, are able to take advantage of uncertainty and ignorance, and also because for the same reason big business is often a lottery, that great inequalities of wealth come about; and these same factors are also the cause of the unemployment of labour, or the disappointment of reasonable business expectations, and of the impairment of efficiency and production. Yet the cure lies outside the operations of individuals; it may even be to the interest of individuals to aggravate the disease. I believe that the cure for these things is partly to be sought in the deliberate control of the currency and of credit by a central institution, and partly in the collection and dissemination on a great scale of data relating to the business situation, including the full publicity, by law if necessary, of all business facts which it is useful to know. These measures would involve society in exercising directive intelligence through some appropriate organ of action over many of the inner intricacies of private business, yet it would leave private initiative and enterprise unhindered. Even if these measures prove insufficient, nevertheless, they will furnish us with better knowledge than we have now for taking the next step.

My second example relates to savings and investment. I believe that some coordinated act of intelligent judgement is required as to the scale on which it is desirable that the community as a whole should save, the scale on which these savings should go abroad in the form of foreign investments, and whether the present organisation of the investment market distributes savings along the most nationally productive channels. I do not think that these matters should be left entirely to the chances of private judgement and private profits, as they are at present.

My third example concerns population. The time has already come when each country needs a considered national policy about what size of population, whether larger or smaller than at present or the same, is most expedient. And having settled this policy, we must take steps to carry it into operation. The time may arrive a little later when the community as a whole must pay attention to the innate quality as well as to the mere numbers of its future members.

V

These reflections have been directed towards possible improvements in the technique of modern capitalism by the agency of collective action. There is nothing in them which is seriously incompatible with what seems to me to be the essential characteristic of capitalism, namely the dependence upon an intense appeal to the money-making and money-loving instincts of individuals as the main motive force of the economic machine. Nor must I, so near to my end, stray towards other fields. Nevertheless, I may do well to remind you, in conclusion, that the fiercest contests and the most deeply felt divisions of opinion are likely to be waged in the coming years not round technical questions, where the arguments on either side are mainly economic, but round those which, for want of better words, may be called psychological or, perhaps, moral.

In Europe, or at least in some parts of Europe - but not, I think, in the United States of America - there is a latent reaction, somewhat widespread, against basing society to the extent that we do upon fostering, encouraging, and protecting the money-motives of individuals. A preference for arranging our affairs in such a way as to appeal to the money-motive as little as possible, rather than as much as possible, need not be entirely *a priori,* but may be based on the comparison of experiences. Different persons, according to their choice of profession, find the money-motive playing a large or a small part in their daily lives, and historians can tell us about other phases of social organisation in which this motive has played a much smaller part than it does now. Most religions and most philosophies deprecate, to say the least of it, a way of life mainly influenced by considerations of personal money profit. On the other hand, most men today reject ascetic notions and do not doubt the real advantages of wealth. Moreover, it seems obvious to them that one cannot do without the money-motive, and that, apart from certain admitted abuses, it does its job well. In the result the average man averts his attention from the problem, and has no clear idea what he really thinks and feels about the whole confounded matter.

Confusion of thought and feeling leads to confusion of speech. Many people, who are really objecting to capitalism as a way of life, argue as though they were objecting to it on the ground of its inefficiency in attaining its own objects. Contrariwise, devotees of capitalism are often unduly conservative, and reject reforms in its technique, which might really strengthen and preserve it, for fear that they may prove to be first steps away from capitalism itself. Nevertheless, a time may be coming when we shall get clearer than at present as to when we are talking about capitalism as an efficient or inefficient technique, and when we are talking about it as desirable or objectionable in itself. For my part I think that capitalism, wisely managed, can probably be made more efficient for attaining economic ends than any alternative system yet in sight, but that in itself it is in many ways extremely objectionable. Our problem is to work out a social organisation which shall be as efficient as possible without offending our notions of a satisfactory way of life.

The next step forward must come, not from political agitation or premature experiments, but from thought. We need by an effort of the mind to elucidate our own feelings. At present our sympathy and our judgement are liable to be on different sides, which is a painful and paralysing state of mind. In the field of action reformers will not be successful until they can steadily pursue a clear and definite object with their intellects and their feelings in tune. There is no party in the world at present which appears to me to be pursuing right aims by right methods. Material poverty provides the incentive to change precisely in situations where there is very little margin for experiments. Material prosperity removes the incentive just when it might be safe to take a chance. Europe lacks the means, America the will, to make a move. We need a new set of convictions which spring naturally from a candid examination of our own inner feelings in relation to the outside facts.

THE ECONOMIC CONSEQUENCES OF THE PEACE

PREFACE

The writer of this book was temporarily attached to the British Treasury during the war and was their official representative at the Paris Peace Conference up to June 7, 1919; he also sat as deputy for the Chancellor of the Exchequer on the Supreme Economic Council. He resigned from these positions when it became evident that hope could no longer be entertained of substantial modification in the draft Terms of Peace. The grounds of his objection to the Treaty, or rather to the whole policy of the Conference towards the economic problems of Europe, will appear in the following chapters. They are entirely of a public character, and are based on facts known to the whole world.

J.M. KEYNES.

KING'S   COLLEGE,   CAMBRIDGE,
November, 1919.

CONTENTS

CHAPTER I

INTRODUCTORY

The power to become habituated to his surroundings is a marked characteristic of mankind. Very few of us realize with conviction the intensely unusual, unstable, complicated, unreliable, temporary nature of the economic organization by which Western Europe has lived for the last half century. We assume some of the most peculiar and temporary of our late advantages as natural, permanent, and to be depended on, and we lay our plans accordingly. On this sandy and false foundation we scheme for social improvement and dress our political platforms, pursue our animosities and particular ambitions, and feel ourselves with enough margin in hand to foster, not assuage, civil conflict in the European family. Moved by insane delusion and reckless self-regard, the German people overturned the foundations on which we all lived and built. But the spokesmen of the French and British peoples have run the risk of completing the ruin, which Germany began, by a Peace which, if it is carried into effect, must impair yet further, when it might have restored, the delicate, complicated organization, already shaken and broken by war, through which alone the European peoples can employ themselves and live.

In England the outward aspect of life does not yet teach us to feel or realize in the least that an age is over. We are busy picking up the threads of our life where we dropped them, with this difference only, that many of us seem a good deal richer than we were before. Where we spent millions before the war, we have now learnt that we can spend hundreds of millions and apparently not suffer for it. Evidently we did not exploit to the utmost the possibilities of our economic life. We look, therefore, not only to a return to the comforts of 1914, but to an immense broadening and intensification of them. All classes alike thus build their plans, the rich to spend more and save less, the poor to spend more and work less.

But perhaps it is only in England (and America) that it is possible to be so unconscious. In continental Europe the earth heaves and no one but is aware of the rumblings. There it is not just a matter of extravagance or "labor troubles"; but of life and death, of starvation and existence, and of the fearful convulsions of a dying civilization.

For one who spent in Paris the greater part of the six months which succeeded the Armistice an occasional visit to London was a strange experience. England still stands outside Europe. Europe's voiceless tremors do not reach her. Europe is apart and England is not of her flesh and body. But Europe is solid with herself. France, Germany, Italy, Austria and Holland, Russia and Roumania and Poland, throb together, and their structure and civilization are essentially one. They flourished together, they have rocked together in a war, which we, in spite of our enormous contributions and sacrifices (like though in a less degree than America), economically stood outside, and they may fall together. In this lies the destructive significance of the Peace of Paris. If the European Civil War is to end with France and Italy abusing their momentary victorious power to destroy Germany and Austria-Hungary now prostrate, they invite their own destruction also, being so deeply and inextricably intertwined with their victims by hidden psychic

24

and economic bonds. At any rate an Englishman who took part in the Conference of Paris and was during those months a member of the Supreme Economic Council of the Allied Powers, was bound to become, for him a new experience, a European in his cares and outlook. There, at the nerve center of the European system, his British preoccupations must largely fall away and he must be haunted by other and more dreadful specters. Paris was a nightmare, and every one there was morbid. A sense of impending catastrophe overhung the frivolous scene; the futility and smallness of man before the great events confronting him; the mingled significance and unreality of the decisions; levity, blindness, insolence, confused cries from without,—all the elements of ancient tragedy were there. Seated indeed amid the theatrical trappings of the French Saloons of State, one could wonder if the extraordinary visages of Wilson and of Clemenceau, with their fixed hue and unchanging characterization, were really faces at all and not the tragi-comic masks of some strange drama or puppet-show.

The proceedings of Paris all had this air of extraordinary importance and unimportance at the same time. The decisions seemed charged with consequences to the future of human society; yet the air whispered that the word was not flesh, that it was futile, insignificant, of no effect, dissociated from events; and one felt most strongly the impression, described by Tolstoy in *War and Peace* or by Hardy in *The Dynasts*, of events marching on to their fated conclusion uninfluenced and unaffected by the cerebrations of Statesmen in Council:

Spirit of the Years

Observe that all wide sight and self-command
Deserts these throngs now driven to demonry
By the Immanent Unrecking. Nought remains
But vindictiveness here amid the strong,
And there amid the weak an impotent rage.

Spirit of the Pities
Why prompts the Will so senseless-shaped a doing?

Spirit of the Years
I have told thee that It works unwittingly,
As one possessed not judging.

In Paris, where those connected with the Supreme Economic Council, received almost hourly the reports of the misery, disorder, and decaying organization of all Central and Eastern Europe, allied and enemy alike, and learnt from the lips of the financial representatives of Germany and Austria unanswerable evidence, of the terrible exhaustion of their countries, an occasional visit to the hot, dry room in the President's house, where the Four fulfilled their destinies in empty and arid intrigue, only added to the sense of nightmare. Yet there in Paris the problems of Europe were terrible and clamant, and an occasional return to the vast unconcern of London a little disconcerting. For in London these questions were very far away, and our own lesser problems alone troubling. London believed that Paris was making a great confusion of its business, but remained uninterested. In this spirit the British people received the Treaty without reading it. But it is under the influence of Paris, not London, that this book has been written by one who, though an Englishman, feels himself a European also, and, because of too vivid recent experience, cannot disinterest himself from the further unfolding of the great historic drama of these days which will destroy great institutions, but may also create a new world.

Chapter II

Europe before the War

Before 1870 different parts of the small continent of Europe had specialized in their own products; but, taken as a whole, it was substantially self-subsistent. And its population was adjusted to this state of affairs.

After 1870 there was developed on a large scale an unprecedented situation, and the economic condition of Europe became during the next fifty years unstable and peculiar. The pressure of population on food, which had already been balanced by the accessibility of supplies from America, became for the first time in recorded history definitely reversed. As numbers increased, food was actually easier to secure. Larger proportional returns from an increasing scale of production became true of agriculture as well as industry. With the growth of the European population there were more emigrants on the one hand to till the soil of the new countries, and, on the other, more workmen were available in Europe to prepare the industrial products and capital goods which were to maintain the emigrant populations in their new homes, and to build the railways and ships which were to make accessible to Europe food and raw products from distant sources. Up to about 1900 a unit of labor applied to industry yielded year by year a purchasing power over an increasing quantity of food. It is possible that about the year 1900 this process began to be reversed, and a diminishing yield of Nature to man's effort was beginning to reassert itself. But the tendency of cereals to rise in real cost was balanced by other improvements; and—one of many novelties—the resources of tropical Africa then for the first time came into large employ, and a great traffic in oil-seeds began to bring to the table of Europe in a new and cheaper form one of the essential foodstuffs of mankind. In this economic Eldorado, in this economic Utopia, as the earlier economists would have deemed it, most of us were brought up.

That happy age lost sight of a view of the world which filled with deep-seated melancholy the founders of our Political Economy. Before the eighteenth century mankind entertained no false hopes. To lay the illusions which grew popular at that age's latter end, Malthus disclosed a Devil. For half a century all serious economical writings held that Devil in clear prospect. For the next half century he was chained up and out of sight. Now perhaps we have loosed him again.

26

What an extraordinary episode in the economic progress of man that age was which came to an end in August, 1914! The greater part of the population, it is true, worked hard and lived at a low standard of comfort, yet were, to all appearances, reasonably contented with this lot. But escape was possible, for any man of capacity or character at all exceeding the average, into the middle and upper classes, for whom life offered, at a low cost and with the least trouble, conveniences, comforts, and amenities beyond the compass of the richest and most powerful monarchs of other ages. The inhabitant of London could order by telephone, sipping his morning tea in bed, the various products of the whole earth, in such quantity as he might see fit, and reasonably expect their early delivery upon his doorstep; he could at the same moment and by the same means adventure his wealth in the natural resources and new enterprises of any quarter of the world, and share, without exertion or even trouble, in their prospective fruits and advantages; or he could decide to couple the security of his fortunes with the good faith of the townspeople of any substantial municipality in any continent that fancy or information might recommend. He could secure forthwith, if he wished it, cheap and comfortable means of transit to any country or climate without passport or other formality, could despatch his servant to the neighboring office of a bank for such supply of the precious metals as might seem convenient, and could then proceed abroad to foreign quarters, without knowledge of their religion, language, or customs, bearing coined wealth upon his person, and would consider himself greatly aggrieved and much surprised at the least interference. But, most important of all, he regarded this state of affairs as normal, certain, and permanent, except in the direction of further improvement, and any deviation from it as aberrant, scandalous, and avoidable. The projects and politics of militarism and imperialism, of racial and cultural rivalries, of monopolies, restrictions, and exclusion, which were to play the serpent to this paradise, were little more than the amusements of his daily newspaper, and appeared to exercise almost no influence at all on the ordinary course of social and economic life, the internationalization of which was nearly complete in practice.

It will assist us to appreciate the character and consequences of the Peace which we have imposed on our enemies, if I elucidate a little further some of the chief unstable elements already present when war broke out, in the economic life of Europe.

I. *Population*

In 1870 Germany had a population of about 40,000,000. By 1892 this figure had risen to 50,000,000, and by June 30, 1914, to about 68,000,000. In the years immediately preceding the war the annual increase was about 850,000, of whom an insignificant proportion emigrated.[1] This great increase was only rendered possible by a far-reaching transformation of the economic structure of the country. From being agricultural and mainly self-supporting, Germany transformed herself into a vast and complicated industrial machine, dependent for its working on the equipoise of many factors outside Germany as well as within. Only by operating this machine, continuously and at full blast, could she find occupation at home for her increasing population and the means of purchasing their subsistence from abroad. The German machine was like a top which to maintain its equilibrium must spin ever faster and faster.

In the Austro-Hungarian Empire, which grew from about 40,000,000 in 1890 to at least 50,000,000 at the outbreak of war, the same tendency was present in a less degree, the annual excess of births over deaths being about half a million, out of which, however, there was an annual emigration of some quarter of a million persons.

To understand the present situation, we must apprehend with vividness what an extraordinary center of population the development of the Germanic system had enabled Central Europe to become. Before the war the population of Germany and Austria-Hungary together not only substantially exceeded that of the United States, but was about equal to that of the whole of North America. In these numbers, situated within a compact territory, lay the military strength of the Central Powers. But these same numbers—for even the war has not appreciably diminished them[2]—if deprived of the means of life, remain a hardly less danger to European order.

European Russia increased her population in a degree even greater than Germany—from less than 100,000,000 in 1890 to about 150,000,000 at the outbreak of war;[3] and in the year immediately preceding 1914 the excess of births over deaths in Russia as a whole was at the prodigious rate of two millions per annum. This inordinate growth in the population of Russia, which has not been widely noticed in England, has been nevertheless one of the most significant facts of recent years.

The great events of history are often due to secular changes in the growth of population and other fundamental economic causes, which, escaping by their gradual character the notice of contemporary observers, are attributed to the follies of statesmen or the fanaticism of atheists. Thus the extraordinary occurrences of the past two years in Russia, that vast upheaval of Society, which has overturned what seemed most stable—religion, the basis of property, the ownership of land, as well as forms of government and the hierarchy of classes—may owe more to the deep influences of expanding numbers than to Lenin or to Nicholas; and the disruptive powers of excessive national fecundity may have played a greater part in bursting the bonds of convention than either the power of ideas or the errors of autocracy.

II. *Organization*

The delicate organization by which these peoples lived depended partly on factors internal to the system.

The interference of frontiers and of tariffs was reduced to a minimum, and not far short of three hundred millions of people lived within the three Empires of Russia, Germany, and Austria-Hungary. The various currencies, which were all maintained on a stable basis in relation to gold and to one another, facilitated the easy flow of capital and of trade to an extent the full value of which we only realize now, when we are deprived of its advantages. Over this great area there was an almost absolute security of property and of person.

These factors of order, security, and uniformity, which Europe had never before enjoyed over so wide and populous a territory or for so long a period, prepared the way for the organization of that vast mechanism of transport, coal distribution, and foreign trade which made possible an industrial order of life in the dense urban centers of new population. This is too well known to require detailed substantiation with figures. But it may be illustrated by the figures for coal, which has been the key to the industrial growth of Central Europe hardly less than of England; the output of German coal grew from 30,000,000 tons in 1871 to 70,000,000 tons in 1890, 110,000,000 tons in 1900, and 190,000,000 tons in 1913.

Round Germany as a central support the rest of the European economic system grouped itself, and on the prosperity and enterprise of Germany the prosperity of the rest of the Continent mainly depended. The increasing pace of Germany gave her neighbors an outlet for their products, in exchange for which the enterprise of the German merchant supplied them with their chief requirements at a low price.

The statistics of the economic interdependence of Germany and her neighbors are overwhelming. Germany was the best customer of Russia, Norway, Holland, Belgium, Switzerland, Italy, and Austria-Hungary; she was the second best customer of Great Britain, Sweden, and Denmark; and the third best customer of France. She was the largest source of supply to Russia, Norway, Sweden, Denmark, Holland, Switzerland, Italy, Austria-Hungary, Roumania, and Bulgaria; and the second largest source of supply to Great Britain, Belgium, and France.

In our own case we sent more exports to Germany than to any other country in the world except India, and we bought more from her than from any other country in the world except the United States.

There was no European country except those west of Germany which did not do more than a quarter of their total trade with her; and in the case of Russia, Austria-Hungary, and Holland the proportion was far greater.

Germany not only furnished these countries with trade, but, in the case of some of them, supplied a great part of the capital needed for their own development. Of Germany's pre-war foreign investments, amounting in all to about $6,250,000,000, not far short of $2,500,000,000 was invested in Russia, Austria-Hungary, Bulgaria, Roumania, and Turkey.[4] And by the system of "peaceful penetration" she gave these countries not only capital, but, what they needed hardly less, organization. The whole of Europe east of the Rhine thus fell into the German industrial orbit, and its economic life was adjusted accordingly.

But these internal factors would not have been sufficient to enable the population to support itself without the co-operation of external factors also and of certain general dispositions common to the whole of Europe. Many of the circumstances already treated were true of Europe as a whole, and were not peculiar to the Central Empires. But all of what follows was common to the whole European system.

III. *The Psychology of Society*

Europe was so organized socially and economically as to secure the maximum accumulation of capital. While there was some continuous improvement in the daily conditions of life of the mass of the population, Society was so framed as to throw a

29

great part of the increased income into the control of the class least likely to consume it. The new rich of the nineteenth century were not brought up to large expenditures, and preferred the power which investment gave them to the pleasures of immediate consumption. In fact, it was precisely the *inequality* of the distribution of wealth which made possible those vast accumulations of fixed wealth and of capital improvements which distinguished that age from all others. Herein lay, in fact, the main justification of the Capitalist System. If the rich had spent their new wealth on their own enjoyments, the world would long ago have found such a régime intolerable. But like bees they saved and accumulated, not less to the advantage of the whole community because they themselves held narrower ends in prospect.

The immense accumulations of fixed capital which, to the great benefit of mankind, were built up during the half century before the war, could never have come about in a Society where wealth was divided equitably. The railways of the world, which that age built as a monument to posterity, were, not less than the Pyramids of Egypt, the work of labor which was not free to consume in immediate enjoyment the full equivalent of its efforts.

Thus this remarkable system depended for its growth on a double bluff or deception. On the one hand the laboring classes accepted from ignorance or powerlessness, or were compelled, persuaded, or cajoled by custom, convention, authority, and the well-established order of Society into accepting, a situation in which they could call their own very little of the cake that they and Nature and the capitalists were co-operating to produce. And on the other hand the capitalist classes were allowed to call the best part of the cake theirs and were theoretically free to consume it, on the tacit underlying condition that they consumed very little of it in practice. The duty of "saving" became nine-tenths of virtue and the growth of the cake the object of true religion. There grew round the non-consumption of the cake all those instincts of puritanism which in other ages has withdrawn itself from the world and has neglected the arts of production as well as those of enjoyment. And so the cake increased; but to what end was not clearly contemplated. Individuals would be exhorted not so much to abstain as to defer, and to cultivate the pleasures of security and anticipation. Saving was for old age or for your children; but this was only in theory,—the virtue of the cake was that it was never to be consumed, neither by you nor by your children after you.

In writing thus I do not necessarily disparage the practices of that generation. In the unconscious recesses of its being Society knew what it was about. The cake was really very small in proportion to the appetites of consumption, and no one, if it were shared all round, would be much the better off by the cutting of it. Society was working not for the small pleasures of to-day but for the future security and improvement of the race,—in fact for "progress." If only the cake were not cut but was allowed to grow in the geometrical proportion predicted by Malthus of population, but not less true of compound interest, perhaps a day might come when there would at last be enough to go round, and when posterity could enter into the enjoyment of *our* labors. In that day overwork, overcrowding, and underfeeding would have come to an end, and men, secure of the comforts and necessities of the body, could proceed to the nobler exercises of their faculties. One geometrical ratio might cancel another, and the nineteenth century was able to forget the fertility of the species in a contemplation of the dizzy virtues of compound interest.

30

There were two pitfalls in this prospect: lest, population still outstripping accumulation, our self-denials promote not happiness but numbers; and lest the cake be after all consumed, prematurely, in war, the consumer of all such hopes.

But these thoughts lead too far from my present purpose. I seek only to point out that the principle of accumulation based on inequality was a vital part of the pre-war order of Society and of progress as we then understood it, and to emphasize that this principle depended on unstable psychological conditions, which it may be impossible to recreate. It was not natural for a population, of whom so few enjoyed the comforts of life, to accumulate so hugely. The war has disclosed the possibility of consumption to all and the vanity of abstinence to many. Thus the bluff is discovered; the laboring classes may be no longer willing to forego so largely, and the capitalist classes, no longer confident of the future, may seek to enjoy more fully their liberties of consumption so long as they last, and thus precipitate the hour of their confiscation.

IV. *The Relation of the Old World to the New*

The accumulative habits of Europe before the war were the necessary condition of the greatest of the external factors which maintained the European equipoise.

Of the surplus capital goods accumulated by Europe a substantial part was exported abroad, where its investment made possible the development of the new resources of food, materials, and transport, and at the same time enabled the Old World to stake out a claim in the natural wealth and virgin potentialities of the New. This last factor came to be of the vastest importance. The Old World employed with an immense prudence the annual tribute it was thus entitled to draw. The benefit of cheap and abundant supplies resulting from the new developments which its surplus capital had made possible, was, it is true, enjoyed and not postponed. But the greater part of the money interest accruing on these foreign investments was reinvested and allowed to accumulate, as a reserve (it was then hoped) against the less happy day when the industrial labor of Europe could no longer purchase on such easy terms the produce of other continents, and when the due balance would be threatened between its historical civilizations and the multiplying races of other climates and environments. Thus the whole of the European races tended to benefit alike from the development of new resources whether they pursued their culture at home or adventured it abroad.

Even before the war, however, the equilibrium thus established between old civilizations and new resources was being threatened. The prosperity of Europe was based on the facts that, owing to the large exportable surplus of foodstuffs in America, she was able to purchase food at a cheap rate measured in terms of the labor required to produce her own exports, and that, as a result of her previous investments of capital, she was entitled to a substantial amount annually without any payment in return at all. The second of these factors then seemed out of danger, but, as a result of the growth of population overseas, chiefly in the United States, the first was not so secure.

When first the virgin soils of America came into bearing, the proportions of the population of those continents themselves, and consequently of their own local requirements, to those of Europe were very small. As lately as 1890 Europe had a population three times that of North and South America added together. But by 1914 the domestic requirements of the United States for wheat were approaching their production, and the date was evidently near when there would be an exportable surplus only in years of exceptionally favorable harvest. Indeed, the present domestic requirements of the United States are estimated at more than ninety per cent of the average yield of the five years 1909-1913.[5] At that time, however, the tendency towards stringency was showing itself, not so much in a lack of abundance as in a steady increase of real cost. That is to say, taking the world as a whole, there was no deficiency of wheat, but in order to call forth an adequate supply it was necessary to offer a higher real price. The most favorable factor in the situation was to be found in the extent to which Central and Western Europe was being fed from the exportable surplus of Russia and Roumania.

In short, Europe's claim on the resources of the New World was becoming precarious; the law of diminishing returns was at last reasserting itself and was making it necessary year by year for Europe to offer a greater quantity of other commodities to obtain the same amount of bread; and Europe, therefore, could by no means afford the disorganization of any of her principal sources of supply.

Much else might be said in an attempt to portray the economic peculiarities of the Europe of 1914. I have selected for emphasis the three or four greatest factors of instability,—the instability of an excessive population dependent for its livelihood on a complicated and artificial organization, the psychological instability of the laboring and capitalist classes, and the instability of Europe's claim, coupled with the completeness of her dependence, on the food supplies of the New World.

The war had so shaken this system as to endanger the life of Europe altogether. A great part of the Continent was sick and dying; its population was greatly in excess of the numbers for which a livelihood was available; its organization was destroyed, its transport system ruptured, and its food supplies terribly impaired.

It was the task of the Peace Conference to honor engagements and to satisfy justice; but not less to re-establish life and to heal wounds. These tasks were dictated as much by prudence as by the magnanimity which the wisdom of antiquity approved in victors. We will examine in the following chapters the actual character of the Peace.

FOOTNOTES:

[1]In 1913 there were 25,843 emigrants from Germany, of whom 19,124 went to the United States.

[2]The net decrease of the German population at the end of 1918 by decline of births and excess of deaths as compared with the

beginning of 1914, is estimated at about 2,700,000.

[3]Including Poland and Finland, but excluding Siberia, Central Asia, and the Caucasus.

[4]Sums of money mentioned in this book in terms of dollars have been converted from pounds sterling at the rate of $5 to £1.

[5]Even since 1914 the population of the United States has increased by seven or eight millions. As their annual consumption of wheat per head is not less than 6 bushels, the pre-war scale of production in the United States would only show a substantial surplus over present domestic requirements in about one year out of five. We have been saved for the moment by the great harvests of 1918 and 1919, which have been called forth by Mr. Hoover's guaranteed price. But the United States can hardly be expected to continue indefinitely to raise by a substantial figure the cost of living in its own country, in order to provide wheat for a Europe which cannot pay for it.

CHAPTER III

THE CONFERENCE

In Chapters IV. and V. I shall study in some detail the economic and financial provisions of the Treaty of Peace with Germany. But it will be easier to appreciate the true origin of many of these terms if we examine here some of the personal factors which influenced their preparation. In attempting this task, I touch, inevitably, questions of motive, on which spectators are liable to error and are not entitled to take on themselves the responsibilities of final judgment. Yet, if I seem in this chapter to assume sometimes the liberties which are habitual to historians, but which, in spite of the greater knowledge with which we speak, we generally hesitate to assume towards contemporaries, let the reader excuse me when he remembers how greatly, if it is to understand its destiny, the world needs light, even if it is partial and uncertain, on the complex struggle of human will and purpose, not yet finished, which, concentrated in the persons of four individuals in a manner never paralleled, made them, in the first months of 1919, the microcosm of mankind.

In those parts of the Treaty with which I am here concerned, the lead was taken by the French, in the sense that it was generally they who made in the first instance the most definite and the most extreme proposals. This was partly a matter of tactics. When the final result is expected to be a compromise, it is often prudent to start from an extreme position; and the French anticipated at the outset—like most other persons—a double process of compromise, first of all to suit the ideas of their allies and associates, and secondly in the course of the Peace Conference proper with the Germans themselves. These tactics were justified by the event. Clemenceau gained a reputation for moderation with his colleagues in Council by sometimes throwing over with an air of intellectual impartiality the more extreme proposals of his ministers; and much went through where the American and British critics were naturally a little ignorant of the true point at issue, or where too persistent criticism by France's allies put them in a position which they felt as invidious, of always appearing to take the enemy's part and to argue his case. Where, therefore, British and American interests were not seriously involved their criticism grew slack, and some provisions were thus passed which the French themselves did not take very seriously, and for which the eleventh-hour decision to allow no discussion with the Germans removed the opportunity of remedy.

But, apart from tactics, the French had a policy. Although Clemenceau might curtly abandon the claims of a Klotz or a Loucheur, or close his eyes with an air of fatigue when French interests were no longer involved in the discussion, he knew which points were vital, and these he abated little. In so far as the main economic lines of the Treaty represent an intellectual idea, it is the idea of France and of Clemenceau.

Clemenceau was by far the most eminent member of the Council of Four, and he had taken the measure of his colleagues. He alone both had an idea and had considered it in all its consequences. His age, his character, his wit, and his appearance joined to give him objectivity and a, defined outline in an environment of confusion. One could not despise Clemenceau or dislike him, but only take a different view as to the nature of civilized man, or indulge, at least, a different hope.

The figure and bearing of Clemenceau are universally familiar. At the Council of Four he wore a square-tailed coat of very good, thick black broadcloth, and on his hands, which were never uncovered, gray suede gloves; his boots were of thick black leather, very good, but of a country style, and sometimes fastened in front, curiously, by a buckle instead of laces. His seat in the room in the President's house, where the regular meetings of the Council of Four were held (as distinguished from their private and unattended conferences in a smaller chamber below), was on a square brocaded chair in the middle of the semicircle facing the fireplace, with Signor Orlando on his left, the President next by the fireplace, and the Prime Minister opposite on the other side of the fireplace on his right. He carried no papers and no portfolio, and was unattended by any personal secretary, though several French ministers and officials appropriate to the particular matter in hand would be present round him. His walk, his hand, and his voice were not lacking in vigor, but he bore nevertheless, especially after the attempt upon him, the aspect of a very old man conserving his strength for important occasions. He spoke seldom, leaving the initial statement of the French case to his ministers or officials; he closed his eyes often and sat back in his chair with an impassive face of parchment, his gray gloved hands clasped in front of him. A short sentence, decisive or cynical, was generally sufficient, a question, an unqualified abandonment of his ministers, whose face would not be saved, or a display of obstinacy reinforced by a few words in a piquantly delivered English.[6] But speech and passion were not lacking when they were wanted, and the sudden outburst of words, often followed by a fit of deep coughing from the chest, produced their impression rather by force and surprise than by persuasion.

Not infrequently Mr. Lloyd George, after delivering a speech in English, would, during the period of its interpretation into French, cross the hearthrug to the President to reinforce his case by some *ad hominem* argument in private conversation, or to sound the ground for a compromise,—and this would sometimes be the signal for a general upheaval and disorder. The President's advisers would press round him, a moment later the British experts would dribble across to learn the result or see that all was well, and next the French would be there, a little suspicious lest the others were arranging something behind them, until all the room were on their feet and conversation was general in both languages. My last and most vivid impression is of such a scene—the President and the Prime Minister as the center of a surging mob and a babel of sound, a welter of eager, impromptu compromises and counter-compromises, all sound and fury signifying nothing, on what was an unreal question anyhow, the great issues of the morning's meeting forgotten and neglected; and Clemenceau silent and aloof on the outskirts—for nothing which touched the security of France was forward—throned, in his gray gloves, on the brocade chair, dry in soul and empty of hope, very old and tired, but surveying the scene with a cynical and almost impish air; and when at last silence was restored and the company had returned to their places, it was to discover that he had disappeared.

He felt about France what Pericles felt of Athens—unique value in her, nothing else mattering; but his theory of politics was Bismarck's. He had one illusion—France; and one disillusion—mankind, including Frenchmen, and his colleagues not least. His principles for the peace can be expressed simply. In the first place, he was a foremost believer in the view of German psychology that the German understands and can understand nothing but intimidation, that he is without generosity or remorse in negotiation, that there is no advantage he will not take of you, and no extent to which he will not demean himself for profit, that he is without honor, pride, or mercy. Therefore you must never negotiate with a German or conciliate him; you must dictate to him. On no other terms will he respect you, or will you prevent him from cheating you. But it is doubtful how far he thought these characteristics peculiar to Germany, or whether his candid view of some other nations was fundamentally different. His philosophy had, therefore, no place for "sentimentality" in international relations. Nations are real things, of whom you love one and feel for the rest indifference—or hatred. The glory of the nation you love is a desirable end,—but generally to be obtained at your neighbor's expense. The politics of power are inevitable, and there is nothing very new to learn about this war or the end it was fought for; England had destroyed, as in each preceding century, a trade rival; a mighty chapter had been closed in the secular struggle between the glories of Germany and of France. Prudence required some measure of lip service to the "ideals" of foolish Americans and hypocritical Englishmen; but it would be stupid to believe that there is much room in the world, as it really is, for such affairs as the League of Nations, or any sense in the principle of self-determination except as an ingenious formula for rearranging the balance of power in one's own interests.

These, however, are generalities. In tracing the practical details of the Peace which he thought necessary for the power and the security of France, we must go back to the historical causes which had operated during his lifetime. Before the Franco-German war the populations of France and Germany were approximately equal; but the coal and iron and shipping of Germany were in their infancy, and the wealth of France was greatly superior. Even after the loss of Alsace-Lorraine there was no great discrepancy between the real resources of the two countries. But in the intervening period the relative position had changed completely. By 1914 the population of Germany was nearly seventy per cent in excess of that of France; she had become one of the first manufacturing and trading nations of the world; her technical skill and her means for the production of future wealth were unequaled. France on the other hand had a stationary or declining population, and, relatively to others, had fallen seriously behind in wealth and in the power to produce it.

In spite, therefore, of France's victorious issue from the present struggle (with the aid, this time, of England and America), her future position remained precarious in the eyes of one who took the view that European civil war is to be regarded as a normal, or at least a recurrent, state of affairs for the future, and that the sort of conflicts between organized great powers which have occupied the past hundred years will also engage the next. According to this vision of the future, European history is to be a perpetual prize-fight, of which France has won this round, but of which this round is certainly not the last. From the belief that essentially the old order does not change, being based on human nature which is always the same, and from a consequent skepticism of all that class of doctrine which the League of Nations stands for, the policy of France and of Clemenceau followed logically. For a Peace of magnanimity or of fair and equal treatment, based on such "ideology" as the Fourteen Points of the President, could only have the effect of shortening the interval of Germany's recovery and hastening the day when she will once again hurl at France her greater numbers and her superior resources and technical skill. Hence the necessity of "guarantees"; and each guarantee that was

36

taken, by increasing irritation and thus the probability of a subsequent *Revanche* by Germany, made necessary yet further provisions to crush. Thus, as soon as this view of the world is adopted and the other discarded, a demand for a Carthaginian Peace is inevitable, to the full extent of the momentary power to impose it. For Clemenceau made no pretense of considering himself bound by the Fourteen Points and left chiefly to others such concoctions as were necessary from time to time to save the scruples or the face of the President.

So far as possible, therefore, it was the policy of France to set the clock back and to undo what, since 1870, the progress of Germany had accomplished. By loss of territory and other measures her population was to be curtailed; but chiefly the economic system, upon which she depended for her new strength, the vast fabric built upon iron, coal, and transport must be destroyed. If France could seize, even in part, what Germany was compelled to drop, the inequality of strength between the two rivals for European hegemony might be remedied for many generations.

Hence sprang those cumulative provisions for the destruction of highly organized economic life which we shall examine in the next chapter.

This is the policy of an old man, whose most vivid impressions and most lively imagination are of the past and not of the future. He sees the issue in terms, of France and Germany not of humanity and of European civilization struggling forwards to a new order. The war has bitten into his consciousness somewhat differently from ours, and he neither expects nor hopes that we are at the threshold of a new age.

It happens, however, that it is not only an ideal question that is at issue. My purpose in this book is to show that the Carthaginian Peace is not *practically* right or possible. Although the school of thought from which it springs is aware of the economic factor, it overlooks, nevertheless, the deeper economic tendencies which are to govern the future. The clock cannot be set back. You cannot restore Central Europe to 1870 without setting up such strains in the European structure and letting loose such human and spiritual forces as, pushing beyond frontiers and races, will overwhelm not only you and your "guarantees," but your institutions, and the existing order of your Society.

By what legerdemain was this policy substituted for the Fourteen Points, and how did the President come to accept it? The answer to these questions is difficult and depends on elements of character and psychology and on the subtle influence of surroundings, which are hard to detect and harder still to describe. But, if ever the action of a single individual matters, the collapse of The President has been one of the decisive moral events of history; and I must make an attempt to explain it. What a place the President held in the hearts and hopes of the world when he sailed to us in the *George Washington!* What a great man came to Europe in those early days of our victory!

In November, 1918, the armies of Foch and the words of Wilson had brought us sudden escape from what was swallowing up all we cared for. The conditions seemed favorable beyond any expectation. The victory was so complete that fear need play no part in the settlement. The enemy had laid down his arms in reliance on a solemn compact as to the general character of the Peace, the terms of which seemed to assure a settlement of justice and magnanimity and a fair hope for a restoration of the broken current of life. To make assurance certain the President was coming himself to set the seal on his work.

When President Wilson left Washington he enjoyed a prestige and a moral influence throughout the world unequaled in history. His bold and measured words carried to the peoples of Europe above and beyond the voices of their own politicians. The enemy peoples trusted him to carry out the compact he had made with them; and the Allied peoples acknowledged him not as a victor only but almost as a prophet. In addition to this moral influence the realities of power were in his hands. The American armies were at the height of their numbers, discipline, and equipment. Europe was in complete dependence on the food supplies of the United States; and financially she was even more absolutely at their mercy. Europe not only already owed the United States more than she could pay; but only a large measure of further assistance could save her from starvation and bankruptcy. Never had a philosopher held such weapons wherewith to bind the princes of this world. How the crowds of the European capitals pressed about the carriage of the President! With what curiosity, anxiety, and hope we sought a glimpse of the features and bearing of the man of destiny who, coming from the West, was to bring healing to the wounds of the ancient parent of his civilization and lay for us the foundations of the future.

The disillusion was so complete, that some of those who had trusted most hardly dared speak of it. Could it be true? they asked of those who returned from Paris. Was the Treaty really as bad as it seemed? What had happened to the President? What weakness or what misfortune had led to so extraordinary, so unlooked-for a betrayal?

Yet the causes were very ordinary and human. The President was not a hero or a prophet; he was not even a philosopher; but a generously intentioned man, with many of the weaknesses of other human beings, and lacking that dominating intellectual equipment which would have been necessary to cope with the subtle and dangerous spellbinders whom a tremendous clash of forces and personalities had brought to the top as triumphant masters in the swift game of give and take, face to face in Council,—a game of which he had no experience at all.

We had indeed quite a wrong idea of the President. We knew him to be solitary and aloof, and believed him very strong-willed and obstinate. We did not figure him as a man of detail, but the clearness with which he had taken hold of certain main ideas would, we thought, in combination with his tenacity, enable him to sweep through cobwebs. Besides these qualities he would have the objectivity, the cultivation, and the wide knowledge of the student. The great distinction of language which had marked his famous Notes seemed to indicate a man of lofty and powerful imagination. His portraits indicated a fine presence and a commanding delivery. With all this he had attained and held with increasing authority the first position in a country where the arts of the politician are not neglected. All of which, without expecting the impossible, seemed a fine combination of qualities for the matter in hand.

The first impression of Mr. Wilson at close quarters was to impair some but not all of these illusions. His head and features were finely cut and exactly like his photographs, and the muscles of his neck and the carriage of his head were distinguished. But, like Odysseus, the President looked wiser when he was seated; and his hands, though capable and fairly strong, were wanting in sensitiveness and finesse. The first glance at the President suggested not only that, whatever else he might be, his temperament was not primarily that of the student or the scholar, but that he had not much even of that culture of the world which marks M. Clemenceau and Mr. Balfour as exquisitely cultivated gentlemen of their class and generation. But more serious than this, he was not only insensitive to his surroundings in the external sense, he was not sensitive to his environment at all. What chance could such a man have against Mr. Lloyd George's unerring, almost medium-like, sensibility to every one immediately round him? To see the British Prime Minister watching the company, with six or seven senses not available to ordinary men, judging character, motive, and subconscious impulse, perceiving what each was thinking and even what each was going to say next, and compounding with telepathic instinct the argument or appeal best suited to the vanity, weakness, or self-interest of his immediate auditor, was to realize that the poor President would be playing blind man's buff in that party. Never could a man have stepped into the parlor a more perfect and predestined victim to the finished accomplishments of the Prime Minister. The Old World was tough in wickedness anyhow; the Old World's heart of stone might blunt the sharpest blade of the bravest knight-errant. But this blind and deaf Don Quixote was entering a cavern where the swift and glittering blade was in the hands of the adversary.

But if the President was not the philosopher-king, what was he? After all he was a man who had spent much of his life at a University. He was by no means a business man or an ordinary party politician, but a man of force, personality, and importance. What, then, was his temperament?

The clue once found was illuminating. The President was like a Nonconformist minister, perhaps a Presbyterian. His thought and his temperament wore essentially theological not intellectual, with all the strength and the weakness of that manner of thought, feeling, and expression. It is a type of which there are not now in England and Scotland such magnificent specimens as formerly; but this description, nevertheless, will give the ordinary Englishman the distinctest impression of the President.

With this picture of him in mind, we can return to the actual course of events. The President's program for the World, as set forth in his speeches and his Notes, had displayed a spirit and a purpose so admirable that the last desire of his sympathizers was to criticize details,—the details, they felt, were quite rightly not filled in at present, but would be in due course. It was commonly believed at the commencement of the Paris Conference that the President had thought out, with the aid of a large body of advisers, a comprehensive scheme not only for the League of Nations, but for the embodiment of the Fourteen Points in an actual Treaty of Peace. But in fact the President had thought out nothing; when it came to practice his ideas were nebulous and incomplete. He had no plan, no scheme, no constructive ideas whatever for clothing with the flesh of life the commandments which he had thundered from the White House. He could have preached a sermon on any of them or have addressed a stately prayer to the Almighty for their fulfilment; but he could not frame their concrete application to the actual state of Europe.

He not only had no proposals in detail, but he was in many respects, perhaps inevitably, ill-informed as to European conditions. And not only was he ill-informed—that was true of Mr. Lloyd George also—but his mind was slow and unadaptable. The President's slowness amongst the Europeans was noteworthy. He could not, all in a minute, take in what the rest were saying, size up the situation with a glance, frame a reply, and meet the case by a slight change of ground; and he was liable, therefore, to defeat by the mere swiftness, apprehension, and agility of a Lloyd George. There can seldom have been a statesman of the first rank more incompetent than the President in the agilities of the council chamber. A moment often arrives when substantial victory is yours if by some slight appearance of a concession you can save the face of the opposition or conciliate them by a restatement of your proposal helpful to them and not injurious to anything essential to yourself. The President was not equipped with this simple and usual artfulness. His mind was too slow and unresourceful to be ready with *any* alternatives. The President was capable of digging his toes in and refusing to budge, as he did over Fiume. But he had no other mode of defense, and it needed as a rule but little manoeuvering by his opponents to prevent matters from coming to such a head until it was too late. By pleasantness and an appearance of conciliation, the President would be manoeuvered off his ground, would miss the moment for digging his toes in, and, before he knew where he had been got to, it was too late. Besides, it is impossible month after month in intimate and ostensibly friendly converse between close associates, to be digging the toes in all the time. Victory would only have been possible to one who had always a sufficiently lively apprehension of the position as a whole to reserve his fire and know for certain the rare exact moments for decisive action. And for that the President was far too slow-minded and bewildered.

He did not remedy these defects by seeking aid from the collective wisdom of his lieutenants. He had gathered round him for the economic chapters of the Treaty a very able group of business men; but they were inexperienced in public affairs, and knew (with one or two exceptions) as little of Europe as he did, and they were only called in irregularly as he might need them for a particular purpose. Thus the aloofness which had been found effective in Washington was maintained, and the abnormal reserve of his nature did not allow near him any one who aspired to moral equality or the continuous exercise of influence. His fellow-plenipotentiaries were dummies; and even the trusted Colonel House, with vastly more knowledge of men and of Europe than the President, from whose sensitiveness the President's dullness had gained so much, fell into the background as time went on. All this was encouraged by his colleagues on the Council of Four, who, by the break-up of the Council of Ten, completed the isolation which the President's own temperament had initiated. Thus day after day and week after week, he allowed himself to be closeted, unsupported, unadvised, and alone, with men much sharper than himself, in situations of supreme difficulty, where he needed for success every description of resource, fertility, and knowledge. He allowed himself to be drugged by their atmosphere, to discuss on the basis of their plans and of their data, and to be led along their paths.

These and other various causes combined to produce the following situation. The reader must remember that the processes which are here compressed into a few pages took place slowly, gradually, insidiously, over a period of about five months.

As the President had thought nothing out, the Council was generally working on the basis of a French or British draft. He had to take up, therefore, a persistent attitude of obstruction, criticism, and negation, if the draft was to become at all in line with his own ideas and purpose. If he was met on some points with apparent generosity (for there was always a safe margin of quite preposterous suggestions which no one took seriously), it was difficult for him not to yield on others. Compromise was inevitable, and never to compromise on the essential, very difficult. Besides, he was soon made to appear to be taking the German part and laid himself open to the suggestion (to which he was foolishly and unfortunately sensitive) of being "pro-German."

After a display of much principle and dignity in the early days of the Council of Ten, he discovered that there were certain very important points in the program of his French, British, or Italian colleague, as the case might be, of which he was incapable of securing the surrender by the methods of secret diplomacy. What then was he to do in the last resort? He could let the Conference drag on an endless length by the exercise of sheer obstinacy. He could break it up and return to America in a rage with nothing settled. Or he could attempt an appeal to the world over the heads of the Conference. These were wretched alternatives, against each of which a great deal could be said. They were also very risky,—especially for a politician. The President's mistaken policy over the Congressional election had weakened his personal position in his own country, and it was by no means certain that the American public would support him in a position of intransigency. It would mean a campaign in which the issues would be clouded by every sort of personal and party consideration, and who could say if right would triumph in a struggle which would certainly not be decided on its merits? Besides, any open rupture with his colleagues would certainly bring upon his head the blind passions of "anti-German" resentment with which the public of all allied countries were still inspired. They would not listen to his arguments. They would not be cool enough to treat the issue as one of international morality or of the right governance of Europe. The cry would simply be that, for various sinister and selfish reasons, the President wished "to let the Hun off." The almost unanimous voice of the French and British Press could be anticipated. Thus, if he threw down the gage publicly he might be defeated. And if he were defeated, would not the final Peace be far worse than if he were to retain his prestige and endeavor to make it as good as the limiting conditions of European politics would allow, him? But above all, if he were defeated, would he not lose the League of Nations? And was not this, after all, by far the most important issue for the future happiness of the world? The Treaty would be altered and softened by time. Much in it which now seemed so vital would become trifling, and much which was impracticable would for that very reason never happen. But the League, even in an imperfect form, was permanent; it was the first commencement of a new principle in the government of the world; Truth and Justice in international relations could not be established in a few months,—they must be born in due course by the slow gestation of the League. Clemenceau had been clever enough to let it be seen that he would swallow the League at a price.

At the crisis of his fortunes the President was a lonely man. Caught up in the toils of the Old World, he stood in great need of sympathy, of moral support, of the enthusiasm of masses. But buried in the Conference, stifled in the hot and poisoned atmosphere of Paris, no echo reached him from the outer world, and no throb of passion, sympathy, or encouragement from his silent constituents in all countries. He felt that the blaze of popularity which had greeted his arrival in Europe was already dimmed; the Paris Press jeered at him openly; his political opponents at home were taking advantage of his absence to create an atmosphere against him; England was cold, critical, and unresponsive. He had so formed his *entourage* that he did not receive through private channels the current of faith and enthusiasm of which the public sources seemed

41

dammed up. He needed, but lacked, the added strength of collective faith. The German terror still overhung us, and even the sympathetic public was very cautious; the enemy must not be encouraged, our friends must be supported, this was not the time for discord or agitations, the President must be trusted to do his best. And in this drought the flower of the President's faith withered and dried up.

Thus it came to pass that the President countermanded the *George Washington*, which, in a moment of well-founded rage, he had ordered to be in readiness to carry him from the treacherous halls of Paris back to the seat of his authority, where he could have felt himself again. But as soon, alas, as he had taken the road of compromise, the defects, already indicated, of his temperament and of his equipment, were fatally apparent. He could take the high line; he could practise obstinacy; he could write Notes from Sinai or Olympus; he could remain unapproachable in the White House or even in the Council of Ten and be safe. But if he once stepped down to the intimate equality of the Four, the game was evidently up.

Now it was that what I have called his theological or Presbyterian temperament became dangerous. Having decided that some concessions were unavoidable, he might have sought by firmness and address and the use of the financial power of the United States to secure as much as he could of the substance, even at some sacrifice of the letter. But the President was not capable of so clear an understanding with himself as this implied. He was too conscientious. Although compromises were now necessary, he remained a man of principle and the Fourteen Points a contract absolutely binding upon him. He would do nothing that was not honorable; he would do nothing that was not just and right; he would do nothing that was contrary to his great profession of faith. Thus, without any abatement of the verbal inspiration of the Fourteen Points, they became a document for gloss and interpretation and for all the intellectual apparatus of self-deception, by which, I daresay, the President's forefathers had persuaded themselves that the course they thought it necessary to take was consistent with every syllable of the Pentateuch.

The President's attitude to his colleagues had now become: I want to meet you so far as I can; I see your difficulties and I should like to be able to agree to what you propose; but I can do nothing that is not just and right, and you must first of all show me that what you want does really fall within the words of the pronouncements which are binding on me. Then began the weaving of that web of sophistry and Jesuitical exegesis that was finally to clothe with insincerity the language and substance of the whole Treaty. The word was issued to the witches of all Paris:

> Fair   is   foul,   and   foul   is   fair,
> Hover through the fog and filthy air.

The subtlest sophisters and most hypocritical draftsmen were set to work, and produced many ingenious exercises which might have deceived for more than an hour a cleverer man than the President.

Thus instead of saying that German-Austria is prohibited from uniting with Germany except by leave of France (which would be inconsistent with the principle of self-determination), the Treaty, with delicate draftsmanship, states that "Germany acknowledges and will respect strictly the independence of Austria, within the frontiers which may be fixed in a Treaty between that State and the Principal Allied and Associated Powers; she agrees that this independence shall be inalienable, except with the consent of the Council of the League of Nations," which sounds, but is not, quite different. And who knows but that the President forgot that another part of the Treaty provides that for this purpose the Council of the League must be *unanimous*.

Instead of giving Danzig to Poland, the Treaty establishes Danzig as a "Free" City, but includes this "Free" City within the Polish Customs frontier, entrusts to Poland the control of the river and railway system, and provides that "the Polish Government shall undertake the conduct of the foreign relations of the Free City of Danzig as well as the diplomatic protection of citizens of that city when abroad."

In placing the river system of Germany under foreign control, the Treaty speaks of declaring international those "river systems which naturally provide more than one State with access to the sea, with or without transhipment from one vessel to another."

Such instances could be multiplied. The honest and intelligible purpose of French policy, to limit the population of Germany and weaken her economic system, is clothed, for the President's sake, in the august language of freedom and international equality.

But perhaps the most decisive moment, in the disintegration of the President's moral position and the clouding of his mind, was when at last, to the dismay of his advisers, he allowed himself to be persuaded that the expenditure of the Allied Governments on pensions and separation allowances could be fairly regarded as "damage done to the civilian population of the Allied and Associated Powers by German aggression by land, by sea, and from the air," in a sense in which the other expenses of the war could not be so regarded. It was a long theological struggle in which, after the rejection of many different arguments, the President finally capitulated before a masterpiece of the sophist's art.

At last the work was finished; and the President's conscience was still intact. In spite of everything, I believe that his temperament allowed him to leave Paris a really sincere man; and it is probable that to this day he is genuinely convinced that the Treaty contains practically nothing inconsistent with his former professions.

But the work was too complete, and to this was due the last tragic episode of the drama. The reply of Brockdorff-Rantzau inevitably took the line that Germany had laid down her arms on the basis of certain assurances, and that the Treaty in many particulars was not consistent with these assurances. But this was exactly what the President could not admit; in the sweat of solitary contemplation and with prayers to God he had done *nothing* that was not just and right; for the President to admit that the German reply had force in it was to destroy his self-respect and to disrupt the inner equipoise of his soul; and every instinct of his stubborn nature rose in self-protection. In the language of medical psychology, to suggest to the President that the Treaty was an abandonment of his professions was to touch on the raw a Freudian complex. It was a subject intolerable to discuss, and every subconscious instinct plotted to defeat its further exploration.

Thus it was that Clemenceau brought to success, what had seemed to be, a few months before, the extraordinary and impossible proposal that the Germans should not be heard. If only the President had not been so conscientious, if only he had not concealed from himself what he had been doing, even at the last moment he was in, a position to have recovered lost ground and to have achieved some very considerable successes. But the President was set. His arms and legs had been spliced by the surgeons to a certain posture, and they must be broken again before they could be altered. To his horror, Mr. Lloyd George, desiring at the last moment all the moderation he dared, discovered that he could not in five days persuade the President of error in what it had taken five months to prove to him to be just and right. After all, it was harder to de-bamboozle this old Presbyterian than it had been to bamboozle him; for the former involved his belief in and respect for himself.

Thus in the last act the President stood for stubbornness and a refusal of conciliations.

FOOTNOTES:

[6]He alone amongst the Four could speak and understand both languages, Orlando knowing only French and the Prime Minister and President only English; and it is of historical importance that Orlando and the President had no direct means of communication.

CHAPTER IV

THE TREATY

The thoughts which I have expressed in the second chapter were not present to the mind of Paris. The future life of Europe was not their concern; its means of livelihood was not their anxiety. Their preoccupations, good and bad alike, related to frontiers and nationalities, to the balance of power, to imperial aggrandizements, to the future enfeeblement of a strong and dangerous enemy, to revenge, and to the shifting by the victors of their unbearable financial burdens on to the shoulders of the defeated.

Two rival schemes for the future polity of the world took the field,—the Fourteen Points of the President, and the Carthaginian Peace of M. Clemenceau. Yet only one of these was entitled to take the field; for the enemy had not surrendered unconditionally, but on agreed terms as to the general character of the Peace.

This aspect of what happened cannot, unfortunately, be passed over with a word, for in the minds of many Englishmen at least it has been a subject of very great misapprehension. Many persons believe that the Armistice Terms constituted the first

Contract concluded between the Allied and Associated Powers and the German Government, and that we entered the Conference with our hands, free, except so far as these Armistice Terms might bind us. This was not the case. To make the position plain, it is necessary briefly to review the history, of the negotiations which began with the German Note of October 5, 1918, and concluded with President Wilson's Note of November 5, 1918.

On October 5, 1918, the German Government addressed a brief Note to the President accepting the Fourteen Points and asking for Peace negotiations. The President's reply of October 8 asked if he was to understand definitely that the German Government accepted "the terms laid down" in Fourteen Points and in his subsequent Addresses and "that its object in entering into discussion would be only to agree upon the practical details of their application." He added that the evacuation of invaded territory must be a prior condition of an Armistice. On October 12 the German Government returned an unconditional affirmative to these questions;-"its object in entering into discussions would be only to agree upon practical details of the application of these terms." On October 14, having received this affirmative answer, the President made a further communication to make clear the points: (1) that the details of the Armistice would have to be left to the military advisers of the United States and the Allies, and must provide absolutely against the possibility of Germany's resuming hostilities; (2) that submarine warfare must cease if these conversations were to continue; and (3) that he required further guarantees of the representative character of the Government with which he was dealing. On October 20 Germany accepted points (1) and (2), and pointed out, as regards (3), that she now had a Constitution and a Government dependent for its authority on the Reichstag. On October 23 the President announced that, "having received the solemn and explicit assurance of the German Government that it unreservedly accepts the terms of peace laid down in his Address to the Congress of the United States on January 8, 1918 (the Fourteen Points), and the principles of settlement enunciated in his subsequent Addresses, particularly the Address of September 27, and that it is ready to discuss the details of their application," he has communicated the above correspondence to the Governments of the Allied Powers "with the suggestion that, if these Governments are disposed to effect peace upon the terms and principles indicated," they will ask their military advisers to draw up Armistice Terms of such a character as to "ensure to the Associated Governments the unrestricted power to safeguard and enforce the details of the peace to which the German Government has agreed." At the end of this Note the President hinted more openly than in that of October 14 at the abdication of the Kaiser. This completes the preliminary negotiations to which the President alone was a party, adding without the Governments of the Allied Powers.

On November 5, 1918, the President transmitted to Germany the reply he had received from the Governments associated with him, and added that Marshal Foch had been authorized to communicate the terms of an armistice to properly accredited representatives. In this reply the Allied Governments, "subject to the qualifications which follow, declare their willingness to make peace with the Government of Germany on the terms of peace laid down in the President's Address to Congress of January 8, 1918, and the principles of settlement enunciated in his subsequent Addresses." The qualifications in question were two in number. The first related to the Freedom of the

Seas, as to which they "reserved to themselves complete freedom." The second related to Reparation and ran as follows:—"Further, in the conditions of peace laid down in his Address to Congress on the 8th January, 1918 the President declared that invaded territories must be restored as well as evacuated and made free. The Allied Governments feel that no doubt ought to be allowed to exist as to what this provision implies. By it they understand that compensation will be made by Germany for all damage done to the civilian population of the Allies and to their property by the aggression of Germany by land, by sea, and from the air."[7]

The nature of the Contract between Germany and the Allies resulting from this exchange of documents is plain and unequivocal. The terms of the peace are to be in accordance with the Addresses of the President, and the purpose of the Peace Conference is "to discuss the details of their application." The circumstances of the Contract were of an unusually solemn and binding character; for one of the conditions of it was that Germany should agree to Armistice Terms which were to be such as would leave her helpless. Germany having rendered herself helpless in reliance on the Contract, the honor of the Allies was peculiarly involved in fulfilling their part and, if there were ambiguities, in not using their position to take advantage of them.

What, then, was the substance of this Contract to which the Allies had bound themselves? An examination of the documents shows that, although a large part of the Addresses is concerned with spirit, purpose, and intention, and not with concrete solutions, and that many questions requiring a settlement in the Peace Treaty are not touched on, nevertheless, there are certain questions which they settle definitely. It is true that within somewhat wide limits the Allies still had a free hand. Further, it is difficult to apply on a contractual basis those passages which deal with spirit, purpose, and intention;—every man must judge for himself whether, in view of them, deception or hypocrisy has been practised. But there remain, as will be seen below, certain important issues on which the Contract is unequivocal.

In addition to the Fourteen Points of January 18, 1918, the Addresses of the President which form part of the material of the Contract are four in number,—before the Congress on February 11; at Baltimore on April 6; at Mount Vernon on July 4; and at New York on September 27, the last of these being specially referred to in the Contract. I venture to select from these Addresses those engagements of substance, avoiding repetitions, which are most relevant to the German Treaty. The parts I omit add to, rather than detract from, those I quote; but they chiefly relate to intention, and are perhaps too vague and general to be interpreted contractually.[8]

The Fourteen Points.—(3). "The removal, so far as possible, of all economic barriers and the establishment of an equality of trade conditions among *all* the nations consenting to the Peace and associating themselves for its maintenance." (4). "Adequate guarantees *given and taken* that national armaments will be reduced to the lowest point consistent with domestic safety." (5). "A free, open-minded, and absolutely impartial adjustment of all colonial claims," regard being had to the interests of the populations concerned. (6), (7), (8), and (11). The evacuation and "restoration" of all invaded territory, especially of Belgium. To this must be added the rider of the Allies, claiming compensation for all damage done to civilians and their property by land, by sea, and from the air (quoted in full above). (8). The righting of "the wrong done to France by

Prussia in 1871 in the matter of Alsace-Lorraine." (13). An independent Poland, including "the territories inhabited by indisputably Polish populations" and "assured a free and secure access to the sea." (14). The League of Nations.

Before the Congress, February 11.—"There shall be no annexations, *no contributions, no punitive damages*.... Self-determination is not a mere phrase. It is an imperative principle of action which statesmen will henceforth ignore at their peril.... Every territorial settlement involved in this war must be made in the interest and for the benefit of the populations concerned, and not as a part of any mere adjustment or compromise of claims amongst rival States."

New York, September 27.—(1) "The impartial justice meted out must involve no discrimination between those to whom we wish to be just and those to whom we do not wish to be just." (2) "No special or separate interest of any single nation or any group of nations can be made the basis of any part of the settlement which is not consistent with the common interest of all." (3) "There can be no leagues or alliances or special covenants and understandings within the general and common family of the League of Nations." (4) "There can be no special selfish economic combinations within the League and no employment of any form of economic boycott or exclusion, except as the power of economic penalty by exclusion from the markets of the world may be vested in the League of Nations itself as a means of discipline and control." (5) "All international agreements and treaties of every kind must be made known in their entirety to the rest of the world."

This wise and magnanimous program for the world had passed on November 5, 1918 beyond the region of idealism and aspiration, and had become part of a solemn contract to which all the Great Powers of the world had put their signature. But it was lost, nevertheless, in the morass of Paris;—the spirit of it altogether, the letter in parts ignored and in other parts distorted.

The German observations on the draft Treaty of Peace were largely a comparison between the terms of this understanding, on the basis of which the German nation had agreed to lay down its arms, and the actual provisions of the document offered them for signature thereafter. The German commentators had little difficulty in showing that the draft Treaty constituted a breach of engagements and of international morality comparable with their own offense in the invasion of Belgium. Nevertheless, the German reply was not in all its parts a document fully worthy of the occasion, because in spite of the justice and importance of much of its contents, a truly broad treatment and high dignity of outlook were a little wanting, and the general effect lacks the simple treatment, with the dispassionate objectivity of despair which the deep passions of the occasion might have evoked. The Allied governments gave it, in any case, no serious consideration, and I doubt if anything which the German delegation could have said at that stage of the proceedings would have much influenced the result.

The commonest virtues of the individual are often lacking in the spokesmen of nations; a statesman representing not himself but his country may prove, without incurring excessive blame—as history often records—vindictive, perfidious, and egotistic. These qualities are familiar in treaties imposed by victors. But the German delegation did not succeed in exposing in burning and prophetic words the quality which chiefly distinguishes this transaction from all its historical predecessors—its insincerity.

This theme, however, must be for another pen than mine. I am mainly concerned in what follows, not with the justice of the Treaty,—neither with the demand for penal justice against the enemy, nor with the obligation of contractual justice on the victor,—but with its wisdom and with its consequences.

I propose, therefore, in this chapter to set forth baldly the principal economic provisions of the Treaty, reserving, however, for the next my comments on the Reparation Chapter and on Germany's capacity to meet the payments there demanded from her.

The German economic system as it existed before the war depended on three main factors: I. Overseas commerce as represented by her mercantile marine, her colonies, her foreign investments, her exports, and the overseas connections of her merchants; II. The exploitation of her coal and iron and the industries built upon them; III. Her transport and tariff system. Of these the first, while not the least important, was certainly the most vulnerable. The Treaty aims at the systematic destruction of all three, but principally of the first two.

I

(1) Germany has ceded to the Allies *all* the vessels of her mercantile marine exceeding 1600 tons gross, half the vessels between 1000 tons and 1600 tons, and one quarter of her trawlers and other fishing boats.[9] The cession is comprehensive, including not only vessels flying the German flag, but also all vessels owned by Germans but flying other flags, and all vessels under construction as well as those afloat.[10] Further, Germany undertakes, if required, to build for the Allies such types of ships as they may specify up to 200,000 tons[11] annually for five years, the value of these ships being credited to Germany against what is due from her for Reparation.[12]

Thus the German mercantile marine is swept from the seas and cannot be restored for many years to come on a scale adequate to meet the requirements of her own commerce. For the present, no lines will run from Hamburg, except such as foreign nations may find it worth while to establish out of their surplus tonnage. Germany will have to pay to foreigners for the carriage of her trade such charges as they may be able to exact, and will receive only such conveniences as it may suit them to give her. The prosperity of German ports and commerce can only revive, it would seem, in proportion as she succeeds in bringing under her effective influence the merchant marines of Scandinavia and of Holland.

(2) Germany has ceded to the Allies "all her rights and titles over her oversea possessions."[13] This cession not only applies to sovereignty but extends on unfavorable terms to Government property, all of which, including railways, must be surrendered without payment, while, on the other hand, the German Government remains liable for any debt which may have been incurred for the purchase or construction of this property, or for the development of the colonies generally.[14]

In distinction from the practice ruling in the case of most similar cessions in recent history, the property and persons of private German nationals, as distinct from their Government, are also injuriously affected. The Allied Government exercising authority in any former German colony "may make such provisions as it thinks fit with reference to the repatriation from them of German nationals and to the conditions upon which German subjects of European origin shall, or shall not, be allowed to reside, hold property, trade or exercise a profession in them."[15] All contracts and agreements in favor of German nationals for the construction or exploitation of public works lapse to the Allied Governments as part of the payment due for Reparation.

But these terms are unimportant compared with the more comprehensive provision by which "the Allied and Associated Powers reserve the right to retain and liquidate *all* property, rights, and interests belonging at the date of the coming into force of the present Treaty to German nationals, or companies controlled by them," within the former German colonies.[16] This wholesale expropriation of private property is to take place without the Allies affording any compensation to the individuals expropriated, and the proceeds will be employed, first, to meet private debts due to Allied nationals from any German nationals, and second, to meet claims due from Austrian, Hungarian, Bulgarian, or Turkish nationals. Any balance may either be returned by the liquidating Power direct to Germany, or retained by them. If retained, the proceeds must be transferred to the Reparation Commission for Germany's credit in the Reparation account.[17]

In short, not only are German sovereignty and German influence extirpated from the whole of her former oversea possessions, but the persons and property of her nationals resident or owning property in those parts are deprived of legal status and legal security.

(3) The provisions just outlined in regard to the private property of Germans in the ex-German colonies apply equally to private German property in Alsace-Lorraine, except in so far as the French Government may choose to grant exceptions.[18] This is of much greater practical importance than the similar expropriation overseas because of the far higher value of the property involved and the closer interconnection, resulting from the great development of the mineral wealth of these provinces since 1871, of German economic interests there with those in Germany itself. Alsace-Lorraine has been part of the German Empire for nearly fifty years—a considerable majority of its population is German speaking—and it has been the scene of some of Germany's most important economic enterprises. Nevertheless, the property of those Germans who reside there, or who have invested in its industries, is now entirely at the disposal of the French Government without compensation, except in so far as the German Government itself may choose to afford it. The French Government is entitled to expropriate without compensation the personal property of private German citizens and German companies resident or situated within Alsace-Lorraine, the proceeds being credited in part satisfaction of various French claims. The severity of this provision is only mitigated to the extent that the French Government may expressly permit German nationals to continue to reside, in which case the above provision is not applicable. Government, State, and Municipal property, on the other hand, is to be ceded to France without any credit being given for it. This includes the railway system of the two provinces, together with its rolling-stock.[19] But while the property is taken over, liabilities contracted in respect of it in the form of public debts of any kind remain the liability of Germany. [20] The provinces also return to French sovereignty free and quit of their share of German war or pre-war dead-weight debt; nor does Germany receive a credit on this account in respect of Reparation.

(4) The expropriation of German private property is not limited, however, to the ex-German colonies and Alsace-Lorraine. The treatment of such property forms, indeed, a very significant and material section of the Treaty, which has not received as much attention as it merits, although it was the subject of exceptionally violent objection on the part of the German delegates at Versailles. So far as I know, there is no precedent in any peace treaty of recent history for the treatment of private property set forth below, and the German representatives urged that the precedent now established strikes a dangerous and immoral blow at the security of private property everywhere. This is an exaggeration, and the sharp distinction, approved by custom and convention during the past two centuries, between the property and rights of a State and the property and rights of its nationals is an artificial one, which is being rapidly put out of date by many other influences than the Peace Treaty, and is inappropriate to modern socialistic conceptions of the relations between the State and its citizens. It is true, however, that the Treaty strikes a destructive blow at a conception which lies at the root of much of so-called international law, as this has been expounded hitherto.

The principal provisions relating to the expropriation of German private property situated outside the frontiers of Germany, as these are now determined, are overlapping in their incidence, and the more drastic would seem in some cases to render the others unnecessary. Generally speaking, however, the more drastic and extensive provisions are not so precisely framed as those of more particular and limited application. They are as follows:—

(*a*) The Allies "reserve the right to retain and liquidate all property, rights and interests belonging at the date of the coming into force of the present Treaty to German nationals, or companies controlled by them, within their territories, colonies, possessions and protectorates, including territories ceded to them by the present Treaty."[21]

This is the extended version of the provision which has been discussed already in the case of the colonies and of Alsace-Lorraine. The value of the property so expropriated will be applied, in the first instance, to the satisfaction of private debts due from Germany to the nationals of the Allied Government within whose jurisdiction the liquidation takes place, and, second, to the satisfaction of claims arising out of the acts of Germany's former allies. Any balance, if the liquidating Government elects to retain it, must be credited in the Reparation account.[22] It is, however, a point of considerable importance that the liquidating Government is not compelled to transfer the balance to the Reparation Commission, but can, if it so decides, return the proceeds direct to Germany. For this will enable the United States, if they so wish, to utilize the very large balances, in the hands of their enemy-property custodian, to pay for the provisioning of Germany, without regard to the views of the Reparation Commission.

These provisions had their origin in the scheme for the mutual settlement of enemy debts by means of a Clearing House. Under this proposal it was hoped to avoid much trouble and litigation by making each of the Governments lately at war responsible for the collection of private *debts* due from its nationals to the nationals of any of the other Governments (the normal process of collection having been suspended by reason of the war), and for the distribution of the funds so collected to those of its nationals who had *claims* against the nationals of the other Governments, any final balance either way

50

being settled in cash. Such a scheme could have been completely bilateral and reciprocal. And so in part it is, the scheme being mainly reciprocal as regards the collection of commercial debts. But the completeness of their victory permitted the Allied Governments to introduce in their own favor many divergencies from reciprocity, of which the following are the chief: Whereas the property of Allied nationals within German jurisdiction reverts under the Treaty to Allied ownership on the conclusion of Peace, the property of Germans within Allied jurisdiction is to be retained and liquidated as described above, with the result that the whole of German property over a large part of the world can be expropriated, and the large properties now within the custody of Public Trustees and similar officials in the Allied countries may be retained permanently. In the second place, such German assets are chargeable, not only with the liabilities of Germans, but also, if they run to it, with "payment of the amounts due in respect of claims by the nationals of such Allied or Associated Power with regard to their property, rights, and interests in the territory of other Enemy Powers," as, for example, Turkey, Bulgaria, and Austria.[23] This is a remarkable provision, which is naturally non-reciprocal. In the third place, any final balance due to Germany on private account need not be paid over, but can be held against the various liabilities of the German Government.[24] The effective operation of these Articles is guaranteed by the delivery of deeds, titles, and information.[25] In the fourth place, pre-war contracts between Allied and German nationals may be canceled or revived at the option of the former, so that all such contracts which are in Germany's favor will be canceled, while, on the other hand, she will be compelled to fulfil those which are to her disadvantage.

(*b*) So far we have been concerned with German property within Allied jurisdiction. The next provision is aimed at the elimination of German interests in the territory of her neighbors and former allies, and of certain other countries. Under Article 260 of the Financial Clauses it is provided that the Reparation Commission may, within one year of the coming into force of the Treaty, demand that the German Government expropriate its nationals and deliver to the Reparation Commission "any rights and interests of German nationals in any public utility undertaking or in any concession[26] operating in Russia, China, Turkey, Austria, Hungary, and Bulgaria, or in the possessions or dependencies of these States, or in any territory formerly belonging to Germany or her allies, to be ceded by Germany or her allies to any Power or to be administered by a Mandatory under the present Treaty." This is a comprehensive description, overlapping in part the provisions dealt with under (*a*) above, but including, it should be noted, the new States and territories carved out of the former Russian, Austro-Hungarian, and Turkish Empires. Thus Germany's influence is eliminated and her capital confiscated in all those neighboring countries to which she might naturally look for her future livelihood, and for an outlet for her energy, enterprise, and technical skill.

The execution of this program in detail will throw on the Reparation Commission a peculiar task, as it will become possessor of a great number of rights and interests over a vast territory owing dubious obedience, disordered by war, disruption, and Bolshevism. The division of the spoils between the victors will also provide employment for a powerful office, whose doorsteps the greedy adventurers and jealous concession-hunters of twenty or thirty nations will crowd and defile.

Lest the Reparation Commission fail by ignorance to exercise its rights to the full, it is further provided that the German Government shall communicate to it within six months of the Treaty's coming into force a list of all the rights and interests in question, "whether already granted, contingent or not yet exercised," and any which are not so communicated within this period will automatically lapse in favor of the Allied Governments.[27] How far an edict of this character can be made binding on a German national, whose person and property lie outside the jurisdiction of his own Government, is an unsettled question; but all the countries specified in the above list are open to pressure by the Allied authorities, whether by the imposition of an appropriate Treaty clause or otherwise.

(c) There remains a third provision more sweeping than either of the above, neither of which affects German interests in *neutral* countries. The Reparation Commission is empowered up to May 1, 1921, to demand payment up to $5,000,000,000 *in such manner as they may fix*, "whether in gold, commodities, ships, securities or otherwise."[28] This provision has the effect of intrusting to the Reparation Commission for the period in question dictatorial powers over all German property of every description whatever. They can, under this Article, point to any specific business, enterprise, or property, whether within or outside Germany, and demand its surrender; and their authority would appear to extend not only to property existing at the date of the Peace, but also to any which may be created or acquired at any time in the course of the next eighteen months. For example, they could pick out—as presumably they will as soon as they are established—the fine and powerful German enterprise in South America known as the *Deutsche Ueberseeische Elektrizitätsgesellschaft* (the D.U.E.G.), and dispose of it to Allied interests. The clause is unequivocal and all-embracing. It is worth while to note in passing that it introduces a quite novel principle in the collection of indemnities. Hitherto, a sum has been fixed, and the nation mulcted has been left free to devise and select for itself the means of payment. But in this case the payees can (for a certain period) not only demand a certain sum but specify the particular kind of property in which payment is to be effected. Thus the powers of the Reparation Commission, with which I deal more particularly in the next chapter, can be employed to destroy Germany's commercial and economic organization as well as to exact payment.

The cumulative effect of (a), (b), and (c) (as well as of certain other minor provisions on which I have not thought it necessary to enlarge) is to deprive Germany (or rather to empower the Allies so to deprive her at their will—it is not yet accomplished) of everything she possesses outside her own frontiers as laid down in the Treaty. Not only are her oversea investments taken and her connections destroyed, but the same process of extirpation is applied in the territories of her former allies and of her immediate neighbors by land.

(5) Lest by some oversight the above provisions should overlook any possible contingencies, certain other Articles appear in the Treaty, which probably do not add very much in practical effect to those already described, but which deserve brief mention as showing the spirit of completeness in which the victorious Powers entered upon the economic subjection of their defeated enemy.

First of all there is a general clause of barrer and renunciation: "In territory outside her European frontiers as fixed by the present Treaty, Germany renounces all rights, titles and privileges whatever in or over territory which belonged to her or to her allies, and all rights, titles and privileges whatever their origin which she held as against the Allied and Associated Powers...."[29]

There follow certain more particular provisions. Germany renounces all rights and privileges she may have acquired in China.[30] There are similar provisions for Siam, [31] for Liberia,[32] for Morocco,[33] and for Egypt.[34] In the case of Egypt not only are special privileges renounced, but by Article 150 ordinary liberties are withdrawn, the Egyptian Government being accorded "complete liberty of action in regulating the status of German nationals and the conditions under which they may establish themselves in Egypt."

By Article 258 Germany renounces her right to any participation in any financial or economic organizations of an international character "operating in any of the Allied or Associated States, or in Austria, Hungary, Bulgaria or Turkey, or in the dependencies of these States, or in the former Russian Empire."

Generally speaking, only those pre-war treaties and conventions are revived which it suits the Allied Governments to revive, and those in Germany's favor may be allowed to lapse.[35]

It is evident, however, that none of these provisions are of any real importance, as compared with those described previously. They represent the logical completion of Germany's outlawry and economic subjection to the convenience of the Allies; but they do not add substantially to her effective disabilities.

II

The provisions relating to coal and iron are more important in respect of their ultimate consequences on Germany's internal industrial economy than for the money value immediately involved. The German Empire has been built more truly on coal and iron than on blood and iron. The skilled exploitation of the great coalfields of the Ruhr, Upper Silesia, and the Saar, alone made possible the development of the steel, chemical, and electrical industries which established her as the first industrial nation of continental Europe. One-third of Germany's population lives in towns of more than 20,000 inhabitants, an industrial concentration which is only possible on a foundation of coal and iron. In striking, therefore, at her coal supply, the French politicians were not mistaking their target. It is only the extreme immoderation, and indeed technical impossibility, of the Treaty's demands which may save the situation in the long-run.

(1) The Treaty strikes at Germany's coal supply in four ways:—

(i.) "As compensation for the destruction of the coal-mines in the north of France, and as part payment towards the total reparation due from Germany for the damage resulting from the war, Germany cedes to France in full and absolute possession, with exclusive rights of exploitation, unencumbered, and free from all debts and charges of any kind, the coal-mines situated in the Saar Basin."[36] While the administration of this district is vested for fifteen years in the League of Nations, it is to be observed that the mines are ceded to France absolutely. Fifteen years hence the population of the district will be called upon to indicate by plebiscite their desires as to the future sovereignty of the territory; and, in the event of their electing for union with Germany, Germany is to be entitled to repurchase the mines at a price payable in gold.[37]

The judgment of the world has already recognized the transaction of the Saar as an act of spoliation and insincerity. So far as compensation for the destruction of French coal-mines is concerned, this is provided for, as we shall see in a moment, elsewhere in the Treaty. "There is no industrial region in Germany," the German representatives have said without contradiction, "the population of which is so permanent, so homogeneous, and so little complex as that of the Saar district. Among more than 650,000 inhabitants, there were in 1918 less than 100 French. The Saar district has been German for more than 1,000 years. Temporary occupation as a result of warlike operations on the part of the French always terminated in a short time in the restoration of the country upon the conclusion of peace. During a period of 1048 years France has possessed the country for not quite 68 years in all. When, on the occasion of the first Treaty of Paris in 1814, a small portion of the territory now coveted was retained for France, the population raised the most energetic opposition and demanded 'reunion with their German fatherland,' to which they were 'related by language, customs, and religion.' After an occupation of one year and a quarter, this desire was taken into account in the second Treaty of Paris in 1815. Since then the country has remained uninterruptedly attached to Germany, and owes its economic development to that connection."

The French wanted the coal for the purpose of working the ironfields of Lorraine, and in the spirit of Bismarck they have taken it. Not precedent, but the verbal professions of the Allies, have rendered it indefensible.[38]

(ii.) Upper Silesia, a district without large towns, in which, however, lies one of the major coalfields of Germany with a production of about 23 per cent of the total German output of hard coal, is, subject to a plebiscite,[39] to be ceded to Poland. Upper Silesia was never part of historic Poland; but its population is mixed Polish, German, and Czecho-Slovakian, the precise proportions of which are disputed.[40] Economically it is intensely German; the industries of Eastern Germany depend upon it for their coal; and its loss would be a destructive blow at the economic structure of the German State.[41]

With the loss of the fields of Upper Silesia and the Saar, the coal supplies of Germany are diminished by not far short of one-third.

(iii.) Out of the coal that remains to her, Germany is obliged to make good year by year the estimated loss which France has incurred by the destruction and damage of war in the coalfields of her northern Provinces. In para. 2 of Annex V. to the Reparation Chapter, "Germany undertakes to deliver to France annually, for a period not exceeding ten years, an amount of coal equal to the difference between the annual production before the war of the coal-mines of the Nord and Pas de Calais, destroyed as a result of the war, and the production of the mines of the same area during the year in question: such delivery not to exceed 20,000,000 tons in any one year of the first five years, and 8,000,000 tons in any one year of the succeeding five years."

This is a reasonable provision if it stood by itself, and one which Germany should be able to fulfil if she were left her other resources to do it with.

(iv.) The final provision relating to coal is part of the general scheme of the Reparation Chapter by which the sums due for Reparation are to be partly paid in kind instead of in cash. As a part of the payment due for Reparation, Germany is to make the following deliveries of coal or equivalent in coke (the deliveries to France being wholly additional to the amounts available by the cession of the Saar or in compensation for destruction in Northern France):—

(i.) To France 7,000,000 tons annually for ten years;[42]

(ii.) To Belgium 8,000,000 tons annually for ten years;

(iii.) To Italy an annual quantity, rising by annual increments from 4,500,000 tons in 1919-1920 to 8,500,000 tons in each of the six years, 1923-1924 to 1928-1929;

(iv.) To Luxemburg, if required, a quantity of coal equal to the pre-war annual consumption of German coal in Luxemburg.

This amounts in all to an annual average of about 25,000,000 tons.

These figures have to be examined in relation to Germany's probable output. The maximum pre-war figure was reached in 1913 with a total of 191,500,000 tons. Of this, 19,000,000 tons were consumed at the mines, and on balance (*i.e.* exports less imports) 33,500,000 tons were exported, leaving 139,000,000 tons for domestic consumption. It is estimated that this total was employed as follows:—

Railways	18,000,000	tons.
Gas, water, and electricity	12,500,000	"
Bunkers	6,500,000	"
House-fuel, small industry and agriculture	24,000,000	"
Industry	78,000,000	"
	139,000,000	"

The diminution of production due to loss of territory is:—

Alsace-Lorraine	3,800,000	tons.
Saar Basin	13,200,000	"
Upper Silesia	43,800,000	"
	60,800,000	"

There would remain, therefore, on the basis of the 1913 output, 130,700,000 tons, or, deducting consumption at the mines themselves, (say) 118,000,000 tons. For some years there must be sent out of this supply upwards of 20,000,000 tons to France as compensation for damage done to French mines, and 25,000,000 tons to France,

Belgium, Italy, and Luxemburg;[43] as the former figure is a maximum, and the latter figure is to be slightly less in the earliest years, we may take the total export to Allied countries which Germany has undertaken to provide as 40,000,000 tons, leaving, on the above basis, 78,000,000 tons for her own use as against a pre-war consumption of 139,000,000 tons.

This comparison, however, requires substantial modification to make it accurate. On the one hand, it is certain that the figures of pre-war output cannot be relied on as a basis of present output. During 1918 the production was 161,500,000 tons as compared with 191,500,000 tons in 1913; and during the first half of 1919 it was less than 50,000,000 tons, exclusive of Alsace-Lorraine and the Saar but including Upper Silesia, corresponding to an annual production of about 100,000,000 tons.[44] The causes of so low an output were in part temporary and exceptional but the German authorities agree, and have not been confuted, that some of them are bound to persist for some time to come. In part they are the same as elsewhere; the daily shift has been shortened from 8-1/2 to 7 hours, and it is improbable that the powers of the Central Government will be adequate to restore them to their former figure. But in addition, the mining plant is in bad condition (due to the lack of certain essential materials during the blockade), the physical efficiency of the men is greatly impaired by malnutrition (which cannot be cured if a tithe of the reparation demands are to be satisfied,—the standard of life will have rather to be lowered), and the casualties of the war have diminished the numbers of efficient miners. The analogy of English conditions is sufficient by itself to tell us that a pre-war level of output cannot be expected in Germany. German authorities put the loss of output at somewhat above 30 per cent, divided about equally between the shortening of the shift and the other economic influences. This figure appears on general grounds to be plausible, but I have not the knowledge to endorse or to criticize it.

The pre-war figure of 118,000,000 tons net (*i.e.* after allowing for loss of territory and consumption at the mines) is likely to fall, therefore, at least as low as to 100,000,000[45] tons, having regard to the above factors. If 40,000,000 tons of this are to be exported to the Allies, there remain 60,000,000 tons for Germany herself to meet her own domestic consumption. Demand as well as supply will be diminished by loss of territory, but at the most extravagant estimate this could not be put above 29,000,000 tons.[46] Our hypothetical calculations, therefore, leave us with post-war German domestic requirements, on the basis of a pre-war efficiency of railways and industry, of 110,000,000 tons against an output not exceeding 100,000,000 tons, of which 40,000,000 tons are mortgaged to the Allies.

The importance of the subject has led me into a somewhat lengthy statistical analysis. It is evident that too much significance must not be attached to the precise figures arrived at, which are hypothetical and dubious.[47] But the general character of the facts presents itself irresistibly. Allowing for the loss of territory and the loss of efficiency, Germany cannot export coal in the near future (and will even be dependent on her Treaty rights to purchase in Upper Silesia), if she is to continue as an industrial nation. Every million tons she is forced to export must be at the expense of closing down an industry. With results to be considered later this within certain limits is *possible*. But it is evident that Germany cannot and will not furnish the Allies with a contribution of 40,000,000 tons annually. Those Allied Ministers, who have told their peoples that she can, have certainly deceived them for the sake of allaying for the moment the misgivings of the European peoples as to the path along which they are being led.

The presence of these illusory provisions (amongst others) in the clauses of the Treaty of Peace is especially charged with danger for the future. The more extravagant expectations as to Reparation receipts, by which Finance Ministers have deceived their publics, will be heard of no more when they have served their immediate purpose of postponing the hour of taxation and retrenchment. But the coal clauses will not be lost sight of so easily,—for the reason that it will be absolutely vital in the interests of France and Italy that these countries should do everything in their power to exact their bond. As a result of the diminished output due to German destruction in France, of the diminished output of mines in the United Kingdom and elsewhere, and of many secondary causes, such as the breakdown of transport and of organization and the inefficiency of new governments, the coal position of all Europe is nearly desperate; [48] and France and Italy, entering the scramble with certain Treaty rights, will not lightly surrender them.

As is generally the case in real dilemmas, the French and Italian case will possess great force, indeed unanswerable force from a certain point of view. The position will be truly represented as a question between German industry on the one hand and French and Italian industry on the other. It may be admitted that the surrender of the coal will destroy German industry, but it may be equally true that its non-surrender will jeopardize French and Italian industry. In such a case must not the victors with their Treaty rights prevail, especially when much of the damage has been ultimately due to the wicked acts of those who are now defeated? Yet if these feelings and these rights are allowed to prevail beyond what wisdom would recommend, the reactions on the social and economic life of Central Europe will be far too strong to be confined within their original limits.

But this is not yet the whole problem. If France and Italy are to make good their own deficiencies in coal from the output of Germany, then Northern Europe, Switzerland, and Austria, which previously drew their coal in large part from Germany's exportable surplus, must be starved of their supplies. Before the war 13,600,000 tons of Germany's coal exports went to Austria-Hungary. Inasmuch as nearly all the coalfields of the former Empire lie outside what is now German-Austria, the industrial ruin of this latter state, if she cannot obtain coal from Germany, will be complete. The case of Germany's neutral neighbors, who were formerly supplied in part from Great Britain but in large part from Germany, will be hardly less serious. They will go to great lengths in the direction of making their own supplies to Germany of materials which are essential to her, conditional on these being paid for in coal. Indeed they are already doing so. [49] With the breakdown of money economy the practice of international barter is becoming prevalent. Nowadays money in Central and South-Eastern Europe is seldom a true measure of value in exchange, and will not necessarily buy anything, with the consequence that one country, possessing a commodity essential to the needs of another, sells it not for cash but only against a reciprocal engagement on the part of the latter country to furnish in return some article not less necessary to the former. This is an extraordinary complication as compared with the former almost perfect simplicity of international trade. But in the no less extraordinary conditions of to-day's industry it is not without advantages as a means of stimulating production. The butter-shifts of the

Ruhr[50] show how far modern Europe has retrograded in the direction of barter, and afford a picturesque illustration of the low economic organization to which the breakdown of currency and free exchange between individuals and nations is quickly leading us. But they may produce the coal where other devices would fail.[51]

Yet if Germany can find coal for the neighboring neutrals, France and Italy may loudly claim that in this case she can and must keep her treaty obligations. In this there will be a great show of justice, and it will be difficult to weigh against such claims the possible facts that, while German miners will work for butter, there is no available means of compelling them to get coal, the sale of which will bring in nothing, and that if Germany has no coal to send to her neighbors she may fail to secure imports essential to her economic existence.

If the distribution of the European coal supplies is to be a scramble in which France is satisfied first, Italy next, and every one else takes their chance, the industrial future of Europe is black and the prospects of revolution very good. It is a case where particular interests and particular claims, however well founded in sentiment or in justice, must yield to sovereign expediency. If there is any approximate truth in Mr. Hoover's calculation that the coal output of Europe has fallen by one-third, a situation confronts us where distribution must be effected with even-handed impartiality in accordance with need, and no incentive can be neglected towards increased production and economical methods of transport. The establishment by the Supreme Council of the Allies in August, 1919, of a European Coal Commission, consisting of delegates from Great Britain, France, Italy, Belgium, Poland, and Czecho-Slovakia was a wise measure which, properly employed and extended, may prove of great assistance. But I reserve constructive proposals for Chapter VII. Here I am only concerned with tracing the consequences, *per impossibile*, of carrying out the Treaty *au pied de lettre*.[52]

(2) The provisions relating to iron-ore require less detailed attention, though their effects are destructive. They require less attention, because they are in large measure inevitable. Almost exactly 75 per cent of the iron-ore raised in Germany in 1913 came from Alsace-Lorraine.[53] In this the chief importance of the stolen provinces lay.

There is no question but that Germany must lose these ore-fields. The only question is how far she is to be allowed facilities for purchasing their produce. The German Delegation made strong efforts to secure the inclusion of a provision by which coal and coke to be furnished by them to France should be given in exchange for *minette* from Lorraine. But they secured no such stipulation, and the matter remains at France's option.

The motives which will govern France's eventual policy are not entirely concordant. While Lorraine comprised 75 per cent of Germany's iron-ore, only 25 per cent of the blast furnaces lay within Lorraine and the Saar basin together, a large proportion of the ore being carried into Germany proper. Approximately the same proportion of Germany's iron and steel foundries, namely 25 per cent, were situated in Alsace-Lorraine. For the moment, therefore, the most economical and profitable course would certainly be to export to Germany, as hitherto, a considerable part of the output of the mines.

On the other hand, France, having recovered the deposits of Lorraine, may be expected to aim at replacing as far as possible the industries, which Germany had based on them, by industries situated within her own frontiers. Much time must elapse before the plant and the skilled labor could be developed within France, and even so she could hardly deal with the ore unless she could rely on receiving the coal from Germany. The uncertainty, too, as to the ultimate fate of the Saar will be disturbing to the calculations of capitalists who contemplate the establishment of new industries in France.

In fact, here, as elsewhere, political considerations cut disastrously across economic. In a régime of Free Trade and free economic intercourse it would be of little consequence that iron lay on one side of a political frontier, and labor, coal, and blast furnaces on the other. But as it is, men have devised ways to impoverish themselves and one another; and prefer collective animosities to individual happiness. It seems certain, calculating on the present passions and impulses of European capitalistic society, that the effective iron output of Europe will be diminished by a new political frontier (which sentiment and historic justice require), because nationalism and private interest are thus allowed to impose a new economic frontier along the same lines. These latter considerations are allowed, in the present governance of Europe, to prevail over the intense need of the Continent for the most sustained and efficient production to repair the destructions of war, and to satisfy the insistence of labor for a larger reward.[54]

The same influences are likely to be seen, though on a lesser scale, in the event of the transference of Upper Silesia to Poland. While Upper Silesia contains but little iron, the presence of coal has led to the establishment of numerous blast furnaces. What is to be the fate of these? If Germany is cut off from her supplies of ore on the west, will she export beyond her frontiers on the east any part of the little which remains to her? The efficiency and output of the industry seem certain to diminish.

Thus the Treaty strikes at organization, and by the destruction of organization impairs yet further the reduced wealth of the whole community. The economic frontiers which are to be established between the coal and the iron, upon which modern industrialism is founded, will not only diminish the production of useful commodities, but may possibly occupy an immense quantity of human labor in dragging iron or coal, as the case may be, over many useless miles to satisfy the dictates of a political treaty or because obstructions have been established to the proper localization of industry.

III

There remain those Treaty provisions which relate to the transport and the tariff systems of Germany. These parts of the Treaty have not nearly the importance and the significance of those discussed hitherto. They are pin-pricks, interferences and vexations, not so much objectionable for their solid consequences, as dishonorable to the Allies in the light of their professions. Let the reader consider what follows in the light of the assurances already quoted, in reliance on which Germany laid down her arms.

(i.) The miscellaneous Economic Clauses commence with a number of provisions which would be in accordance with the spirit of the third of the Fourteen Points,—if they were reciprocal. Both for imports and exports, and as regards tariffs, regulations, and prohibitions, Germany binds herself for five years to accord most-favored-nation treatment to the Allied and Associated States.[55] But she is not entitled herself to receive such treatment.

For five years Alsace-Lorraine shall be free to export into Germany, without payment of customs duty, up to the average amount sent annually into Germany from 1911 to 1913. [56] But there is no similar provision for German exports into Alsace-Lorraine.

For three years Polish exports to Germany, and for five years Luxemburg's exports to Germany, are to have a similar privilege,[57]— but not German exports to Poland or to Luxemburg. Luxemburg also, which for many years has enjoyed the benefits of inclusion within the German Customs Union, is permanently excluded from it henceforward.[58]

For six months after the Treaty has come into force Germany may not impose duties on imports from the Allied and Associated States higher than the most favorable duties prevalent before the war and for a further two years and a half (making three years in all) this prohibition continues to apply to certain commodities, notably to some of those as to which special agreements existed before the war, and also to wine, to vegetable oils, to artificial silk, and to washed or scoured wool.[59] This is a ridiculous and injurious provision, by which Germany is prevented from taking those steps necessary to conserve her limited resources for the purchase of necessaries and the discharge of Reparation. As a result of the existing distribution of wealth in Germany, and of financial wantonness amongst individuals, the offspring of uncertainty, Germany is threatened with a deluge of luxuries and semi-luxuries from abroad, of which she has been starved for years, which would exhaust or diminish her small supplies of foreign exchange. These provisions strike at the authority of the German Government to ensure economy in such consumption, or to raise taxation during a critical period. What an example of senseless greed overreaching itself, to introduce, after taking from Germany what liquid wealth she has and demanding impossible payments for the future, a special and particularized injunction that she must allow as readily as in the days of her prosperity the import of champagne and of silk!

One other Article affects the Customs Régime of Germany which, if it was applied, would be serious and extensive in its consequences. The Allies have reserved the right to apply a special customs régime to the occupied area on the bank of the Rhine, "in the event of such a measure being necessary in their opinion in order to safeguard the economic interests of the population of these territories."[60] This provision was probably introduced as a possibly useful adjunct to the French policy of somehow detaching the left bank provinces from Germany during the years of their occupation. The project of establishing an independent Republic under French clerical auspices, which would act as a buffer state and realize the French ambition of driving Germany proper beyond the Rhine, has not yet been abandoned. Some believe that much may be accomplished by a régime of threats, bribes, and cajolery extended over a period of fifteen years or longer.[61] If this Article is acted upon, and the economic system of the left bank of the Rhine is effectively severed from the rest of Germany, the effect would be far-reaching. But the dreams of designing diplomats do not always prosper, and we must trust the future.

(ii.) The clauses relating to Railways, as originally presented to Germany, were substantially modified in the final Treaty, and are now limited to a provision by which goods, coming from Allied territory to Germany, or in transit through Germany, shall receive the most favored treatment as regards rail freight rates, etc., applied to goods of the same kind carried on *any* German lines "under similar conditions of transport, for example, as regards length of route."[62] As a non-reciprocal provision this is an act of interference in internal arrangements which it is difficult to justify, but the practical effect of this,[63] and of an analogous provision relating to passenger traffic,[64] will much depend on the interpretation of the phrase, "similar conditions of transport."[65]

For the time being Germany's transport system will be much more seriously disordered by the provisions relating to the cession of rolling-stock. Under paragraph 7 of the Armistice conditions Germany was called on to surrender 5000 locomotives and 150,000 wagons, "in good working order, with all necessary spare parts and fittings." Under the Treaty Germany is required to confirm this surrender and to recognize the title of the Allies to the material.[66] She is further required, in the case of railway systems in ceded territory, to hand over these systems complete with their full complement of rolling-stock "in a normal state of upkeep" as shown in the last inventory before November 11, 1918.[67]That is to say, ceded railway systems are not to bear any share in the general depletion and deterioration of the German rolling-stock as a whole.

This is a loss which in course of time can doubtless be made good. But lack of lubricating oils and the prodigious wear and tear of the war, not compensated by normal repairs, had already reduced the German railway system to a low state of efficiency. The further heavy losses under the Treaty will confirm this state of affairs for some time to come, and are a substantial aggravation of the difficulties of the coal problem and of export industry generally.

(iii.) There remain the clauses relating to the river system of Germany. These are largely unnecessary and are so little related to the supposed aims of the Allies that their purport is generally unknown. Yet they constitute an unprecedented interference with a country's domestic arrangements and are capable of being so operated as to take from Germany all effective control over her own transport system. In their present form they are incapable of justification; but some simple changes might transform them into a reasonable instrument.

Most of the principal rivers of Germany have their source or their outlet in non-German territory. The Rhine, rising in Switzerland, is now a frontier river for a part of its course, and finds the sea in Holland; the Danube rises in Germany but flows over its greater length elsewhere; the Elbe rises in the mountains of Bohemia, now called Czecho-Slovakia; the Oder traverses Lower Silesia; and the Niemen now bounds the frontier of East Prussia and has its source in Russia. Of these, the Rhine and the Niemen are frontier rivers, the Elbe is primarily German but in its upper reaches has much importance for Bohemia, the Danube in its German parts appears to have little concern for any country but Germany, and the Oder is an almost purely German river unless the result of the plebiscite is to detach all Upper Silesia.

Rivers which, in the words of the Treaty, "naturally provide more than one State with access to the sea," properly require some measure of international regulation and adequate guarantees against discrimination. This principle has long been recognized in the International Commissions which regulate the Rhine and the Danube. But on such Commissions the States concerned should be represented more or less in proportion to their interests. The Treaty, however, has made the international character of these rivers a pretext for taking the river system of Germany out of German control.

After certain Articles which provide suitably against discrimination and interference with freedom of transit,[68] the Treaty proceeds to hand over the administration of the Elbe, the Oder, the Danube, and the Rhine to International Commissions.[69] The ultimate powers of these Commissions are to be determined by "a General Convention drawn up by the Allied and Associated Powers, and approved by the League of Nations."[70] In the meantime the Commissions are to draw up their own constitutions and are apparently to enjoy powers of the most extensive description, "particularly in regard to the execution of works of maintenance, control, and improvement on the river system, the financial régime, the fixing and collection of charges, and regulations for navigation."[71]

So far there is much to be said for the Treaty. Freedom of through transit is a not unimportant part of good international practice and should be established everywhere. The objectionable feature of the Commissions lies in their membership. In each case the voting is so weighted as to place Germany in a clear minority. On the Elbe Commission Germany has four votes out of ten; on the Oder Commission three out of nine; on the Rhine Commission four out of nineteen; on the Danube Commission, which is not yet definitely constituted, she will be apparently in a small minority. On the government of all these rivers France and Great Britain are represented; and on the Elbe for some undiscoverable reason there are also representatives of Italy and Belgium.

Thus the great waterways of Germany are handed over to foreign bodies with the widest powers; and much of the local and domestic business of Hamburg, Magdeburg, Dresden, Stettin, Frankfurt, Breslau, and Ulm will be subject to a foreign jurisdiction. It is almost as though the Powers of Continental Europe were to be placed in a majority on the Thames Conservancy or the Port of London.

Certain minor provisions follow lines which in our survey of the Treaty are now familiar. Under Annex III. of the Reparation Chapter Germany is to cede up to 20 per cent of her inland navigation tonnage. Over and above this she must cede such proportion of her river craft upon the Elbe, the Oder, the Niemen, and the Danube as an American arbitrator may determine, "due regard being had to the legitimate needs of the parties concerned, and particularly to the shipping traffic during the five years preceding the war," the craft so ceded to be selected from those most recently built. [72] The same course is to be followed with German vessels and tugs on the Rhine and with German property in the port of Rotterdam.[73] Where the Rhine flows between France and Germany, France is to have all the rights of utilizing the water for irrigation or for power and Germany is to have none;[74] and all the bridges are to be French property as to their whole length.[75] Finally the administration of the purely German Rhine port of Kehl lying on the eastern bank of the river is to be united to that of

Strassburg for seven years and managed by a Frenchman to be nominated by the new Rhine Commission.

Thus the Economic Clauses of the Treaty are comprehensive, and little has been overlooked which might impoverish Germany now or obstruct her development in future. So situated, Germany is to make payments of money, on a scale and in a manner to be examined in the next chapter.

FOOTNOTES:

[7]The precise force of this reservation is discussed in detail in Chapter V.

[8]I also omit those which have no special relevance to the German Settlement. The second of the Fourteen Points, which relates to the Freedom of the Seas, is omitted because the Allies did not accept it. Any italics are mine.

[9]Part VIII. Annex III. (1).

[10]Part VIII. Annex III. (3).

[11]In the years before the war the average shipbuilding output of Germany was about 350,000 tons annually, exclusive of warships.

[12]Part VIII. Annex III. (5).

[13]Art. 119.

[14]Arts. 120 and 257.

[15]Art. 122.

[16]Arts. 121 and 297(b). The exercise or non-exercise of this

option of expropriation appears to lie, not with the Reparation Commission, but with the particular Power in whose territory the property has become situated by cession or mandation.

[17]Art. 297 (h) and para. 4 of Annex to Part X. Section IV.

[18]Arts. 53 and 74.

[19]In 1871 Germany granted France credit for the railways of Alsace-Lorraine but not for State property. At that time, however, the railways were private property. As they afterwards became the property of the German Government, the French Government have held, in spite of the large additional capital which Germany has sunk in them, that their treatment must follow the precedent of State property generally.

[20]Arts. 55 and 255. This follows the precedent of 1871.

[21]Art. 297 (*b*).

[22]Part X. Sections III. and IV. and Art. 243.

[23]The interpretation of the words between inverted commas is a little dubious. The phrase is so wide as to

seem to include private debts. But in the final draft of the Treaty private debts are not explicitly referred to.

[24]This provision is mitigated in the case of German property in Poland and the other new States, the proceeds of liquidation in these areas being payable direct to the owner (Art. 92.)

[25]Part X. Section IV. Annex, para. 10: "Germany will, within six months from the coming into force of the present Treaty, deliver to each Allied or Associated Power all securities, certificates, deeds, or other documents of title held by its nationals and relating to property, rights, or interests situated in the territory of that Allied or Associated Power.... Germany will at any time on demand of any Allied or Associated Power furnish such information as may be required with regard to the territory, rights, and interests of German nationals within the territory of such Allied or Associated Power, or with regard to any transactions concerning such property, rights, or

interests effected since July 1, 1914."

[26]"Any public utility undertaking or concession" is a vague phrase, the precise interpretation of which is not provided for.

[27]Art. 260.

[28]Art. 235.

[29]Art. 118.

[30]Arts. 129 and 132.

[31]Arts. 135-137.

[32]Arts. 135-140.

[33]Art. 141: "Germany renounces all rights, titles and privileges conferred on her by the General Act of Algeciras of April 7, 1906, and by the Franco-German Agreements, of Feb. 9, 1909, and Nov. 4, 1911...."

[34]Art. 148: "All treaties, agreements, arrangements and contracts concluded by Germany with Egypt are regarded as abrogated from Aug. 4, 1914." Art. 153: "All property and possessions in Egypt of the German Empire and the German States pass to the Egyptian Government without payment."

[35]Art. 289.

[36]Art. 45.

[37]Part IV. Section IV. Annex, Chap. III.

[38]"We take over the ownership of the Sarre mines, and in order not to be inconvenienced in the exploitation of these coal deposits, we constitute a distinct little estate for the 600,000 Germans who inhabit this coal basin, and in fifteen years we shall endeavor by a plebiscite to bring them to declare that they want to be French. We know what that means. During fifteen years we are going to work on them, to attack them from every point, till we obtain from them a declaration of love. It is evidently a less brutal proceeding than the *coup de force* which detached from us our Alsatians and Lorrainers. But if less brutal, it is more hypocritical. We know quite well between ourselves that it is an attempt to annex these 600,000 Germans. One can understand very well the reasons of an economic nature which have led Clemenceau to wish to give us these Sarre coal deposits, but in order to acquire them must we give ourselves the appearance of

wanting to juggle with 600,000 Germans in order to make Frenchmen of them in fifteen years?" (M. Hervé in *La Victorie*, May 31, 1919).

[39]This plebiscite is the most important of the concessions accorded to Germany in the Allies' Final Note, and one for which Mr. Lloyd George, who never approved the Allies' policy on the Eastern frontiers of Germany, can claim the chief credit. The vote cannot take place before the spring of 1920, and may be postponed until 1921. In the meantime the province will be governed by an Allied Commission. The vote will be taken by communes, and the final frontiers will be determined by the Allies, who shall have regard, partly to the results of the vote in each commune, and partly "to the geographical and economic conditions of the locality." It would require great local knowledge to predict the result. By voting Polish, a locality can escape liability for the indemnity, and for the crushing taxation consequent on voting German, a factor not to

be neglected. On the other hand, the bankruptcy and incompetence of the new Polish State might deter those who were disposed to vote on economic rather than on racial grounds. It has also been stated that the conditions of life in such matters as sanitation and social legislation are incomparably better in Upper Silesia than in the adjacent districts of Poland, where similar legislation is in its infancy. The argument in the text assumes that Upper Silesia will cease to be German. But much may happen in a year, and the assumption is not certain. To the extent that it proves erroneous the conclusions must be modified.

[40]German authorities claim, not without contradiction, that to judge from the votes cast at elections, one-third of the population would elect in the Polish interest, and two-thirds in the German.

[41]It must not be overlooked, however, that, amongst the other concessions relating to Silesia accorded in the Allies' Final Note, there has been included

Article 90, by which "Poland undertakes to permit for a period of fifteen years the exportation to Germany of the products of the mines in any part of Upper Silesia transferred to Poland in accordance with the present Treaty. Such products shall be free from all export duties or other charges or restrictions on exportation. Poland agrees to take such steps as may be necessary to secure that any such products shall be available for sale to purchasers in Germany on terms as favorable as are applicable to like products sold under similar conditions to purchasers in Poland or in any other country." This does not apparently amount to a right of preemption, and it is not easy to estimate its effective practical consequences. It is evident, however, that in so far as the mines are maintained at their former efficiency, and in so far as Germany is in a position to purchase substantially her former supplies from that source, the loss is limited to the effect on her balance of trade, and is without the more serious repercussions on her economic life which are contemplated in the text. Here is an opportunity for the Allies to render more tolerable the actual operation of the settlement. The Germans, it should be added, have pointed out that the same economic argument which adds the Saar fields to France allots Upper Silesia to Germany. For whereas the Silesian mines are essential to the economic life of Germany, Poland does not need them. Of Poland's pre-war annual demand of 10,500,000 tons, 6,800,000 tons were supplied by the indisputably Polish districts adjacent to Upper Silesia. 1,500,000 tons from Upper Silesia (out of a total Upper Silesian output of 43,500,000 tons), and the balance from what is now Czecho-Slovakia. Even without any supply from Upper Silesia and Czecho-Slovakia, Poland could probably meet her requirements by the fuller exploitation of her own coalfields which are not yet scientifically developed, or from the deposits of Western Galicia which are now to be annexed to her.

[42]France is also to receive annually for three years 35,000 tons of benzol, 60,000 tons of coal tar, and 30,000 tons of sulphate of ammonia.

[43]The Reparation Commission is authorized under the Treaty (Part VIII Annex V. para. 10) "to postpone or to cancel deliveries" if they consider "that the full exercise of the foregoing options would interfere unduly with the industrial requirements of Germany." In the event of such postponements or cancellations "the coal to replace coal from destroyed mines shall receive priority over other deliveries." This concluding clause is of the greatest importance, if, as will be seen, it is physically impossible for Germany to furnish the full 45,000,000; for it means that France will receive 20,000,000 tons before Italy receives anything. The Reparation Commission has no discretion to modify this. The Italian Press has not failed to notice the significance of the provision, and alleges that this clause was inserted during the absence of the Italian

representatives from Paris (*Corriere della Sera*, July 19, 1919).

[44]It follows that the current rate of production in Germany has sunk to about 60 per cent of that of 1913. The effect on reserves has naturally been disastrous, and the prospects for the coming winter are dangerous.

[45]This assumes a loss of output of 15 per cent as compared with the estimate of 30 per cent quoted above.

[46]This supposes a loss of 23 per cent of Germany's industrial undertaking and a diminution of 13 per cent in her other requirements.

[47]The reader must be reminded in particular that the above calculations take no account of the German production of lignite, which yielded in 1913 13,000,000 tons of rough lignite in addition to an amount converted into 21,000,000 tons of briquette. This amount of lignite, however, was required in Germany before the war *in addition* *to* the quantities of coal assumed above. I am not competent to speak

on the extent to which the loss of coal can be made good by the extended use of lignite or by economies in its present employment; but some authorities believe that Germany may obtain substantial compensation for her loss of coal by paying more attention to her deposits of lignite.

[48]Mr. Hoover, in July, 1919, estimated that the coal output of Europe, excluding Russia and the Balkans, had dropped from 679,500,000 tons to 443,000,000 tons,—as a result in a minor degree of loss of material and labor, but owing chiefly to a relaxation of physical effort after the privations and sufferings of the war, a lack of rolling-stock and transport, and the unsettled political fate of some of the mining districts.

[49]Numerous commercial agreements during the war ware arranged on these lines. But in the month of June, 1919, alone, minor agreements providing for payment in coal were made by Germany with Denmark, Norway, and Switzerland. The amounts involved were

not large, but without them Germany could not have obtained butter from Denmark, fats and herrings from Norway, or milk and cattle from Switzerland.

[50]"Some 60,000 Ruhr miners have agreed to work extra shifts—so-called butter-shifts—for the purpose of furnishing coal for export to Denmark hence butter will be exported in return. The butter will benefit the miners in the first place, as they have worked specially to obtain it" (*Kölnische Zeitung*, June 11, 1919).

[51]What of the prospects of whisky-shifts in England?

[52]As early as September, 1919, the Coal Commission had to face the physical impracticability of enforcing the demands of the Treaty, and agreed to modify them as follows:—"Germany shall in the next six months make deliveries corresponding to an annual delivery of 20 million tons as compared with 43 millions as provided in the Peace Treaty. If Germany's total production exceeds the present level of about 108 millions a year, 60

per cent of extra production, up to 128 millions, shall be delivered to the Entente and 50 per cent of any extra beyond that, until the figure provided in the Peace Treaty is reached. If the total production falls below 108 millions the Entente will examine the situation, after hearing Germany, and take account of it."

[53]21,136,265 tons out of a total of 28,607,903 tons. The loss of iron-ore in respect of Upper Silesia is insignificant. The exclusion of the iron and steel of Luxemburg from the German Customs Union is, however, important, especially when this loss is added to that of Alsace-Lorraine. It may be added in passing that Upper Silesia includes 75 per cent of the zinc production of Germany.

[54]In April, 1919, the British Ministry of Munitions despatched an expert Commission to examine the conditions of the iron and steel works in Lorraine and the occupied areas of Germany. The Report states that the iron and steel works in Lorraine, and to a lesser extent in the Saar Valley, are

dependent on supplies of coal and coke from Westphalia. It is necessary to mix Westphalian coal with Saar coal to obtain a good furnace coke. The entire dependence of all the Lorraine iron and steel works upon Germany for fuel supplies "places them," says the Report, "in a very unenviable position."

[55]Arts. 264, 265, 266, and 267. These provisions can only be extended beyond five years by the Council of the League of Nations.

[56]Art. 268 (*a*).

[57]Art. 268 (*b*) and (*c*).

[58]The Grand Duchy is also deneutralized and Germany binds herself to "accept in advance all international arrangements which may be concluded by the Allied and Associated Powers relating to the Grand Duchy" (Art. 40). At the end of September, 1919, a plebiscite was held to determine whether Luxemburg should join the French or the Belgian Customs Union, which decided by a substantial majority in favour of the former. The third alternative of the

77

maintenance of the union with Germany was not left open to the electorate.

[59]Art. 269.

[60]Art. 270.

[61]The occupation provisions may be conveniently summarized at this point. German territory situated west of the Rhine, together with the bridge-heads, is subject to occupation for a period of fifteen years (Art. 428). If, however, "the conditions of the present Treaty are faithfully carried out by Germany," the Cologne district will be evacuated after five years, and the Coblenz district after ten years (Art. 429). It is, however, further provided that if at the expiration of fifteen years "the guarantees against unprovoked aggression by Germany are not considered sufficient by the Allied and Associated Governments, the evacuation of the occupying troops may be delayed to the extent regarded as necessary for the purpose of obtaining the required guarantees" (Art. 429); and also that "in case either during the occupation or after the

78

expiration of the fifteen years, the Reparation Commission finds that Germany refuses to observe the whole or part of her obligations under the present Treaty with regard to Reparation, the whole or part of the areas specified in Article 429 will be re-occupied immediately by the Allied and Associated Powers" (Art. 430). Since it will be impossible for Germany to fulfil the whole of her Reparation obligations, the effect of the above provisions will be in practice that the Allies will occupy the left bank of the Rhine just so long as they choose. They will also govern it in such manner as they may determine (*e.g.* not only as regards customs, but such matters as the respective authority of the local German representatives and the Allied Governing Commission), since "all matters relating to the occupation and not provided for by the present Treaty shall be regulated by subsequent agreements, which Germany hereby undertakes to observe" (Art. 432). The actual Agreement under which the occupied areas are to be administered for the present has been published as a White Paper [Cd. 222]. The supreme authority is to be in the hands of an Inter-Allied Rhineland Commission, consisting of a Belgian, a French, a British, and an American member. The articles of this Agreement are very fairly and reasonably drawn.

[62]Art. 365. After five years this Article is subject to revision by the Council of the League of Nations.

[63]The German Government withdrew, as from September 1, 1919, all preferential railway tariffs for the export of iron and steel goods, on the ground that these privileges would have been more than counterbalanced by the corresponding privileges which, under this Article of the Treaty, they would have been forced to give to Allied traders.

[64]Art. 367.

[65]Questions of interpretation and application are to be referred to the League of Nations (Art. 376).

[66]Art. 250.

[67]Art 371. This provision is even applied "to the lines of former Russian Poland converted by Germany to the German gage, such lines being regarded as detached from the Prussian State System."

[68]Arts. 332-337. Exception may be taken, however, to the second paragraph of Art. 332, which allows the vessels of other nations to trade between German towns but forbids German vessels to trade between non-German towns except with special permission; and Art. 333, which prohibits Germany from making use of her river system as a source of revenue, may be injudicious.

[69]The Niemen and the Moselle are to be similarly treated at a later date if required.

[70]Art. 338.

[71]Art. 344. This is with particular reference to the Elbe and the Oder; the Danube and the Rhine are dealt with in relation to the existing Commissions.

[72]Art. 339.

[73]Art. 357.

[74]Art. 358. Germany is, however, to be allowed some payment or credit in respect of power so taken by France.

[75]Art. 66.

CHAPTER V

REPARATION

I. *Undertakings given prior to the Peace Negotiations*

The categories of damage in respect of which the Allies were entitled to ask for Reparation are governed by the relevant passages in President Wilson's Fourteen Points of January 8, 1918, as modified by the Allied Governments in their qualifying Note, the text of which the President formally communicated to the German Government as the basis of peace on November 5, 1918. These passages have been quoted in full at the beginning of Chapter IV. That is to say, "compensation will be made by Germany for all damage done to the civilian population of the Allies and to their property by the aggression of Germany by land, by sea, and from the air." The limiting quality of this sentence is reinforced by the passage in the President's speech before Congress on February 11, 1918 (the terms of this speech being an express part of the contract with the enemy), that there shall be "no contributions" and "no punitive damages."

It has sometimes been argued that the preamble to paragraph 19[76] of the Armistice Terms, to the effect "that any future claims and demands of the Allies and the United States of America remain unaffected," wiped out all precedent conditions, and left the Allies free to make whatever demands they chose. But it is not possible to maintain that this casual protective phrase, to which no one at the time attached any particular importance, did away with all the formal communications which passed between the President and the German Government as to the basis of the Terms of Peace during the days preceding the Armistice, abolished the Fourteen Points, and converted the German acceptance of the Armistice Terms into unconditional surrender, so far as it affects the Financial Clauses. It is merely the usual phrase of the draftsman, who, about to rehearse a list of certain claims, wishes to guard himself from the implication that such list is exhaustive. In any case, this contention is disposed of by the Allied reply to the German observations on the first draft of the Treaty, where it is admitted that the terms of the Reparation Chapter must be governed by the President's Note of November 5.

Assuming then that the terms of this Note are binding, we are left to elucidate the precise force of the phrase—"all damage done to the civilian population of the Allies and to their property by the aggression of Germany by land, by sea, and from the air."

Few sentences in history have given so much work to the sophists and the lawyers, as we shall see in the next section of this chapter, as this apparently simple and unambiguous statement. Some have not scrupled to argue that it covers the entire cost of the war; for, they point out, the entire cost of the war has to be met by taxation, and such taxation is "damaging to the civilian population." They admit that the phrase is cumbrous, and that it would have been simpler to have said "all loss and expenditure of whatever description"; and they allow that the apparent emphasis of damage to the persons and property of *civilians* is unfortunate; but errors of draftsmanship should not, in their opinion, shut off the Allies from the rights inherent in victors.

But there are not only the limitations of the phrase in its natural meaning and the emphasis on civilian damages as distinct from military expenditure generally; it must also be remembered that the context of the term is in elucidation of the meaning of the term "restoration" in the President's Fourteen Points. The Fourteen Points provide for damage in invaded territory—Belgium, France, Roumania, Serbia, and Montenegro (Italy being unaccountably omitted)—but they do not cover losses at sea by submarine, bombardments from the sea (as at Scarborough), or damage done by air raids. It was to repair these omissions, which involved losses to the life and property of civilians not really distinguishable in kind from those effected in occupied territory, that the Supreme Council of the Allies in Paris proposed to President Wilson their qualifications. At that time—the last days of October, 1918—I do not believe that any responsible statesman had in mind the exaction from Germany of an indemnity for the general costs of the war. They sought only to make it clear (a point of considerable importance to Great Britain) that reparation for damage done to non-combatants and their property was not limited to invaded territory (as it would have been by the Fourteen Points unqualified), but applied equally to *all* such damage, whether "by land, by sea, or from the air" It was only at a later stage that a general popular demand for an indemnity, covering the full costs of the war, made it politically desirable to practise dishonesty and to try to discover in the written word what was not there.

What damages, then, can be claimed from the enemy on a strict interpretation of our engagements?[77] In the case of the United Kingdom the bill would cover the following items:—

(a) Damage to civilian life and property by the acts of an enemy Government including damage by air raids, naval bombardments, submarine warfare, and mines.

(b) Compensation for improper treatment of interned civilians.

It would not include the general costs of the war, or (*e.g.*) indirect damage due to loss of trade.

The French claim would include, as well as items corresponding to the above:—

(c) Damage done to the property and persons of civilians in the war area, and by aerial warfare behind the enemy lines.

(d) Compensation for loot of food, raw materials, live-stock, machinery, household effects, timber, and the like by the enemy Governments or their nationals in territory occupied by them.

(e) Repayment of fines and requisitions levied by the enemy Governments or their officers on French municipalities or nationals.

(f) Compensation to French nationals deported or compelled to do forced labor.

In addition to the above there is a further item of more doubtful character, namely—

(g) The expenses of the Relief Commission in providing necessary food and clothing to maintain the civilian French population in the enemy-occupied districts.

The Belgian claim would include similar items.[78] If it were argued that in the case of Belgium something more nearly resembling an indemnity for general war costs can be justified, this could only be on the ground of the breach of International Law involved in the invasion of Belgium, whereas, as we have seen, the Fourteen Points include no special demands on this ground.[79] As the cost of Belgian Belief under (g), as well as her general war costs, has been met already by advances from the British, French, and United States Governments, Belgium would presumably employ any repayment of them by Germany in part discharge of her debt to these Governments, so that any such demands are, in effect, an addition to the claims of the three lending Governments.

The claims of the other Allies would be compiled on similar lines. But in their case the question arises more acutely how far Germany can be made contingently liable for damage done, not by herself, but by her co-belligerents, Austria-Hungary, Bulgaria, and Turkey. This is one of the many questions to which the Fourteen Points give no clear answer; on the one hand, they cover explicitly in Point 11 damage done to Roumania, Serbia, and Montenegro, without qualification as to the nationality of the troops inflicting the damage; on the other hand, the Note of the Allies speaks of "German" aggression when it might have spoken of the aggression of "Germany and her allies." On a strict and literal interpretation, I doubt if claims lie against Germany for damage done,—e.g. by the Turks to the Suez Canal, or by Austrian submarines in the Adriatic. But it is a case where, if the Allies wished to strain a point, they could impose contingent liability on Germany without running seriously contrary to the general intention of their engagements.

As between the Allies themselves the case is quite different. It would be an act of gross unfairness and infidelity if France and Great Britain were to take what Germany could pay and leave Italy and Serbia to get what they could out of the remains of Austria-Hungary. As amongst the Allies themselves it is clear that assets should be pooled and shared out in proportion to aggregate claims.

In this event, and if my estimate is accepted, as given below, that Germany's capacity to pay will be exhausted by the direct and legitimate claims which the Allies hold against her, the question of her contingent liability for her allies becomes academic. Prudent and honorable statesmanship would therefore have given her the benefit of the doubt, and claimed against her nothing but the damage she had herself caused.

What, on the above basis of claims, would the aggregate demand amount to? No figures exist on which to base any scientific or exact estimate, and I give my own guess for what it is worth, prefacing it with the following observations.

The amount of the material damage done in the invaded districts has been the subject of enormous, if natural, exaggeration. A journey through the devastated areas of France is impressive to the eye and the imagination beyond description. During the winter of 1918-19, before Nature had cast over the scene her ameliorating mantle, the horror and desolation of war was made visible to sight on an extraordinary scale of blasted grandeur. The completeness of the destruction was evident. For mile after mile nothing was left. No building was habitable and no field fit for the plow. The sameness was also striking. One devastated area was exactly like another—a heap of rubble, a morass of shell-holes, and a tangle of wire.[80] The amount of human labor which would be required to restore such a countryside seemed incalculable; and to the returned traveler any number of milliards of dollars was inadequate to express in matter the destruction thus impressed upon his spirit. Some Governments for a variety of intelligible reasons have not been ashamed to exploit these feelings a little.

Popular sentiment is most at fault, I think, in the case of Belgium. In any event Belgium is a small country, and in its case the actual area of devastation is a small proportion of the whole. The first onrush of the Germans in 1914 did some damage locally; after that the battle-line in Belgium did not sway backwards and forwards, as in France, over a deep belt of country. It was practically stationary, and hostilities were confined to a small corner of the country, much of which in recent times was backward, poor, and sleepy, and did not include the active industry of the country. There remains some injury in the small flooded area, the deliberate damage done by the retreating Germans to buildings, plant, and transport, and the loot of machinery, cattle, and other movable property. But Brussels, Antwerp, and even Ostend are substantially intact, and the great bulk of the land, which is Belgium's chief wealth, is nearly as well cultivated as before. The traveler by motor can pass through and from end to end of the devastated area of Belgium almost before he knows it; whereas the destruction in France is on a different kind of scale altogether. Industrially, the loot has been serious and for the moment paralyzing; but the actual money cost of replacing machinery mounts up slowly, and a few tens of millions would have covered the value of every machine of every possible description that Belgium ever possessed. Besides, the cold statistician must not overlook the fact that the Belgian people possess the instinct of individual self-protection unusually well developed; and the great mass of German bank-notes[81] held in the country at the date of the Armistice, shows that certain classes of them at least found a way, in spite of all the severities and barbarities of German rule, to profit at the expense of the invader. Belgian claims against Germany such as I have seen, amounting to a sum in excess of the total estimated pre-war wealth of the whole country, are simply irresponsible.[82]

It will help to guide our ideas to quote the official survey of Belgian wealth, published in 1913 by the Finance Ministry of Belgium, which was as follows:

Land	$1,320,000,000	tons.
Buildings	1,175,000,000	"
Personal wealth	2,725,000,000	"
Cash	85,000,000	"
Furniture, etc.	600,000,000	"

This total yields an average of $780 per inhabitant, which Dr. Stamp, the highest authority on the subject, is disposed to consider as *prima facie* too low (though he does not accept certain much higher estimates lately current), the corresponding wealth per head (to take Belgium's immediate neighbors) being $835 for Holland, $1,220 for Germany, and $1,515 for France.[83] A total of $7,500,000,000, giving an average of about $1,000 per head, would, however, be fairly liberal. The official estimate of land and buildings is likely to be more accurate than the rest. On the other hand, allowance has to be made for the increased costs of construction.

Having regard to all these considerations, I do not put the money value of the actual *physical* loss of Belgian property by destruction and loot above $750,000,000 *as a maximum*, and while I hesitate to put yet lower an estimate which differs so widely from those generally current, I shall be surprised if it proves possible to substantiate claims even to this amount. Claims in respect of levies, fines, requisitions, and so forth might possibly amount to a further $500,000,000. If the sums advanced to Belgium by her allies for the general costs of the war are to be included, a sum of about $1,250,000,000 has to be added (which includes the cost of relief), bringing the total to $2,500,000,000.

The destruction in France was on an altogether more significant scale, not only as regards the length of the battle line, but also on account of the immensely deeper area of country over which the battle swayed from time to time. It is a popular delusion to think of Belgium as the principal victim of the war; it will turn out, I believe, that taking account of casualties, loss of property and burden of future debt, Belgium has made the least relative sacrifice of all the belligerents except the United States. Of the Allies, Serbia's sufferings and loss have been proportionately the greatest, and after Serbia, France. France in all essentials was just as much the victim of German ambition as was Belgium, and France's entry into the war was just as unavoidable. France, in my judgment, in spite of her policy at the Peace Conference, a policy largely traceable to her sufferings, has the greatest claims on our generosity.

The special position occupied by Belgium in the popular mind is due, of course, to the fact that in 1914 her sacrifice was by far the greatest of any of the Allies. But after 1914 she played a minor rôle. Consequently, by the end of 1918, her relative sacrifices, apart from those sufferings from invasion which cannot be measured in money, had fallen behind, and in some respects they were not even as great, for example, as Australia's. I say this with no wish to evade the obligations towards Belgium under which the pronouncements of our responsible statesmen at many different dates have certainly laid us. Great Britain ought not to seek any payment at all from Germany for herself until the just claims of Belgium have been fully satisfied. But this is no reason why we or they should not tell the truth about the amount.

While the French claims are immensely greater, here too there has been excessive exaggeration, as responsible French statisticians have themselves pointed out. Not above 10 per cent of the area of France was effectively occupied by the enemy, and not above 4 per cent lay within the area of substantial devastation. Of the sixty French towns having a population exceeding 35,000, only two were destroyed—Reims (115,178) and St. Quentin (55,571); three others were occupied—Lille, Roubaix, and Douai—and suffered from loot of machinery and other property, but were not substantially injured otherwise. Amiens, Calais, Dunkerque, and Boulogne suffered secondary damage by bombardment and from the air; but the value of Calais and Boulogne must have been increased by the new works of various kinds erected for the use of the British Army.

The *Annuaire Statistique de la France, 1917,* values the entire house property of France at $11,900,000,000 (59.5 milliard francs).[84] An estimate current in France of $4,000,000,000 (20 milliard francs) for the destruction of house property alone is, therefore, obviously wide of the mark.[85] $600,000,000 at pre-war prices, or say $1,250,000,000 at the present time, is much nearer the right figure. Estimates of the value of the land of France (apart from buildings) vary from $12,400,000,000 to $15,580,000,000, so that it would be extravagant to put the damage on this head as high as $500,000,000. Farm Capital for the whole of France has not been put by responsible authorities above $2,100,000,000.[86] There remain the loss of furniture and machinery, the damage to the coal-mines and the transport system, and many other minor items. But these losses, however serious, cannot be reckoned in value by hundreds of millions of dollars in respect of so small a part of France. In short, it will be difficult to establish a bill exceeding $2,500,000,000 for *physical and material* damage in the occupied and devastated areas of Northern France.[87] I am confirmed in this estimate by the opinion of M. René Pupin, the author of the most comprehensive and scientific estimate of the pre-war wealth of France,[88] which I did not come across until after my own figure had been arrived at. This authority estimates the material losses of the invaded regions at from $2,000,000,000 to $3,000,000,000 (10 to 15 milliards),[89] between which my own figure falls half-way.

Nevertheless, M. Dubois, speaking on behalf of the Budget Commission of the Chamber, has given the figure of $13,000,000,000 (65 milliard francs) "as a minimum" without counting "war levies, losses at sea, the roads, or the loss of public monuments." And M. Loucheur, the Minister of Industrial Reconstruction, stated before the Senate on the 17th February, 1919, that the reconstitution of the devastated regions would involve an expenditure of $15,000,000,000 (75 milliard francs),—more than double M. Pupin's estimate of the entire wealth of their inhabitants. But then at that time M. Loucheur was taking a prominent part in advocating the claims of France before the Peace Conference, and, like others, may have found strict veracity inconsistent with the demands of patriotism.[90]

The figure discussed so far is not, however, the totality of the French claims. There remain, in particular, levies and requisitions on the occupied areas and the losses of the French mercantile marine at sea from the attacks of German cruisers and submarines. Probably $1,000,000,000 would be ample to cover all such claims; but to be on the safe side, we will, somewhat arbitrarily, make an addition to the French claim of $1,500,000,000 on all heads, bringing it to $4,000,000,000 in all.

The statements of M. Dubois and M. Loucheur were made in the early spring of 1919. A speech delivered by M. Klotz before the French Chamber six months later (Sept. 5, 1919) was less excusable. In this speech the French Minister of Finance estimated the total French claims for damage to property (presumably inclusive of losses at sea, etc., but apart from pensions and allowances) at $26,800,000,000 (134 milliard francs), or more than six times my estimate. Even if my figure prove erroneous, M. Klotz's can never have been justified. So grave has been the deception practised on the French people by their Ministers that when the inevitable enlightenment comes, as it soon must (both as to their own claims and as to Germany's capacity to meet them), the repercussions will strike at more than M. Klotz, and may even involve the order of Government and Society for which he stands.

British claims on the present basis would be practically limited to losses by sea—losses of hulls and losses of cargoes. Claims would lie, of course, for damage to civilian property in air raids and by bombardment from the sea, but in relation to such figures as we are now dealing with, the money value involved is insignificant,—$25,000,000 might cover them all, and $50,000,000 would certainly do so.

The British mercantile vessels lost by enemy action, excluding fishing vessels, numbered 2479, with an aggregate of 7,759,090 tons gross.[91] There is room for considerable divergence of opinion as to the proper rate to take for replacement cost; at the figure of $150 per gross ton, which with the rapid growth of shipbuilding may soon be too high but can be replaced by any other which better authorities[92] may prefer, the aggregate claim is $1,150,000,000. To this must be added the loss of cargoes, the value of which is almost entirely a matter of guesswork. An estimate of $200 per ton of shipping lost may be as good an approximation as is possible, that is to say $1,550,000,000, making $2,700,000,000 altogether.

An addition to this of $150,000,000, to cover air raids, bombardments, claims of interned civilians, and miscellaneous items of every description, should be more than sufficient,—making a total claim for Great Britain of $2,850,000,000. It is surprising, perhaps, that the money value of Great Britain's claim should be so little short of that of France and actually in excess of that of Belgium. But, measured either by pecuniary loss or real loss to the economic power of the country, the injury to her mercantile marine was enormous.

There remain the claims of Italy, Serbia, and Roumania for damage by invasion and of these and other countries, as for example Greece,[93] for losses at sea. I will assume for the present argument that these claims rank against Germany, even when they were directly caused not by her but by her allies; but that it is not proposed to enter any such claims on behalf of Russia.[94] Italy's losses by invasion and at sea cannot be very heavy, and a figure of from $250,000,000 to $500,000,000 would be fully adequate to cover them. The losses of Serbia, although from a human point of view her sufferings were the greatest of all,[95] are not measured *pecuniarily* by very great figures, on account of her low economic development. Dr. Stamp (*loc. cit.*) quotes an estimate by the Italian statistician Maroi, which puts the national wealth of Serbia at $2,400,000,000 or $525 per head,[96] and the greater part of this would be represented by land which has sustained no permanent damage.[97] In view of the very inadequate data for guessing at more than the *general magnitude* of the legitimate claims of this group of countries, I prefer to make one guess rather than several and to put the figure for the whole group at the round sum of $1,250,000,000.

We are finally left with the following—

Belgium	$2,500,000,000	[98]
France	4,000,000,000	
Great Britain	2,850,000,000	
Other Allies	1,250,000,000	
Total	$10,600,000,000	

I need not impress on the reader that there is much guesswork in the above, and the figure for France in particular is likely to be criticized. But I feel some confidence that the *general magnitude*, as distinct from the precise figures, is not hopelessly erroneous; and this may be expressed by the statement that a claim against Germany, based on the interpretation of the pre-Armistice engagements of the Allied Powers which is adopted above, would assuredly be found to exceed $8,000,000,000 and to fall short of $15,000,000,000.

This is the amount of the claim which we were entitled to present to the enemy. For reasons which will appear more fully later on, I believe that it would have been a wise and just act to have asked the German Government at the Peace Negotiations to agree to a sum of $10,000,000,000 in final settlement, without further examination of particulars. This would have provided an immediate and certain solution, and would have required from Germany a sum which, if she were granted certain indulgences, it might not have proved entirely impossible for her to pay. This sum should have been divided up amongst the Allies themselves on a basis of need and general equity.

But the question was not settled on its merits.

II. *The Conference and the Terms of the Treaty*

I do not believe that, at the date of the Armistice, responsible authorities in the Allied countries expected any indemnity from Germany beyond the cost of reparation for the direct material damage which had resulted from the invasion of Allied territory and from the submarine campaign. At that time there were serious doubts as to whether Germany intended to accept our terms, which in other respects were inevitably very severe, and it would have been thought an unstatesmanlike act to risk a continuance of the war by demanding a money payment which Allied opinion was not then anticipating and which probably could not be secured in any case. The French, I think, never quite accepted this point of view; but it was certainly the British attitude; and in this atmosphere the pre-Armistice conditions were framed.

A month later the atmosphere had changed completely. We had discovered how hopeless the German position really was, a discovery which some, though not all, had anticipated, but which no one had dared reckon on as a certainty. It was evident that we could have secured unconditional surrender if we had determined to get it.

But there was another new factor in the situation which was of greater local importance. The British Prime Minister had perceived that the conclusion of hostilities might soon bring with it the break-up of the political *bloc* upon which he was depending for his personal ascendency, and that the domestic difficulties which would be attendant on demobilization, the turn-over of industry from war to peace conditions, the financial situation, and the general psychological reactions of men's minds, would provide his enemies with powerful weapons, if he were to leave them time to mature. The best chance, therefore, of consolidating his power, which was personal and exercised, as such, independently of party or principle, to an extent unusual in British politics, evidently lay in active hostilities before the prestige of victory had abated, and in an attempt to found on the emotions of the moment a new basis of power which might outlast the inevitable reactions of the near future. Within a brief period, therefore, after the Armistice, the popular victor, at the height of his influence and his authority, decreed a General Election. It was widely recognized at the time as an act of political immorality. There were no grounds of public interest which did not call for a short delay until the issues of the new age had a little defined themselves and until the country had something more specific before it on which to declare its mind and to instruct its new representatives. But the claims of private ambition determined otherwise.

For a time all went well. But before the campaign was far advanced Government candidates were finding themselves handicapped by the lack of an effective cry. The War Cabinet was demanding a further lease of authority on the ground of having won the war. But partly because the new issues had not yet defined themselves, partly out of regard for the delicate balance of a Coalition Party, the Prime Minister's future policy was the subject of silence or generalities. The campaign seemed, therefore, to fall a little flat. In the light of subsequent events it seems improbable that the Coalition Party was ever in real danger. But party managers are easily "rattled." The Prime Minister's more neurotic advisers told him that he was not safe from dangerous surprises, and the Prime Minister lent an ear to them. The party managers demanded more "ginger." The Prime Minister looked about for some.

On the assumption that the return of the Prime Minister to power was the primary consideration, the rest followed naturally. At that juncture there was a clamor from certain quarters that the Government had given by no means sufficiently clear undertakings that they were not going "to let the Hun off." Mr. Hughes was evoking a good deal of attention by his demands for a very large indemnity,[99] and Lord Northcliffe was lending his powerful aid to the same cause. This pointed the Prime Minister to a stone for two birds. By himself adopting the policy of Mr. Hughes and Lord Northcliffe, he could at the same time silence those powerful critics and provide his party managers with an effective platform cry to drown the increasing voices of criticism from other quarters.

The progress of the General Election of 1918 affords a sad, dramatic history of the essential weakness of one who draws his chief inspiration not from his own true impulses, but from the grosser effluxions of the atmosphere which momentarily surrounds him. The Prime Minister's natural instincts, as they so often are, were right and reasonable. He himself did not believe in hanging the Kaiser or in the wisdom or the possibility of a great indemnity. On the 22nd of November he and Mr. Bonar Law issued their Election Manifesto. It contains no allusion of any kind either to the one or to the other but, speaking, rather, of Disarmament and the League of Nations, concludes that "our first task must be to conclude a just and lasting peace, and so to establish the foundations of a new Europe that occasion for further wars may be for ever averted." In his speech at Wolverhampton on the eve of the Dissolution (November 24), there is no word of Reparation or Indemnity. On the following day at Glasgow, Mr. Bonar Law would promise nothing. "We are going to the Conference," he said, "as one of a number of allies, and you cannot expect a member of the Government, whatever he may think, to state in public before he goes into that Conference, what line he is going to take in regard to any particular question." But a few days later at Newcastle (November 29) the Prime Minister was warming to his work: "When Germany defeated France she made France pay. That is the principle which she herself has established. There is absolutely no doubt about the principle, and that is the principle we should proceed upon—that Germany must pay the costs of the war up to the limit of her capacity to do so." But he accompanied this statement of principle with many "words of warning" as to the practical difficulties of the case: "We have appointed a strong Committee of experts, representing every shade of opinion, to consider this question very carefully and to advise us. There is no doubt as to the justice of the demand. She ought to pay, she must pay as far as she can, but we are not going to allow her to pay in such a way as to wreck our industries." At this stage the Prime Minister sought to indicate that he intended great severity, without raising excessive hopes of actually getting the money, or committing himself to a particular line of action at the Conference. It was rumored that a high city authority had committed himself to the opinion that Germany could certainly pay $100,000,000,000 and that this authority for his part would not care to discredit a figure of twice that sum. The Treasury officials, as Mr. Lloyd George indicated, took a different view. He could, therefore, shelter himself behind the wide discrepancy between the opinions of his different advisers, and regard the precise figure of Germany's capacity to pay as an open question in the treatment of which he must do his best for his country's interests. As to our engagements under the Fourteen Points he was always silent.

On November 30, Mr. Barnes, a member of the War Cabinet, in which he was supposed to represent Labor, shouted from a platform, "I am for hanging the Kaiser."

On December 6, the Prime Minister issued a statement of policy and aims in which he stated, with significant emphasis on the word *European*, that "All the European Allies have accepted the principle that the Central Powers must pay the cost of the war up to the limit of their capacity."

But it was now little more than a week to Polling Day, and still he had not said enough to satisfy the appetites of the moment. On December 8, the *Times*, providing as usual a cloak of ostensible decorum for the lesser restraint of its associates, declared in a leader entitled "Making Germany Pay," that "The public mind was still bewildered by the Prime Minister's various statements." "There is too much suspicion," they added, "of influences concerned to let the Germans off lightly, whereas the only possible motive in determining their capacity to pay must be the interests of the Allies." "It is the candidate who deals with the issues of to-day," wrote their Political Correspondent, "who adopts Mr. Barnes's phrase about 'hanging the Kaiser' and plumps for the payment of the cost of the war by Germany, who rouses his audience and strikes the notes to which they are most responsive."

91

On December 9, at the Queen's Hall, the Prime Minister avoided the subject. But from now on, the debauchery of thought and speech progressed hour by hour. The grossest spectacle was provided by Sir Eric Geddes in the Guildhall at Cambridge. An earlier speech in which, in a moment of injudicious candor, he had cast doubts on the possibility of extracting from Germany the whole cost of the war had been the object of serious suspicion, and he had therefore a reputation to regain. "We will get out of her all you can squeeze out of a lemon and a bit more," the penitent shouted, "I will squeeze her until you can hear the pips squeak"; his policy was to take every bit of property belonging to Germans in neutral and Allied countries, and all her gold and silver and her jewels, and the contents of her picture-galleries and libraries, to sell the proceeds for the Allies' benefit. "I would strip Germany," he cried, "as she has stripped Belgium."

By December 11 the Prime Minister had capitulated. His Final Manifesto of Six Points issued on that day to the electorate furnishes a melancholy comparison with his program of three weeks earlier. I quote it in full:

" 1.   Trial   of   the   Kaiser.
2.   Punishment   of   those   responsible   for   atrocities.
3.   Fullest   Indemnities   from   Germany.
4.   Britain   for   the   British,   socially   and   industrially.
5.   Rehabilitation   of   those   broken   in   the   war.
6. A happier country for all."

Here is food for the cynic. To this concoction of greed and sentiment, prejudice and deception, three weeks of the platform had reduced the powerful governors of England, who but a little while before had spoken not ignobly of Disarmament and a League of Nations and of a just and lasting peace which should establish the foundations of a new Europe.

On the same evening the Prime Minister at Bristol withdrew in effect his previous reservations and laid down four principles to govern his Indemnity Policy, of which the chief were: First, we have an absolute right to demand the whole cost of the war; second, we propose to demand the whole cost of the war; and third, a Committee appointed by direction of the Cabinet believe that it can be done.[100] Four days later he went to the polls.

The Prime Minister never said that he himself believed that Germany could pay the whole cost of the war. But the program became in the mouths of his supporters on the hustings a great deal more than concrete. The ordinary voter was led to believe that Germany could certainly be made to pay the greater part, if not the whole cost of the war. Those whose practical and selfish fears for the future the expenses of the war had aroused, and those whose emotions its horrors had disordered, were both provided for. A vote for a Coalition candidate meant the Crucifixion of Anti-Christ and the assumption by Germany of the British National Debt.

It proved an irresistible combination, and once more Mr. George's political instinct was not at fault. No candidate could safely denounce this program, and none did so. The old Liberal Party, having nothing comparable to offer to the electorate, was swept out of existence.[101] A new House of Commons came into being, a majority of whose members had pledged themselves to a great deal more than the Prime Minister's guarded promises. Shortly after their arrival at Westminster I asked a Conservative friend, who had known previous Houses, what he thought of them. "They are a lot of hard-faced men," he said, "who look as if they had done very well out of the war."

This was the atmosphere in which the Prime Minister left for Paris, and these the entanglements he had made for himself. He had pledged himself and his Government to make demands of a helpless enemy inconsistent with solemn engagements on our part, on the faith of which this enemy had laid down his arms. There are few episodes in history which posterity will have less reason to condone,—a war ostensibly waged in defense of the sanctity of international engagements ending in a definite breach of one of the most sacred possible of such engagements on the part of victorious champions of these ideals.[102]

Apart from other aspects of the transaction, I believe that the campaign for securing out of Germany the general costs of the war was one of the most serious acts of political unwisdom for which our statesmen have ever been responsible. To what a different future Europe might have looked forward if either Mr. Lloyd George or Mr. Wilson had apprehended that the most serious of the problems which claimed their attention were not political or territorial but financial and economic, and that the perils of the future lay not in frontiers or sovereignties but in food, coal, and transport. Neither of them paid adequate attention to these problems at any stage of the Conference. But in any event the atmosphere for the wise and reasonable consideration of them was hopelessly befogged by the commitments of the British delegation on the question of Indemnities. The hopes to which the Prime Minister had given rise not only compelled him to advocate an unjust and unworkable economic basis to the Treaty with Germany, but set him at variance with the President, and on the other hand with competing interests to those of France and Belgium. The clearer it became that but little could be expected from Germany, the more necessary it was to exercise patriotic greed and "sacred egotism" and snatch the bone from the juster claims and greater need of France or the well-founded expectations of Belgium. Yet the financial problems which were about to exercise Europe could not be solved by greed. The possibility of *their* cure lay in magnanimity.

Europe, if she is to survive her troubles, will need so much magnanimity from America, that she must herself practice it. It is useless for the Allies, hot from stripping Germany and one another, to turn for help to the United States to put the States of Europe, including Germany, on to their feet again. If the General Election of December, 1918, had been fought on lines of prudent generosity instead of imbecile greed, how much better the financial prospect of Europe might now be. I still believe that before the main Conference, or very early in its proceedings, the representatives of Great Britain should have entered deeply, with those of the United States, into the economic and financial situation as a whole, and that the former should have been authorized to make concrete proposals on the general lines (1) that all inter-allied indebtedness be canceled outright; (2) that the sum to be paid by Germany be fixed at $10,000,000,000; (3) that Great Britain renounce all claim to participation in this sum and that any share to which she proves entitled be placed at the disposal of the Conference for the purpose of aiding the finances of the New States about to be established; (4) that in order to make some basis of credit immediately available an appropriate proportion of the German obligations representing the sum to be paid by her should be guaranteed by all parties to the Treaty; and (5) that the ex-enemy Powers should also be allowed, with a view to their economic restoration, to issue a moderate amount of bonds carrying a similar guarantee. Such proposals involved an appeal to the generosity of the United States. But that was inevitable; and, in view of her far less financial sacrifices, it was an appeal which could fairly have been made to her. Such proposals would have been practicable. There is nothing in them quixotic or Utopian. And they would have opened up for Europe some prospect of financial stability and reconstruction.

The further elaboration of these ideas, however, must be left to Chapter VII., and we must return to Paris. I have described the entanglements which Mr. Lloyd George took with him. The position of the Finance Ministers of the other Allies was even worse. We in Great Britain had not based our financial arrangements on any expectations of an indemnity. Receipts from such a source would have been more or less in the nature of a windfall; and, in spite of subsequent developments, there was an expectation at that time of balancing our budget by normal methods. But this was not the case with France or Italy. Their peace budgets made no pretense of balancing and had no prospects of doing so, without some far-reaching revision of the existing policy. Indeed, the position was and remains nearly hopeless. These countries were heading for national bankruptcy. This fact could only be concealed by holding out the expectation of vast receipts from the enemy. As soon as it was admitted that it was in fact impossible to make Germany pay the expenses of both sides, and that the unloading of their liabilities upon the enemy was not practicable, the position of the Ministers of Finance of France and Italy became untenable.

Thus a scientific consideration of Germany's capacity to pay was from the outset out of court. The expectations which the exigencies of politics had made it necessary to raise were so very remote from the truth that a slight distortion of figures was no use, and it was necessary to ignore the facts entirely. The resulting unveracity was fundamental. On a basis of so much falsehood it became impossible to erect any constructive financial policy which was workable. For this reason amongst others, a magnanimous financial policy was essential. The financial position of France and Italy was so bad that it was impossible to make them listen to reason on the subject of the German Indemnity, unless one could at the same time point out to them some alternative mode of escape from their troubles.[103] The representatives of the United States were greatly at fault, in my judgment, for having no constructive proposals whatever to offer to a suffering and distracted Europe.

It is worth while to point out in passing a further element in the situation, namely, the opposition which existed between the "crushing" policy of M. Clemenceau and the financial necessities of M. Klotz. Clemenceau's aim was to weaken and destroy Germany in every possible way, and I fancy that he was always a little contemptuous about the Indemnity; he had no intention of leaving Germany in a position to practise a vast commercial activity. But he did not trouble his head to understand either the indemnity or poor M. Klotz's overwhelming financial difficulties. If it amused the financiers to put into the Treaty some very large demands, well there was no harm in that; but the satisfaction of these demands must not be allowed to interfere with the essential requirements of a Carthaginian Peace. The combination of the "real" policy of

94

M. Clemenceau on unreal issues, with M. Klotz's policy of pretense on what were very real issues indeed, introduced into the Treaty a whole set of incompatible provisions, over and above the inherent impracticabilities of the Reparation proposals.

I cannot here describe the endless controversy and intrigue between the Allies themselves, which at last after some months culminated in the presentation to Germany of the Reparation Chapter in its final form. There can have been few negotiations in history so contorted, so miserable, so utterly unsatisfactory to all parties. I doubt if any one who took much part in that debate can look back on it without shame. I must be content with an analysis of the elements of the final compromise which is known to all the world.

The main point to be settled was, of course, that of the items for which Germany could fairly be asked to make payment. Mr. Lloyd George's election pledge to the effect that the Allies were *entitled* to demand from Germany the entire costs of the war was from the outset clearly untenable; or rather, to put it more impartially, it was clear that to persuade the President of the conformity of this demand with our pro-Armistice engagements was beyond the powers of the most plausible. The actual compromise finally reached is to be read as follows in the paragraphs of the Treaty as it has been published to the world.

Article 231 reads: "The Allied and Associated Governments affirm and Germany accepts the responsibility of Germany and her allies for causing all the loss and damage to which the Allied and Associated Governments and their nationals have been subjected as a consequence of the war imposed upon them by the aggression of Germany and her allies." This is a well and carefully drafted Article; for the President could read it as statement of admission on Germany's part of *moral* responsibility for bringing about the war, while the Prime Minister could explain it as an admission of *financial* liability for the general costs of the war. Article 232 continues: "The Allied and Associated Governments recognize that the resources of Germany are not adequate, after taking into account permanent diminutions of such resources which will result from other provisions of the present Treaty, to make complete reparation for all such loss and damage." The President could comfort himself that this was no more than a statement of undoubted fact, and that to recognize that Germany *cannot* pay a certain claim does not imply that she is *liable* to pay the claim; but the Prime Minister could point out that in the context it emphasizes to the reader the assumption of Germany's theoretic liability asserted in the preceding Article. Article 232 proceeds: "The Allied and Associated Governments, however, require, and Germany undertakes, that *she will make compensation for all damage done to the civilian population of the Allied and Associated Powers and to their property* during the period of the belligerency of each as an Allied or Associated Power against Germany *by such aggression by land, by sea, and from the air,* and in general all damage as defined in Annex I. hereto."[104] The words italicized being practically a quotation from the pre-Armistice conditions, satisfied the scruples of the President, while the addition of the words "and in general all damage as defined in Annex I. hereto" gave the Prime Minister a chance in Annex I.

So far, however, all this is only a matter of words, of virtuosity in draftsmanship, which does no one any harm, and which probably seemed much more important at the time than it ever will again between now and Judgment Day. For substance we must turn to Annex I.

A great part of Annex I. is in strict conformity with the pre-Armistice conditions, or, at any rate, does not strain them beyond what is fairly arguable. Paragraph 1 claims damage done for injury to the persons of civilians, or, in the case of death, to their dependents, as a direct consequence of acts of war; Paragraph 2, for acts of cruelty, violence, or maltreatment on the part of the enemy towards civilian victims; Paragraph 3, for enemy acts injurious to health or capacity to work or to honor towards civilians in occupied or invaded territory; Paragraph 8, for forced labor exacted by the enemy from civilians; Paragraph 9, for damage done to property "with the exception of naval and military works or materials" as a direct consequence of hostilities; and Paragraph 10, for fines and levies imposed by the enemy upon the civilian population. All these demands are just and in conformity with the Allies' rights.

Paragraph 4, which claims for "damage caused by any kind of maltreatment of prisoners of war," is more doubtful on the strict letter, but may be justifiable under the Hague Convention and involves a very small sum.

In Paragraphs 5, 6, and 7, however, an issue of immensely greater significance is involved. These paragraphs assert a claim for the amount of the Separation and similar Allowances granted during the war by the Allied Governments to the families of mobilized persons, and for the amount of the pensions and compensations in respect of the injury or death of combatants payable by these Governments now and hereafter. Financially this adds to the Bill, as we shall see below, a very large amount, indeed about twice as much again as all the other claims added together.

The reader will readily apprehend what a plausible case can be made out for the inclusion of these items of damage, if only on sentimental grounds. It can be pointed out, first of all, that from the point of view of general fairness it is monstrous that a woman whose house is destroyed should be entitled to claim from the enemy whilst a woman whose husband is killed on the field of battle should not be so entitled; or that a farmer deprived of his farm should claim but that a woman deprived of the earning power of her husband should not claim. In fact the case for including Pensions and Separation Allowances largely depends on exploiting the rather *arbitrary* character of the criterion laid down in the pre-Armistice conditions. Of all the losses caused by war some bear more heavily on individuals and some are more evenly distributed over the community as a whole; but by means of compensations granted by the Government many of the former are in fact converted into the latter. The most logical criterion for a limited claim, falling short of the entire costs of the war, would have been in respect of enemy acts contrary to International engagements or the recognized practices of warfare. But this also would have been very difficult to apply and unduly unfavorable to French interests as compared with Belgium (whose neutrality Germany had guaranteed) and Great Britain (the chief sufferer from illicit acts of submarines).

In any case the appeals to sentiment and fairness outlined above are hollow; for it makes no difference to the recipient of a separation allowance or a pension whether the State which pays them receives compensation on this or on another head, and a recovery by the State out of indemnity receipts is just as much in relief of the general taxpayer as a contribution towards the general costs of the war would have been. But the main consideration is that it was too late to consider whether the pre-Armistice conditions were perfectly judicious and logical or to amend them; the only question at issue was whether these conditions were not in fact limited to such classes of direct damage to civilians and their property as are set forth in Paragraphs 1, 2, 3, 8, 9, and 10 of Annex I. If words have any meaning, or engagements any force, we had no more right to claim for those war expenses of the State, which arose out of Pensions and Separation Allowances, than for any other of the general costs of the war. And who is prepared to argue in detail that we were entitled to demand the latter?

What had really happened was a compromise between the Prime Minister's pledge to the British electorate to claim the entire costs of the war and the pledge to the contrary which the Allies had given to Germany at the Armistice. The Prime Minister could claim that although he had not secured the entire costs of the war, he had nevertheless secured an important contribution towards them, that he had always qualified his promises by the limiting condition of Germany's capacity to pay, and that the bill as now presented more than exhausted this capacity as estimated by the more sober authorities. The President, on the other hand, had secured a formula, which was not too obvious a breach of faith, and had avoided a quarrel with his Associates on an issue where the appeals to sentiment and passion would all have been against him, in the event of its being made a matter of open popular controversy. In view of the Prime Minister's election pledges, the President could hardly hope to get him to abandon them in their entirety without a struggle in public; and the cry of pensions would have had an overwhelming popular appeal in all countries. Once more the Prime Minister had shown himself a political tactician of a high order.

A further point of great difficulty may be readily perceived between the lines of the Treaty. It fixes no definite sum as representing Germany's liability. This feature has been the subject of very general criticism,—that it is equally inconvenient to Germany and to the Allies themselves that she should not know what she has to pay or they what they are to receive. The method, apparently contemplated by the Treaty, of arriving at the final result over a period of many months by an addition of hundreds of thousands of individual claims for damage to land, farm buildings, and chickens, is evidently impracticable; and the reasonable course would have been for both parties to compound for a round sum without examination of details. If this round sum had been named in the Treaty, the settlement would have been placed on a more business-like basis.

But this was impossible for two reasons. Two different kinds of false statements had been widely promulgated, one as to Germany's capacity to pay, the other as to the amount of the Allies' just claims in respect of the devastated areas. The fixing of either of these figures presented a dilemma. A figure for Germany's prospective capacity to pay, not too much in excess of the estimates of most candid and well-informed authorities, would have fallen hopelessly far short of popular expectations both in England and in France. On the other hand, a definitive figure for damage done which would not disastrously disappoint the expectations which had been raised in France and Belgium might have been incapable of substantiation under challenge,[105] and open to damaging criticism on the part of the Germans, who were believed to have been prudent enough to accumulate considerable evidence as to the extent of their own misdoings.

97

By far the safest course for the politicians was, therefore, to mention no figure at all; and from this necessity a great deal of the complication of the Reparation Chapter essentially springs.

The reader may be interested, however, to have my estimate of the claim which can in fact be substantiated under Annex I. of the Reparation Chapter. In the first section of this chapter I have already guessed the claims other than those for Pensions and Separation Allowances at $15,000,000,000 (to take the extreme upper limit of my estimate). The claim for Pensions and Separation Allowances under Annex I. is not to be based on the *actual* cost of these compensations to the Governments concerned, but is to be a computed figure calculated on the basis of the scales in force in France at the date of the Treaty's coming into operation. This method avoids the invidious course of valuing an American or a British life at a higher figure than a French or an Italian. The French rate for Pensions and Allowances is at an intermediate rate, not so high as the American or British, but above the Italian, the Belgian, or the Serbian. The only data required for the calculation are the actual French rates and the numbers of men mobilized and of the casualties in each class of the various Allied Armies. None of these figures are available in detail, but enough is known of the general level of allowances, of the numbers involved, and of the casualties suffered to allow of an estimate which may not be *very wide* of the mark. My guess as to the amount to be added in respect of Pensions and Allowances is as follows:

British Empire	$7,000,000,000	[106]
France	12,000,000,000	[106]
Italy	2,500,000,000	
Others (Including United States)	3,500,000,000	
Total	$25,000,000,000	

I feel much more confidence in the approximate accuracy of the total figure [107] than in its division between the different claimants. The reader will observe that in any case the addition of Pensions and Allowances enormously increases the aggregate claim, raising it indeed by nearly double. Adding this figure to the estimate under other heads, we have a total claim against Germany of $40,000,000,000. [108] I believe that this figure is fully high enough, and that the actual result may fall somewhat short of it. [109] In the next section of this chapter the relation of this figure to Germany's capacity to pay will be examined. It is only necessary here to remind the reader of certain other particulars of the Treaty which speak for themselves:

1. Out of the total amount of the claim, whatever it eventually turns out to be, a sum of $5,000,000,000 must be paid before May 1, 1921. The possibility of this will be discussed below. But the Treaty itself provides certain abatements. In the first place, this sum is to include the expenses of the Armies of Occupation since the Armistice (a large charge of the order of magnitude of $1,000,000,000 which under another Article of the Treaty—No. 249—is laid upon Germany). [110] But further, "such supplies of food and raw materials as may be judged by the Governments of the Principal Allied and Associated Powers to be essential to enable Germany to meet her obligations for

Reparation may also, with the approval of the said Governments, be paid for out of the above sum."[111] This is a qualification of high importance. The clause, as it is drafted, allows the Finance Ministers of the Allied countries to hold out to their electorates the hope of substantial payments at an early date, while at the same time it gives to the Reparation Commission a discretion, which the force of facts will compel them to exercise, to give back to Germany what is required for the maintenance of her economic existence. This discretionary power renders the demand for an immediate payment of $5,000,000,000 less injurious than it would otherwise be, but nevertheless it does not render it innocuous. In the first place, my conclusions in the next section of this chapter indicate that this sum cannot be found within the period indicated, even if a large proportion is in practice returned to Germany for the purpose of enabling her to pay for imports. In the second place, the Reparation Commission can only exercise its discretionary power effectively by taking charge of the entire foreign trade of Germany, together with the foreign exchange arising out of it, which will be quite beyond the capacity of any such body. If the Reparation Commission makes any serious attempt to administer the collection of this sum of $5,000,000,000 and to authorize the return to Germany of a part it, the trade of Central Europe will be strangled by bureaucratic regulation in its most inefficient form.

2. In addition to the early payment in cash or kind of a sum of $5,000,000,000, Germany is required to deliver bearer bonds to a further amount of $10,000,000,000, or, in the event of the payments in cash or kind before May 1, 1921, available for Reparation, falling short of $5,000,000,000 by reason of the permitted deductions, to such further amount as shall bring the total payments by Germany in cash, kind, and bearer bonds up to May 1, 1921, to a figure of $15,000,000,000 altogether.[112] These bearer bonds carry interest at 2-1/2 per cent per annum from 1921 to 1925, and at 5 per cent *plus* 1 per cent for amortization thereafter. Assuming, therefore, that Germany is not able to provide any appreciable surplus towards Reparation before 1921, she will have to find a sum of $375,000,000 annually from 1921 to 1925, and $900,000,000 annually thereafter.[113]

3. As soon as the Reparation Commission is satisfied that Germany can do better than this, 5 per cent bearer bonds are to be issued for a further $10,000,000,000, the rate of amortization being determined by the Commission hereafter. This would bring the annual payment to $1,400,000,000 without allowing anything for the discharge of the capital of the last $10,000,000,000.

4. Germany's liability, however, is not limited to $25,000,000,000, and the Reparation Commission is to demand further instalments of bearer bonds until the total enemy liability under Annex I. has been provided for. On the basis of my estimate of $40,000,000,000 for the total liability, which is more likely to be criticized as being too low than as being too high, the amount of this balance will be $15,000,000,000. Assuming interest at 5 per cent, this will raise the annual payment to $2,150,000,000 without allowance for amortization.

5. But even this is not all. There is a further provision of devastating significance. Bonds representing payments in excess of $15,000,000,000 are not to be issued until the Commission is satisfied that Germany can meet the interest on them. But this does not mean that interest is remitted in the meantime. As from May 1, 1921, interest is to be

debited to Germany on such part of her outstanding debt as has not been covered by payment in cash or kind or by the issue of bonds as above,[114] and "the rate of interest shall be 5 per cent unless the Commission shall determine at some future time that circumstances justify a variation of this rate." That is to say, the capital sum of indebtedness is rolling up all the time at compound interest. The effect of this provision towards increasing the burden is, on the assumption that Germany cannot pay very large sums at first, enormous. At 5 per cent compound interest a capital sum doubles itself in fifteen years. On the assumption that Germany cannot pay more than $750,000,000 annually until 1936 (*i.e.* 5 per cent interest on $15,000,000,000) the $25,000,000,000 on which interest is deferred will have risen to $50,000,000,000, carrying an annual interest charge of $2,500,000,000. That is to say, even if Germany pays $750,000,000 annually up to 1936, she will nevertheless owe us at that date more than half as much again as she does now ($65,000,000,000 as compared with $40,000,000,000). From 1936 onwards she will have to pay to us $3,250,000,000 annually in order to keep pace with the interest alone. At the end of any year in which she pays less than this sum she will owe more than she did at the beginning of it. And if she is to discharge the capital sum in thirty years from 1930, *i.e.* in forty-eight years from the Armistice, she must pay an additional $650,000,000 annually, making $3,900,000,000 in all.[115]

It is, in my judgment, as certain as anything can be, for reasons which I will elaborate in a moment, that Germany cannot pay anything approaching this sum. Until the Treaty is altered, therefore, Germany has in effect engaged herself to hand over to the Allies the whole of her surplus production in perpetuity.

6. This is not less the case because the Reparation Commission has been given discretionary powers to vary the rate of interest, and to postpone and even to cancel the capital indebtedness. In the first place, some of these powers can only be exercised if the Commission or the Governments represented on it are *unanimous*.[116] But also, which is perhaps more important, it will be the *duty* of the Reparation Commission, until there has been a unanimous and far-reaching change of the policy which the Treaty represents, to extract from Germany year after year the maximum sum obtainable. There is a great difference between fixing a definite sum, which though large is within Germany's capacity to pay and yet to retain a little for herself, and fixing a sum far beyond her capacity, which is then to be reduced at the discretion of a foreign Commission acting with the object of obtaining each year the maximum which the circumstances of that year permit. The first still leaves her with some slight incentive for enterprise, energy, and hope. The latter skins her alive year by year in perpetuity, and however skilfully and discreetly the operation is performed, with whatever regard for not killing the patient in the process, it would represent a policy which, if it were really entertained and deliberately practised, the judgment of men would soon pronounce to be one of the most outrageous acts of a cruel victor in civilized history.

There are other functions and powers of high significance which the Treaty accords to the Reparation Commission. But these will be most conveniently dealt with in a separate section.

III. *Germany's Capacity to pay*

The forms in which Germany can discharge the sum which she has engaged herself to pay are three in number—

1. Immediately transferable wealth in the form of gold, ships, and foreign securities;

2. The value of property in ceded territory, or surrendered under the Armistice;

3. Annual payments spread over a term of years, partly in cash and partly in materials such as coal products, potash, and dyes.

There is excluded from the above the actual restitution of property removed from territory occupied by the enemy, as, for example, Russian gold, Belgian and French securities, cattle, machinery, and works of art. In so far as the actual goods taken can be identified and restored, they must clearly be returned to their rightful owners, and cannot be brought into the general reparation pool. This is expressly provided for in Article 238 of the Treaty.

1. *Immediately Transferable Wealth*

(*a*) *Gold.*—After deduction of the gold to be returned to Russia, the official holding of gold as shown in the Reichsbank's return of the 30th November, 1918, amounted to $577,089,500. This was a very much larger amount than had appeared in the Reichsbank's return prior to the war,[117] and was the result of the vigorous campaign carried on in Germany during the war for the surrender to the Reichsbank not only of gold coin but of gold ornaments of every kind. Private hoards doubtless still exist, but, in view of the great efforts already made, it is unlikely that either the German Government or the Allies will be able to unearth them. The return can therefore be taken as probably representing the maximum amount which the German Government are able to extract from their people. In addition to gold there was in the Reichsbank a sum of about $5,000,000 in silver. There must be, however, a further substantial amount in circulation, for the holdings of the Reichsbank were as high as $45,500,000 on the 31st December, 1917, and stood at about $30,000,000 up to the latter part of October, 1918, when the internal run began on currency of every kind.[118]We may, therefore, take a total of (say) $625,000,000 for gold and silver together at the date of the Armistice.

These reserves, however, are no longer intact. During the long period which elapsed between the Armistice and the Peace it became necessary for the Allies to facilitate the provisioning of Germany from abroad. The political condition of Germany at that time and the serious menace of Spartacism rendered this step necessary in the interests of the Allies themselves if they desired the continuance in Germany of a stable Government to treat with. The question of how such provisions were to be paid for presented, however, the gravest difficulties. A series of Conferences was held at Trèves, at Spa, at Brussels, and subsequently at Château Villette and Versailles, between representatives of the Allies and of Germany, with the object of finding some method of payment as little injurious as possible to the future prospects of Reparation payments. The German representatives maintained from the outset that the financial exhaustion of their country was for the time being so complete that a temporary loan from the Allies was the only

101

possible expedient. This the Allies could hardly admit at a time when they were preparing demands for the immediate payment by Germany of immeasurably larger sums. But, apart from this, the German claim could not be accepted as strictly accurate so long as their gold was still untapped and their remaining foreign securities unmarketed. In any case, it was out of the question to suppose that in the spring of 1919 public opinion in the Allied countries or in America would have allowed the grant of a substantial loan to Germany. On the other hand, the Allies were naturally reluctant to exhaust on the provisioning of Germany the gold which seemed to afford one of the few obvious and certain sources for Reparation. Much time was expended in the exploration of all possible alternatives; but it was evident at last that, even if German exports and saleable foreign securities had been available to a sufficient value, they could not be liquidated in time, and that the financial exhaustion of Germany was so complete that nothing whatever was immediately available in substantial amounts except the gold in the Reichsbank. Accordingly a sum exceeding $250,000,000 in all out of the Reichsbank gold was transferred by Germany to the Allies (chiefly to the United States, Great Britain, however, also receiving a substantial sum) during the first six months of 1919 in payment for foodstuffs.

But this was not all. Although Germany agreed, under the first extension of the Armistice, not to export gold without Allied permission, this permission could not be always withheld. There were liabilities of the Reichsbank accruing in the neighboring neutral countries, which could not be met otherwise than in gold. The failure of the Reichsbank to meet its liabilities would have caused a depreciation of the exchange so injurious to Germany's credit as to react on the future prospects of Reparation. In some cases, therefore, permission to export gold was accorded to the Reichsbank by the Supreme Economic Council of the Allies.

The net result of these various measures was to reduce the gold reserve of the Reichsbank by more than half, the figures falling from $575,000,000 to $275,000,000 in September, 1919.

It would be *possible* under the Treaty to take the whole of this latter sum for Reparation purposes. It amounts, however, as it is, to less than 4 per cent of the Reichsbank's Note Issue, and the psychological effect of its total confiscation might be expected (having regard to the very large volume of mark notes held abroad) to destroy the exchange value of the mark almost entirely. A sum of $25,000,000, $50,000,000, or even $100,000,000 might be taken for a special purpose. But we may assume that the Reparation Commission will judge it imprudent, having regard to the reaction on their future prospects of securing payment, to ruin the German currency system altogether, more particularly because the French and Belgian Governments, being holders of a very large volume of mark notes formerly circulating in the occupied or ceded territory, have a great interest in maintaining some exchange value for the mark, quite apart from Reparation prospects.

It follows, therefore, that no sum worth speaking of can be expected in the form of gold or silver towards the initial payment of $5,000,000,000 due by 1921.

(*b*) *Shipping.*—Germany has engaged, as we have seen above, to surrender to the Allies virtually the whole of her merchant shipping. A considerable part of it, indeed, was already in the hands of the Allies prior to the conclusion of Peace, either by detention in their ports or by the provisional transfer of tonnage under the Brussels Agreement in connection with the supply of foodstuffs.[119] Estimating the tonnage of German shipping to be taken over under the Treaty at 4,000,000 gross tons, and the average value per ton at $150 per ton, the total money value involved is $600,000,000.[120]

(c) *Foreign Securities.*—Prior to the census of foreign securities carried out by the German Government in September, 1916,[121] of which the exact results have not been made public, no official return of such investments was ever called for in Germany, and the various unofficial estimates are confessedly based on insufficient data, such as the admission of foreign securities to the German Stock Exchanges, the receipts of the stamp duties, consular reports, etc. The principal German estimates current before the war are given in the appended footnote.[122] This shows a general consensus of opinion among German authorities that their net foreign investments were upwards of $6,250,000,000. I take this figure as the basis of my calculations, although I believe it to be an exaggeration; $5,000,000,000 would probably be a safer figure.

Deductions from this aggregate total have to be made under four heads.

(i.) Investments in Allied countries and in the United States, which between them constitute a considerable part of the world, have been sequestrated by Public Trustees, Custodians of Enemy Property, and similar officials, and are not available for Reparation except in so far as they show a surplus over various private claims. Under the scheme for dealing with enemy debts outlined in Chapter IV., the first charge on these assets is the private claims of Allied against German nationals. It is unlikely, except in the United States, that there will be any appreciable surplus for any other purpose.

(ii.) Germany's most important fields of foreign investment before the war were not, like ours, oversea, but in Russia, Austria-Hungary, Turkey, Roumania, and Bulgaria. A great part of these has now become almost valueless, at any rate for the time being; especially those in Russia and Austria-Hungary. If present market value is to be taken as the test, none of these investments are now saleable above a nominal figure. Unless the Allies are prepared to take over these securities much above their nominal market valuation, and hold them for future realization, there is no substantial source of funds for immediate payment in the form of investments in these countries.

(iii.) While Germany was not in a position to realize her foreign investments during the war to the degree that we were, she did so nevertheless in the case of certain countries and to the extent that she was able. Before the United States came into the war, she is believed to have resold a large part of the pick of her investments in American securities, although some current estimates of these sales (a figure of $300,000,000 has been mentioned) are probably exaggerated. But throughout the war and particularly in its later stages, when her exchanges were weak and her credit in the neighboring neutral countries was becoming very low, she was disposing of such securities as Holland, Switzerland, and Scandinavia would buy or would accept as collateral. It is reasonably certain that by June, 1919, her investments in these countries had been reduced to a negligible figure and were far exceeded by her liabilities in them. Germany has also sold certain overseas securities, such as Argentine cedulas, for which a market could be found.

103

(iv.) It is certain that since the Armistice there has been a great flight abroad of the foreign securities still remaining in private hands. This is exceedingly difficult to prevent. German foreign investments are as a rule in the form of bearer securities and are not registered. They are easily smuggled abroad across Germany's extensive land frontiers, and for some months before the conclusion of peace it was certain that their owners would not be allowed to retain them if the Allied Governments could discover any method of getting hold of them. These factors combined to stimulate human ingenuity, and the efforts both of the Allied and of the German Governments to interfere effectively with the outflow are believed to have been largely futile.

In face of all these considerations, it will be a miracle if much remains for Reparation. The countries of the Allies and of the United States, the countries of Germany's own allies, and the neutral countries adjacent to Germany exhaust between them almost the whole of the civilized world; and, as we have seen, we cannot expect much to be available for Reparation from investments in any of these quarters. Indeed there remain no countries of importance for investments except those of South America.

To convert the significance of these deductions into figures involves much guesswork. I give the reader the best personal estimate I can form after pondering the matter in the light of the available figures and other relevant data.

I put the deduction under (i.) at $1,500,000,000, of which $500,000,000 may be ultimately available after meeting private debts, etc.

As regards (ii.)—according to a census taken by the Austrian Ministry of Finance on the 31st December, 1912, the nominal value of the Austro-Hungarian securities held by Germans was $986,500,000. Germany's pre-war investments in Russia outside Government securities have been estimated at $475,000,000, which is much lower than would be expected, and in 1906 Sartorius v. Waltershausen estimated her investments in Russian Government securities at $750,000,000. This gives a total of $1,225,000,000, which is to some extent borne out by the figure of $1,000,000,000 given in 1911 by Dr. Ischchanian as a deliberately modest estimate. A Roumanian estimate, published at the time of that country's entry in the war, gave the value of Germany's investments in Roumania at $20,000,000 to $22,000,000, of which $14,000,000 to $16,000,000 were in Government securities. An association for the defense of French interests in Turkey, as reported in the *Temps* (Sept. 8, 1919), has estimated the total amount of German capital invested in Turkey at about $295,000,000, of which, according to the latest Report of the Council of Foreign Bondholders, $162,500,000 was held by German nationals in the Turkish External Debt. No estimates are available to me of Germany's investments in Bulgaria. Altogether I venture a deduction of $2,500,000,000 in respect of this group of countries as a whole.

Resales and the pledging as collateral of securities during the war under (iii.) I put at $500,000,000 to $750,000,000, comprising practically all Germany's holding of Scandinavian, Dutch, and Swiss securities, a part of her South American securities, and a substantial proportion of her North American securities sold prior to the entry of the United States into the war.

As to the proper deduction under (iv.) there are naturally no available figures. For months past the European press has been full of sensational stories of the expedients adopted. But if we put the value of securities which have already left Germany or have been safely secreted within Germany itself beyond discovery by the most inquisitorial and powerful methods at $500,000,000, we are not likely to overstate it.

These various items lead, therefore, in all to a deduction of a round figure of about $5,000,000,000, and leave us with an amount of $1,250,000,000 theoretically still available.[123]

To some readers this figure may seem low, but let them remember that it purports to represent the remnant of *saleable* securities upon which the German Government might be able to lay hands for public purposes. In my own opinion it is much too high, and considering the problem by a different method of attack I arrive at a lower figure. For leaving out of account sequestered Allied securities and investments in Austria, Russia, etc., what blocks of securities, specified by countries and enterprises, can Germany possibly still have which could amount to as much as $1,250,000,000? I cannot answer the question. She has some Chinese Government securities which have not been sequestered, a few Japanese perhaps, and a more substantial value of first-class South American properties. But there are very few enterprises of this class still in German hands, and even *their* value is measured by one or two tens of millions, not by fifties or hundreds. He would be a rash man, in my judgment, who joined a syndicate to pay $500,000,000 in cash for the unsequestered remnant of Germany's overseas investments. If the Reparation Commission is to realize even this lower figure, it is probable that they will have to nurse, for some years, the assets which they take over, not attempting their disposal at the present time.

We have, therefore, a figure of from $500,000,000 to $1,250,000,000 as the maximum contribution from Germany's foreign securities.

Her immediately transferable wealth is composed, then, of—

(*a*) Gold and silver—say $300,000,000.

(*b*) Ships—$600,000,000.

(*c*) Foreign securities—$500,000,000 to $1,250,000,000.

Of the gold and silver, it is not, in fact, practicable to take any substantial part without consequences to the German currency system injurious to the interests of the Allies themselves. The contribution from all these sources together which the Reparation Commission can hope to secure by May, 1921, may be put, therefore, at from $1,250,000,000 to $1,750,000,000 *as a maximum*.[124]

2. Property in ceded Territory or surrendered under the Armistice

As the Treaty has been drafted Germany will not receive important credits available towards meeting reparation in respect of her property in ceded territory.

Private property in most of the ceded territory is utilized towards discharging private German debts to Allied nationals, and only the surplus, if any, is available towards

Reparation. The value of such property in Poland and the other new States is payable direct to the owners.

Government property in Alsace-Lorraine, in territory ceded to Belgium, and in Germany's former colonies transferred to a Mandatory, is to be forfeited without credit given. Buildings, forests, and other State property which belonged to the former Kingdom of Poland are also to be surrendered without credit. There remain, therefore, Government properties, other than the above, surrendered to Poland, Government properties in Schleswig surrendered to Denmark,[125] the value of the Saar coalfields, the value of certain river craft, etc., to be surrendered under the Ports, Waterways, and Railways Chapter, and the value of the German submarine cables transferred under Annex VII. of the Reparation Chapter.

Whatever the Treaty may say, the Reparation Commission will not secure any cash payments from Poland. I believe that the Saar coalfields have been valued at from $75,000,000 to $100,000,000. A round figure of $150,000,000 for all the above items, excluding any surplus available in respect of private property, is probably a liberal estimate.

Then remains the value of material surrendered under the Armistice. Article 250 provides that a credit shall be assessed by the Reparation Commission for rolling-stock surrendered under the Armistice as well as for certain other specified items, and generally for any material so surrendered for which the Reparation Commission think that credit should be given, "as having non-military value." The rolling-stock (150,000 wagons and 5,000 locomotives) is the only very valuable item. A round figure of $250,000,000, for all the Armistice surrenders, is probably again a liberal estimate.

We have, therefore, $400,000,000 to add in respect of this heading to our figure of $1,250,000,000 to $1,750,000,000 under the previous heading. This figure differs from the preceding in that it does not represent cash capable of benefiting the financial situation of the Allies, but is only a book credit between themselves or between them and Germany.

The total of $1,650,000,000 to $2,150,000,000 now reached is not, however, available for Reparation. The *first* charge upon it, under Article 251 of the Treaty, is the cost of the Armies of Occupation both during the Armistice and after the conclusion of Peace. The aggregate of this figure up to May, 1921, cannot be calculated until the rate of withdrawal is known which is to reduce the *monthly* cost from the figure exceeding $100,000,000, which prevailed during the first part of 1919, to that of $5,000,000, which is to be the normal figure eventually. I estimate, however, that this aggregate may be about $1,000,000,000. This leaves us with from $500,000,000 to $1,000,000,000 still in hand.

Out of this, and out of exports of goods, and payments in kind under the Treaty prior to May, 1921 (for which I have not as yet made any allowance), the Allies have held out the hope that they will allow Germany to receive back such sums for the purchase of necessary food and raw materials as the former deem it essential for her to have. It is not possible at the present time to form an accurate judgment either as to the money-value of the goods which Germany will require to purchase from abroad in order to re-establish her economic life, or as to the degree of liberality with which the Allies will

106

exercise their discretion. If her stocks of raw materials and food were to be restored to anything approaching their normal level by May, 1921, Germany would probably require foreign purchasing power of from $500,000,000 to $1,000,000,000 at least, in addition to the value of her current exports. While this is not likely to be permitted, I venture to assert as a matter beyond reasonable dispute that the social and economic condition of Germany cannot possibly permit a surplus of exports over imports during the period prior to May, 1921, and that the value of any payments in kind with which she may be able to furnish the Allies under the Treaty in the form of coal, dyes, timber, or other materials will have to be returned to her to enable her to pay for imports essential to her existence.[126]

The Reparation Commission can, therefore, expect no addition from other sources to the sum of from $500,000,000 to $1,000,000,000 with which we have hypothetically credited it after the realization of Germany's immediately transferable wealth, the calculation of the credits due to Germany under the Treaty, and the discharge of the cost of the Armies of Occupation. As Belgium has secured a private agreement with France, the United States, and Great Britain, outside the Treaty, by which she is to receive, towards satisfaction of her claims, the *first* $500,000,000 available for Reparation, the upshot of the whole matter is that Belgium may *possibly* get her $500,000,000 by May, 1921, but none of the other Allies are likely to secure by that date any contribution worth speaking of. At any rate, it would be very imprudent for Finance Ministers to lay their plans on any other hypothesis.

3. *Annual Payments spread over a Term of Years*

It is evident that Germany's pre-war capacity to pay an annual foreign tribute has not been unaffected by the almost total loss of her colonies, her overseas connections, her mercantile marine, and her foreign properties, by the cession of ten per cent of her territory and population, of one-third of her coal and of three-quarters of her iron ore, by two million casualties amongst men in the prime of life, by the starvation of her people for four years, by the burden of a vast war debt, by the depreciation of her currency to less than one-seventh its former value, by the disruption of her allies and their territories, by Revolution at home and Bolshevism on her borders, and by all the unmeasured ruin in strength and hope of four years of all-swallowing war and final defeat.

All this, one would have supposed, is evident. Yet most estimates of a great indemnity from Germany depend on the assumption that she is in a position to conduct in the future a vastly greater trade than ever she has had in the past.

For the purpose of arriving at a figure it is of no great consequence whether payment takes the form of cash (or rather of foreign exchange) or is partly effected in kind (coal, dyes, timber, etc.), as contemplated by the Treaty. In any event, it is only by the export of specific commodities that Germany can pay, and the method of turning the value of these exports to account for Reparation purposes is, comparatively, a matter of detail.

We shall lose ourselves in mere hypothesis unless we return in some degree to first principles, and, whenever we can, to such statistics as there are. It is certain that an annual payment can only be made by Germany over a series of years by diminishing her imports and increasing her exports, thus enlarging the balance in her favor which is available for effecting payments abroad. Germany can pay in the long-run in goods, and in goods only, whether these goods are furnished direct to the Allies, or whether they are sold to neutrals and the neutral credits so arising are then made over to the Allies. The most solid basis for estimating the extent to which this process can be carried is to be found, therefore, in an analysis of her trade returns before the war. Only on the basis of such an analysis, supplemented by some general data as to the aggregate wealth-producing capacity of the country, can a rational guess be made as to the maximum degree to which the exports of Germany could be brought to exceed her imports.

In the year 1913 Germany's imports amounted to $2,690,000,000, and her exports to $2,525,000,000, exclusive of transit trade and bullion. That is to say, imports exceeded exports by about $165,000,000. On the average of the five years ending 1913, however, her imports exceeded her exports by a substantially larger amount, namely, $370,000,000. It follows, therefore, that more than the whole of Germany's pre-war balance for new foreign investment was derived from the interest on her existing foreign securities, and from the profits of her shipping, foreign banking, etc. As her foreign properties and her mercantile marine are now to be taken from her, and as her foreign banking and other miscellaneous sources of revenue from abroad have been largely destroyed, it appears that, on the pre-war basis of exports and imports, Germany, so far from having a surplus wherewith to make a foreign payment, would be not nearly self-supporting. Her first task, therefore, must be to effect a readjustment of consumption and production to cover this deficit. Any further economy she can effect in the use of imported commodities, and any further stimulation of exports will then be available for Reparation.

Two-thirds of Germany's import and export trade is enumerated under separate headings in the following tables. The considerations applying to the enumerated portions may be assumed to apply more or less to the remaining one-third, which is composed of commodities of minor importance individually.

German Exports, 1913	Amount: Million Dollars	Percentage of Total Exports
Iron goods (including tin plates, etc.)	330.65	13.2
Machinery and parts (including motor-cars)	187.75	7.5
Coal, coke, and briquettes	176.70	7.0
Woolen goods (including raw and combed wool and clothing)	147.00	5.9
Cotton goods (including raw cotton, yarn, and thread)	140.75	5.6
	982.85	39.2
Cereals, etc. (including rye, oats, wheat, hops)	105.90	4.1
Leather and leather goods	77.35	3.0

Sugar	66.00	2.6
Paper, etc.	65.50	2.6
Furs	58.75	2.2
Electrical goods (installations, ma-chinery, lamps, cables)	54.40	2.2
Silk goods	50.50	2.0
Dyes	48.80	1.9
Copper goods	32.50	1.3
Toys	25.75	1.0
Rubber and rubber goods	21.35	0.9
Books, maps, and music	18.55	0.8
Potash	15.90	0.6
Glass	15.70	0.6
Potassium chloride	14.55	0.6
Pianos, organs, and parts	13.85	0.6
Raw zinc	13.70	0.5
Porcelain	12.65	0.5
	711.70	67.2
Other goods, unenumerated	829.69	32.8
Total	2,524.15	100.0

German Imports, 1913	Amount: Million Dollars	Percentage of Total Exports
I. Raw materials:—		
Cotton	151.75	5.6
Hides and skins	124.30	4.6
Wool	118.35	4.4
Copper	83.75	3.1
Coal	68.30	2.5
Timber	58.00	2.2
Iron ore	56.75	2.1
Furs	46.75	1.7
Flax and flaxseed	46.65	1.7
Saltpetre	42.75	1.6
Silk	39.50	1.5
Rubber	36.50	1.4
Jute	23.50	0.9
Petroleum	17.45	0.7
Tin	14.55	0.5
Phosphorus chalk	11.60	0.4
Lubricating oil	11.45	0.4
	951.90	35.3
II. Food, tobacco, etc.:—		
Cereals, etc. (wheat, barley, bran, rice, maize, oats, rye,	327.55	12.2

clover)

Oil seeds and cake, etc. (including palm kernels, copra, cocoa beans)	102.65	3.8
Cattle, lamb fat, bladders	73.10	2.8
Coffee	54.75	2.0
Eggs	48.50	1.8
Tobacco	33.50	1.2
Butter	29.65	1.1
Horses	29.05	1.1
Fruit	18.25	0.7
Fish	14.95	0.6
Poultry	14.00	0.6
Wine	13.35	0.5
	759.30	28.3
III. Manufactures:—		
Cotton yarn and thread and cotton goods	47.05	1.8
Woolen yarn and woolen goods	37.85	1.4
Machinery	20.10	0.7
	105.00	3.9
IV. Unenumerated	876.40	32.5
Total	2,692.60	100.0

These tables show that the most important exports consisted of:—

1. Iron Goods, including tin plates (13.2 per cent),
2. Machinery, etc. (7.5 per cent),
3. Coal, coke, and briquettes (7 per cent),
4. Woolen goods, including raw and combed wool (5.9 per cent), and
5. Cotton goods, including cotton yarn and thread and raw cotton (5.6 per cent),

these five classes between them accounting for 39.2 per cent. of the total exports. It will be observed that all these goods are of a kind in which before the war competition between Germany and the United Kingdom was very severe. If, therefore, the volume of such exports to overseas or European destinations is very largely increased the effect upon British export trade must be correspondingly serious. As regards two of the categories, namely, cotton and woolen goods, the increase of an export trade is dependent upon an increase of the import of the raw material, since Germany produces no cotton and practically no wool. These trades are therefore incapable of expansion unless Germany is given facilities for securing these raw materials (which can only be at the expense of the Allies) in excess of the pre-war standard of consumption, and even then the effective increase is not the gross value of the exports, but only the difference between the value of the manufactured exports and of the imported raw material. As regards the other three categories, namely, machinery, iron goods, and coal, Germany's capacity to increase her exports will have been taken from her by the cessions of territory in Poland, Upper Silesia, and Alsace-Lorraine. As has been pointed out already, these districts accounted for nearly one-third of Germany's production of coal. But they also supplied no less than three-quarters of her iron-ore production, 38 per cent of her blast furnaces, and 9.5 per cent of her iron and steel foundries. Unless, therefore, Alsace-Lorraine and Upper Silesia send their iron ore to Germany proper, to be worked up, which will involve an increase in the imports for which she will have to find payment, so far from any increase in export trade being possible, a decrease is inevitable.[127]

Next on the list come cereals, leather goods, sugar, paper, furs, electrical goods, silk goods, and dyes. Cereals are not a net export and are far more than balanced by imports of the same commodities. As regards sugar, nearly 90 per cent of Germany's pre-war exports came to the United Kingdom.[128] An increase in this trade might be stimulated by a grant of a preference in this country to German sugar or by an arrangement by which sugar was taken in part payment for the indemnity on the same lines as has been proposed for coal, dyes, etc. Paper exports also might be capable of some increase. Leather goods, furs, and silks depend upon corresponding imports on the other side of the account. Silk goods are largely in competition with the trade of France and Italy. The remaining items are individually very small. I have heard it suggested that the indemnity might be paid to a great extent in potash and the like. But potash before the war represented 0.6 per cent of Germany's export trade, and about $15,000,000 in aggregate value. Besides, France, having secured a potash field in the territory which has been restored to her, will not welcome a great stimulation of the German exports of this material.

An examination of the import list shows that 63.6 per cent are raw materials and food. The chief items of the former class, namely, cotton, wool, copper, hides, iron-ore, furs, silk, rubber, and tin, could not be much reduced without reacting on the export trade, and might have to be increased if the export trade was to be increased. Imports of food, namely, wheat, barley, coffee, eggs, rice, maize, and the like, present a different problem. It is unlikely that, apart from certain comforts, the consumption of food by the German laboring classes before the war was in excess of what was required for maximum efficiency; indeed, it probably fell short of that amount. Any substantial decrease in the imports of food would therefore react on the efficiency of the industrial population, and consequently on the volume of surplus exports which they could be forced to produce. It is hardly possible to insist on a greatly increased productivity of German industry if the workmen are to be underfed. But this may not be equally true of barley, coffee, eggs, and tobacco. If it were possible to enforce a régime in which for the future no German drank beer or coffee, or smoked any tobacco, a substantial saving could be effected. Otherwise there seems little room for any significant reduction.

The following analysis of German exports and imports, according to destination and origin, is also relevant. From this it appears that of Germany's exports in 1913, 18 per cent went to the British Empire, 17 per cent to France, Italy, and Belgium, 10 per cent to Russia and Roumania, and 7 per cent to the United States; that is to say, more than half of the exports found their market in the countries of the Entente nations. Of the balance, 12 per cent went to Austria-Hungary, Turkey, and Bulgaria, and 35 per cent elsewhere. Unless, therefore, the present Allies are prepared to encourage the importation of

German products, a substantial increase in total volume can only be effected by the wholesale swamping of neutral markets.

GERMAN TRADE (1913) ACCORDING TO DESTINATION AND ORIGIN

	Destination of Germany's Exports		Origin of Germany's Imports	
	Million Dollars	Per cent	Million Dollars	Per cent
Great Britain	359.65	14.2	219.00	8.1
India	37.65	1.5	135.20	5.0
Egypt	10.85	0.4	29.60	1.1
Canada	15.10	0.6	16.00	0.6
Australia	22.10	0.9	74.00	2.8
South Africa	11.70	0.5	17.40	0.6
Total: British Empire	456.95	18.1	491.20	18.2
France	197.45	7.8	146.65	5.4
Belgium	137.75	5.5	86.15	3.2
Italy	98.35	3.9	79.40	3.0
U. S. A.	178.30	7.1	427.80	15.9
Russia	220.00	8.7	356.15	13.2
Roumania	35.00	1.4	19.95	0.7
Austria-Hungary	276.20	10.9	206.80	7.7
Turkey	24.60	1.0	18.40	0.7
Bulgaria	7.55	0.3	2.00	...
Other countries	800.20	35.3	858.70	32.0
	2,522.35	100.0	2,692.60	100.0

The above analysis affords some indication of the possible magnitude of the maximum modification of Germany's export balance under the conditions which will prevail after the Peace. On the assumptions (1) that we do not specially favor Germany over ourselves in supplies of such raw materials as cotton and wool (the world's supply of which is limited), (2) that France, having secured the iron-ore deposits, makes a serious attempt to secure the blast-furnaces and the steel trade also, (3) that Germany is not encouraged and assisted to undercut the iron and other trades of the Allies in overseas market, and (4) that a substantial preference is not given to German goods in the British Empire, it is evident by examination of the specific items that not much is practicable.

Let us run over the chief items again: (1) Iron goods. In view of Germany's loss of resources, an increased net export seems impossible and a large decrease probable. (2) Machinery. Some increase is possible. (3) Coal and coke. The value of Germany's net export before the war was $110,000,000; the Allies have agreed that for the time being 20,000,000 tons is the maximum possible export with a problematic (and in fact) impossible increase to 40,000,000 tons at some future time; even on the basis of 20,000,000 tons we have virtually no increase of value, measured in pre-war prices;

112

[129] whilst, if this amount is exacted, there must be a decrease of far greater value in the export of manufactured articles requiring coal for their production. (4) Woolen goods. An increase is impossible without the raw wool, and, having regard to the other claims on supplies of raw wool, a decrease is likely. (5) Cotton goods. The same considerations apply as to wool. (6) Cereals. There never was and never can be a net export. (7) Leather goods. The same considerations apply as to wool.

We have now covered nearly half of Germany's pre-war exports, and there is no other commodity which formerly represented as much as 3 per cent of her exports. In what commodity is she to pay? Dyes?—their total value in 1913 was $50,000,000. Toys? Potash?—1913 exports were worth $15,000,000. And even if the commodities could be specified, in what markets are they to be sold?—remembering that we have in mind goods to the value not of tens of millions annually, but of hundreds of millions.

On the side of imports, rather more is possible. By lowering the standard of life, an appreciable reduction of expenditure on imported commodities may be possible. But, as we have already seen, many large items are incapable of reduction without reacting on the volume of exports.

Let us put our guess as high as we can without being foolish, and suppose that after a time Germany will be able, in spite of the reduction of her resources, her facilities, her markets, and her productive power, to increase her exports and diminish her imports so as to improve her trade balance altogether by $500,000,000 annually, measured in pre-war prices. This adjustment is first required to liquidate the adverse trade balance, which in the five years before the war averaged $370,000,000; but we will assume that after allowing for this, she is left with a favorable trade balance of $250,000,000 a year. Doubling this to allow for the rise in pre-war prices, we have a figure of $500,000,000. Having regard to the political, social, and human factors, as well as to the purely economic, I doubt if Germany could be made to pay this sum annually over a period of 30 years; but it would not be foolish to assert or to hope that she could.

Such a figure, allowing 5 per cent for interest, and 1 per cent for repayment of capital, represents a capital sum having a present value of about $8,500,000,000.[130]

I reach, therefore, the final conclusion that, including all methods of payment— immediately transferable wealth, ceded property, and an annual tribute— $10,000,000,000 is a safe maximum figure of Germany's capacity to pay. In all the actual circumstances, I do not believe that she can pay as much. Let those who consider this a very low figure, bear in mind the following remarkable comparison. The wealth of France in 1871 was estimated at a little less than half that of Germany in 1913. Apart from changes in the value of money, an indemnity from Germany of $2,500,000,000 would, therefore, be about comparable to the sum paid by France in 1871; and as the real burden of an indemnity increases more than in proportion to its amount, the payment of $10,000,000,000 by Germany would have far severer consequences than the $1,000,000,000 paid by France in 1871.

There is only one head under which I see a possibility of adding to the figure reached on the line of argument adopted above; that is, if German labor is actually transported to the devastated areas and there engaged in the work of reconstruction. I have heard that a limited scheme of this kind is actually in view. The additional contribution thus

113

obtainable depends on the number of laborers which the German Government could contrive to maintain in this way and also on the number which, over a period of years, the Belgian and French inhabitants would tolerate in their midst. In any case, it would seem very difficult to employ on the actual work of reconstruction, even over a number of years, imported labor having a net present value exceeding (say) $1,250,000,000; and even this would not prove in practice a net addition to the annual contributions obtainable in other ways.

A capacity of $40,000,000,000 or even of $25,000,000,000 is, therefore, not within the limits of reasonable possibility. It is for those who believe that Germany can make an annual payment amounting to hundreds of millions sterling to say *in what specific commodities* they intend this payment to be made and *in what markets* the goods are to be sold. Until they proceed to some degree of detail, and are able to produce some tangible argument in favor of their conclusions, they do not deserve to be believed.[131]

I make three provisos only, none of which affect the force of my argument for immediate practical purposes.

First: if the Allies were to "nurse" the trade and industry of Germany for a period of five or ten years, supplying her with large loans, and with ample shipping, food, and raw materials during that period, building up markets for her, and deliberately applying all their resources and goodwill to making her the greatest industrial nation in Europe, if not in the world, a substantially larger sum could probably be extracted thereafter; for Germany is capable of very great productivity.

Second: whilst I estimate in terms of money, I assume that there is no revolutionary change in the purchasing power of our unit of value. If the value of gold were to sink to a half or a tenth of its present value, the real burden of a payment fixed in terms of gold would be reduced proportionately. If a sovereign comes to be worth what a shilling is worth now, then, of course, Germany can pay a larger sum than I have named, measured in gold sovereigns.

Third: I assume that there is no revolutionary change in the yield of Nature and material to man's labor. It is not *impossible* that the progress of science should bring within our reach methods and devices by which the whole standard of life would be raised immeasurably, and a given volume of products would represent but a portion of the human effort which it represents now. In this case all standards of "capacity" would be changed everywhere. But the fact that all things are *possible* is no excuse for talking foolishly.

It is true that in 1870 no man could have predicted Germany's capacity in 1910. We cannot expect to legislate for a generation or more. The secular changes in man's economic condition and the liability of human forecast to error are as likely to lead to mistake in one direction as in another. We cannot as reasonable men do better than base our policy on the evidence we have and adapt it to the five or ten years over which we may suppose ourselves to have some measure of prevision; and we are not at fault if we leave on one side the extreme chances of human existence and of revolutionary changes in the order of Nature or of man's relations to her. The fact that we have no adequate knowledge of Germany's capacity to pay over a long period of years is no justification (as I have heard some people claim that, it is) for the statement that she can pay $50,000,000,000.

Why has the world been so credulous of the unveracities of politicians? If an explanation is needed, I attribute this particular credulity to the following influences in part.

In the first place, the vast expenditures of the war, the inflation of prices, and the depreciation of currency, leading up to a complete instability of the unit of value, have made us lose all sense of number and magnitude in matters of finance. What we believed to be the limits of possibility have been so enormously exceeded, and those who founded their expectations on the past have been so often wrong, that the man in the street is now prepared to believe anything which is told him with some show of authority, and the larger the figure the more readily he swallows it.

But those who look into the matter more deeply are sometimes misled by a fallacy, much more plausible to reasonableness. Such a one might base his conclusions on Germany's total surplus of annual productivity as distinct from her export surplus. Helfferich's estimate of Germany's annual increment of wealth in 1913 was $2,000,000,000 to $2,125,000,000 (exclusive of increased money value of existing land and property). Before the war, Germany spent between $250,000,000 and $500,000,000 on armaments, with which she can now dispense. Why, therefore, should she not pay over to the Allies an annual sum of $2,500,000,000? This puts the crude argument in its strongest and most plausible form.

But there are two errors in it. First of all, Germany's annual savings, after what she has suffered in the war and by the Peace, will fall far short of what they were before, and, if they are taken from her year by year in future, they cannot again reach their previous level. The loss of Alsace-Lorraine, Poland, and Upper Silesia could not be assessed in terms of surplus productivity at less than $250,000,000 annually. Germany is supposed to have profited about $500,000,000 per annum from her ships, her foreign investments, and her foreign banking and connections, all of which have now been taken from her. Her saving on armaments is far more than balanced by her annual charge for pensions now estimated at $1,250,000,000,[132] which represents a real loss of productive capacity. And even if we put on one side the burden of the internal debt, which amounts to 24 milliards of marks, as being a question of internal distribution rather than of productivity, we must still allow for the foreign debt incurred by Germany during the war, the exhaustion of her stock of raw materials, the depletion of her live-stock, the impaired productivity of her soil from lack of manures and of labor, and the diminution in her wealth from the failure to keep up many repairs and renewals over a period of nearly five years. Germany is not as rich as she was before the war, and the diminution in her future savings for these reasons, quite apart from the factors previously allowed for, could hardly be put at less than ten per cent, that is $200,000,000 annually.

These factors have already reduced Germany's annual surplus to less than the $500,000,000 at which we arrived on other grounds as the maximum of her annual payments. But even if the rejoinder be made, that we have not yet allowed for the lowering of the standard of life and comfort in Germany which may reasonably be imposed on a defeated enemy,[133] there is still a fundamental fallacy in the method of calculation. An annual surplus available for home investment can only be converted into a surplus available for export abroad by a radical change in the kind of work performed. Labor, while it may be available and efficient for domestic services in Germany, may yet be able to find no outlet in foreign trade. We are back on the same question which faced us in our examination of the export trade—in *what* export trade is German labor going to find a greatly increased outlet? Labor can only he diverted into new channels with loss of efficiency, and a large expenditure of capital. The annual surplus which German labor can produce for capital improvements at home is no measure, either theoretically or practically, of the annual tribute which she can pay abroad.

IV. *The Reparation Commission.*

This body is so remarkable a construction and may, if it functions at all, exert so wide an influence on the life of Europe, that its attributes deserve a separate examination.

There are no precedents for the indemnity imposed on Germany under the present Treaty; for the money exactions which formed part of the settlement after previous wars have differed in two fundamental respects from this one. The sum demanded has been determinate and has been measured in a lump sum of money; and so long as the defeated party was meeting the annual instalments of cash no consequential interference was necessary.

But for reasons already elucidated, the exactions in this case are not yet determinate, and the sum when fixed will prove in excess of what can be paid in cash and in excess also of what can be paid at all. It was necessary, therefore, to set up a body to establish the bill of claim, to fix the mode of payment, and to approve necessary abatements and delays. It was only possible to place this body in a position to exact the utmost year by year by giving it wide powers over the internal economic life of the enemy countries, who are to be treated henceforward as bankrupt estates to be administered by and for the benefit of the creditors. In fact, however, its powers and functions have been enlarged even beyond what was required for this purpose, and the Reparation Commission has been established as the final arbiter on numerous economic and financial issues which it was convenient to leave unsettled in the Treaty itself.[134]

The powers and constitution of the Reparation Commission are mainly laid down in Articles 233-241 and Annex II. of the Reparation Chapter of the Treaty with Germany. But the same Commission is to exercise authority over Austria and Bulgaria, and possibly over Hungary and Turkey, when Peace is made with these countries. There are, therefore, analogous articles *mutatis mudandis* in the Austrian Treaty[135] and in the Bulgarian Treaty.[136]

The principal Allies are each represented by one chief delegate. The delegates of the United States, Great Britain, France, and Italy take part in all proceedings; the delegate of Belgium in all proceedings except those attended by the delegates of Japan or the Serb-Croat- Slovene State; the delegate of Japan in all proceedings affecting maritime or specifically Japanese questions; and the delegate of the Serb-Croat-Slovene State when questions relating to Austria, Hungary, or Bulgaria are under consideration. Other allies are to be represented by delegates, without the power to vote, whenever their respective claims and interests are under examination.

In general the Commission decides by a majority vote, except in certain specific cases where unanimity is required, of which the most important are the cancellation of German indebtedness, long postponement of the instalments, and the sale of German bonds of indebtedness. The Commission is endowed with full executive authority to carry out its decisions. It may set up an executive staff and delegate authority to its officers. The Commission and its staff are to enjoy diplomatic privileges, and its salaries are to be paid by Germany, who will, however, have no voice in fixing them, If the Commission is to discharge adequately its numerous functions, it will be necessary for it to establish a vast polyglot bureaucratic organization, with a staff of hundreds. To this organization, the headquarters of which will be in Paris, the economic destiny of Central Europe is to be entrusted.

Its main functions are as follows:—

1. The Commission will determine the precise figure of the claim against the enemy Powers by an examination in detail of the claims of each of the Allies under Annex I. of the Reparation Chapter. This task must be completed by May, 1921. It shall give to the German Government and to Germany's allies "a just opportunity to be heard, but not to take any part whatever in the decisions of the Commission." That is to say, the Commission will act as a party and a judge at the same time.

2. Having determined the claim, it will draw up a schedule of payments providing for the discharge of the whole sum with interest within thirty years. From time to time it shall, with a view to modifying the schedule within the limits of possibility, "consider the resources and capacity of Germany . . . giving her representatives a just opportunity to be heard."

"In periodically estimating Germany's capacity to pay, the Commission shall examine the German system of taxation, first, to the end that the sums for reparation which Germany is required to pay shall become a charge upon all her revenues prior to that for the service or discharge of any domestic loan, and secondly, so as to satisfy itself that, in general, the German scheme of taxation is fully as heavy proportionately as that of any of the Powers represented on the Commission."

3. Up to May, 1921, the Commission has power, with a view to securing the payment of $5,000,000,000, to demand the surrender of any piece of German property whatever, wherever situated: that is to say, "Germany shall pay in such installments and in such manner, whether in gold, commodities, ships, securities, or otherwise, as the Reparation Commission may fix."

4. The Commission will decide which of the rights and interests of German nationals in public utility undertakings operating in Russia, China, Turkey, Austria, Hungary, and Bulgaria, or in any territory formerly belonging to Germany or her allies, are to be expropriated and transferred to the Commission itself; it will assess the value of the interests so transferred; and it will divide the spoils.

5 The Commission will determine how much of the resources thus stripped from Germany must be returned to her to keep enough life in her economic organization to enable her to continue to make Reparation payments in future.[137]

6. The Commission will assess the value, without appeal or arbitration, of the property and rights ceded under the Armistice, and under the Treaty,—roiling-stock, the mercantile marine, river craft, cattle, the Saar mines, the property in ceded territory for which credit is to be given, and so forth.

7. The Commission will determine the amounts and values (within certain defined limits) of the contributions which Germany is to make in kind year by year under the various Annexes to the Reparation Chapter.

8. The Commission will provide for the restitution by Germany of property which can be identified.

9. The Commission will receive, administer, and distribute all receipts from Germany in cash or in kind. It will also issue and market German bonds of indebtedness.

10. The Commission will assign the share of the pre-war public debt to be taken over by the ceded areas of Schleswig, Poland, Danzig, and Upper Silesia. The Commission will also distribute the public debt of the late Austro-Hungarian Empire between its constituent parts.

11. The Commission will liquidate the Austro-Hungarian Bank, and will supervise the withdrawal and replacement of the currency system of the late Austro-Hungarian Empire.

12. It is for the Commission to report if, in their judgment, Germany is falling short in fulfillment of her obligations, and to advise methods of coercion.

13. In general, the Commission, acting through a subordinate body, will perform the same functions for Austria and Bulgaria as for Germany, and also, presumably, for Hungary and Turkey.[138]

There are also many other relatively minor duties assigned to the Commission. The above summary, however, shows sufficiently the scope and significance of its authority. This authority is rendered of far greater significance by the fact that the demands of the Treaty generally exceed Germany's capacity. Consequently the clauses which allow the Commission to make abatements, if in their judgment the economic conditions of Germany require it, will render it in many different particulars the arbiter of Germany's economic life. The Commission is not only to inquire into Germany's general capacity to pay, and to decide (in the early years) what import of foodstuffs and raw materials is necessary; it is authorized to exert pressure on the German system of taxation (Annex II. para. 12(*b*))[139] and on German internal expenditure, with a view to insuring that Reparation payments are a first charge on the country's entire resources; and it is to decide on the effect on German economic life of demands for machinery, cattle, etc., and of the scheduled deliveries of coal.

By Article 240 of the Treaty Germany expressly recognizes the Commission and its powers "as the same may be constituted by the Allied and Associated Governments," and "agrees irrevocably to the possession and exercise by such Commission of the power and authority given to it under the present Treaty." She undertakes to furnish the Commission with all relevant information. And finally in Article 241, "Germany undertakes to pass, issue, and maintain in force any legislation, orders, and decrees that may be necessary to give complete effect to these provisions."

The comments on this of the German Financial Commission at Versailles were hardly an exaggeration:—"German democracy is thus annihilated at the very moment when the German people was about to build it up after a severe struggle—annihilated by the very persons who throughout the war never tired of maintaining that they sought to bring democracy to us.... Germany is no longer a people and a State, but becomes a mere trade concern placed by its creditors in the hands of a receiver, without its being granted so much as the opportunity to prove its willingness to meet its obligations of its own accord. The Commission, which is to have its permanent headquarters outside Germany, will possess in Germany incomparably greater rights than the German Emperor ever possessed, the German people under its régime would remain for decades to come shorn of all rights, and deprived, to a far greater extent than any people in the days of absolutism, of any independence of action, of any individual aspiration in its economic or even in its ethical progress."

In their reply to these observations the Allies refused to admit that there was any substance, ground, or force in them. "The observations of the German Delegation," they pronounced, "present a view of this Commission so distorted and so inexact that it is difficult to believe that the clauses of the Treaty have been calmly or carefully examined. It is not an engine of oppression or a device for interfering with German sovereignty. It has no forces at its command; it has no executive powers within the territory of Germany; it cannot, as is suggested, direct or control the educational or other systems of the country. Its business is to ask what is to be paid; to satisfy itself that Germany can pay; and to report to the Powers, whose delegation it is, in case Germany makes default. If Germany raises the money required in her own way, the Commission cannot order that it shall be raised in some other way; if Germany offers payment in kind, the Commission may accept such payment, but, except as specified in the Treaty itself, the Commission cannot require such a payment."

This is not a candid statement of the scope and authority of the Reparation Commission, as will be seen by a comparison of its terms with the summary given above or with the Treaty itself. Is not, for example, the statement that the Commission "has no forces at its command" a little difficult to justify in view of Article 430 of the Treaty, which runs: —"In case, either during the occupation or after the expiration of the fifteen years referred to above, the Reparation Commission finds that Germany refuses to observe the whole or part of her obligations under the present Treaty with regard to Reparation, the whole or part of the areas specified in Article 429 will be reoccupied immediately by the Allied and Associated Powers"? The decision, as to whether Germany has kept her engagements and whether it is possible for her to keep them, is left, it should be observed, not to the League of Nations, but to the Reparation Commission itself; and an adverse ruling on the part of the Commission is to be followed "immediately" by the use of armed force. Moreover, the depreciation of the powers of the Commission attempted in the Allied reply largely proceeds from the assumption that it is quite open to Germany to "raise the money required in her own way," in which case it is true that many of the powers of the Reparation Commission would not come into practical effect; whereas in truth one of the main reasons for setting up the Commission at all is the expectation that Germany will not be able to carry the burden nominally laid upon her.

It is reported that the people of Vienna, hearing that a section of the Reparation Commission is about to visit them, have decided characteristically to pin their hopes on it. A financial body can obviously take nothing from them, for they have nothing; therefore this body must be for the purpose of assisting and relieving them. Thus do the Viennese argue, still light-headed in adversity. But perhaps they are right. The Reparation Commission will come into very close contact with the problems of Europe; and it will bear a responsibility proportionate to its powers. It may thus come to fulfil a very different rôle from that which some of its authors intended for it. Transferred to the League of Nations, an appanage of justice and no longer of interest, who knows that by a change of heart and object the Reparation Commission may not yet be transformed from an instrument of oppression and rapine into an economic council of Europe, whose object is the restoration of life and of happiness, even in the enemy countries?

V. The German Counter-Proposals

The German counter-proposals were somewhat obscure, and also rather disingenuous. It will be remembered that those clauses of the Reparation Chapter which dealt with the issue of bonds by Germany produced on the public mind the impression that the Indemnity had been fixed at $25,000,000,000, or at any rate at this figure as a minimum. The German Delegation set out, therefore, to construct their reply on the basis of this figure, assuming apparently that public opinion in Allied countries would not be satisfied with less than the appearance of $25,000,000,000; and, as they were not really prepared to offer so large a figure, they exercised their ingenuity to produce a formula which might be represented to Allied opinion as yielding this amount, whilst really representing a much more modest sum. The formula produced was transparent to any one who read it carefully and knew the facts, and it could hardly have been expected by its authors to deceive the Allied negotiators. The German tactic assumed, therefore, that the latter were secretly as anxious as the Germans themselves to arrive at a settlement which bore some relation to the facts, and that they would therefore be willing, in view of the entanglements which they had got themselves into with their own publics, to practise a little collusion in drafting the Treaty,—a supposition which in slightly different circumstances might have had a good deal of foundation. As matters actually were, this subtlety did not benefit them, and they would have done much better with a straightforward and candid estimate of what they believed to be the amount of their liabilities on the one hand, and their capacity to pay on the other.

The German offer of an alleged sum of $25,000,000,000 amounted to the following. In the first place it was conditional on concessions in the Treaty insuring that "Germany shall retain the territorial integrity corresponding to the Armistice Convention,[140] that she shall keep her colonial possessions and merchant ships, including those of large tonnage, that in her own country and in the world at large she shall enjoy the same freedom of action as all other peoples, that all war legislation shall be at once annulled, and that all interferences during the war with her economic rights and with German private property, etc., shall be treated in accordance with the principle of reciprocity";— that is to say, the offer is conditional on the greater part of the rest of the Treaty being abandoned. In the second place, the claims are not to exceed a maximum of $25,000,000,000, of which $5,000,000,000 is to be discharged by May 1, 1926; and no part of this sum is to carry interest pending the payment of it.[141] In the third place, there are to be allowed as credit against it (amongst other things): (*a*) the value of all deliveries under the Armistice, including military material (*e.g.*Germany's navy); (*b*) the value of all railways and State property in ceded territory; (*c*) the *pro rata* share of all ceded territory in the German public debt (including the war debt) and in the Reparation payments which this territory would have had to bear if it had remained part of Germany; and (*d*) the value of the cession of Germany's claims for sums lent by her to her allies in the war.[142]

The credits to be deducted under (*a*), (*b*), (*c*), and (*d*) might be in excess of those allowed in the actual Treaty, according to a rough estimate, by a sum of as much as $10,000,000,000, although the sum to be allowed under (*d*) can hardly be calculated.

If, therefore, we are to estimate the real value of the German offer of $25,000,000,000 on the basis laid down by the Treaty, we must first of all deduct $10,000,000,000 claimed for offsets which the Treaty does not allow, and then halve the remainder in order to obtain the present value of a deferred payment on which interest is not chargeable. This reduces the offer to $7,500,000,000, as compared with the $40,000,000,000 which, according to my rough estimate, the Treaty demands of her.

This in itself was a very substantial offer—indeed it evoked widespread criticism in Germany—though, in view of the fact that it was conditional on the abandonment of the greater part of the rest of the Treaty, it could hardly be regarded as a serious one. [143] But the German Delegation would have done better if they had stated in less equivocal language how far they felt able to go.

In the final reply of the Allies to this counter-proposal there is one important provision, which I have not attended to hitherto, but which can be conveniently dealt with in this place. Broadly speaking, no concessions were entertained on the Reparation Chapter as it was originally drafted, but the Allies recognized the inconvenience of the *indeterminacy* of the burden laid upon Germany and proposed a method by which the final total of claim might be established at an earlier date than May 1, 1921. They promised, therefore, that at any time within four months of the signature of the Treaty (that is to say, up to the end of October, 1919), Germany should be at liberty to submit an offer of a lump sum in settlement of her whole liability as defined in the Treaty, and within two months thereafter (that is to say, before the end of 1919) the Allies "will, so far as may be possible, return their answers to any proposals that may be made."

This offer is subject to three conditions. "Firstly, the German authorities will be expected, before making such proposals, to confer with the representatives of the Powers directly concerned. Secondly, such offers must be unambiguous and must be precise and clear. Thirdly, they must accept the categories and the Reparation clauses as matters settled beyond discussion."

The offer, as made, does not appear to contemplate any opening up of the problem of Germany's capacity to pay. It is only concerned with the establishment of the total bill of claims as defined in the Treaty—whether (*e.g.*) it is $35,000,000,000, $40,000,000,000, or $50,000,000,000. "The questions," the Allies' reply adds, "are bare questions of fact, namely, the amount of the liabilities, and they are susceptible of being treated in this way."

If the promised negotiations are really conducted on these lines, they are not likely to be fruitful. It will not be much easier to arrive at an agreed figure before the end of 1919 that it was at the time of the Conference; and it will not help Germany's financial position to know for certain that she is liable for the huge sum which on any computation the Treaty liabilities must amount to. These negotiations do offer, however, an opportunity of reopening the whole question of the Reparation payments, although it is hardly to be hoped that at so very early a date, public opinion in the countries of the Allies has changed its mood sufficiently.[144]

I cannot leave this subject as though its just treatment wholly depended either on our own pledges or on economic facts. The policy of reducing Germany to servitude for a generation, of degrading the lives of millions of human beings, and of depriving a whole nation of happiness should be abhorrent and detestable,—abhorrent and detestable, even if it were possible, even if it enriched ourselves, even if it did not sow the decay of the whole civilized life of Europe. Some preach it in the name of Justice. In the great events of man's history, in the unwinding of the complex fates of nations Justice is not so simple. And if it were, nations are not authorized, by religion or by natural morals, to visit on the children of their enemies the misdoings of parents or of rulers.

FOOTNOTES:

[76]"With reservation that any future claims and demands of the Allies and the United States of America remain unaffected, the following financial conditions are required: Reparation for damage done. Whilst Armistice lasts, no public securities shall be removed by the enemy which can serve as a pledge to the Allies for recovery or reparation of war losses.

Immediate restitution of cash deposit in National Bank of Belgium, and, in general, immediate return of all documents, of specie, stock, shares, paper money, together with plant for issue thereof, touching public or private interests in invaded countries. Restitution of Russian and Roumanian gold yielded to Germany or taken by that Power. This gold to be delivered in trust to the Allies until signature of peace."

[77]It is to be noticed, in passing, that they contain nothing which limits the damage to damage inflicted contrary to the recognized rules of warfare. That is to say, it is permissible to include claims arising out of the legitimate capture of a merchantman at sea, as well as the costs of illegal submarine warfare.

[78]Mark-paper or mark-credits owned in ex-occupied territory by Allied nationals should be included, if at all, in the settlement of enemy debts, along with other sums owed to Allied nationals, and not in connection with reparation.

[79]A special claim on behalf of Belgium was actually included In the Peace Treaty, and was accepted by the German representatives without demur.

[80]To the British observer, one scene, however, stood out distinguished from the rest—the field of Ypres. In that desolate and ghostly spot, the natural color and humors of the landscape and the climate seemed designed to express to the traveler the memories of the ground. A visitor to the salient early in November, 1918, when a few German bodies still added a touch of realism and human horror, and the great struggle was not yet certainly ended, could feel there, as nowhere else, the present outrage of war, and at the same time the tragic and sentimental purification which to the future will in some degree transform its harshness.

[81]These notes, estimated to amount to no less than six thousand million marks, are now a source of embarrassment and great potential loss to the Belgian Government, inasmuch

124

as on their recovery of the country they took them over from their nationals in exchange for Belgian notes at the rate of Fr. 120 = Mk. 1. This rate of exchange, being substantially in excess of the value of the mark-notes at the rate of exchange current at the time (and enormously in excess of the rate to which the mark notes have since fallen, the Belgian franc being now worth more than three marks), was the occasion of the smuggling of mark-notes into Belgium on an enormous scale, to take advantage of the profit obtainable. The Belgian Government took this very imprudent step, partly because they hoped to persuade the Peace Conference to make the redemption of these bank-notes, at the par of exchange, a first charge on German assets. The Peace Conference held, however, that Reparation proper must take precedence of the adjustment of improvident banking transactions effected at an excessive rate of exchange. The possession by the Belgian Government of this great mass of German currency, in addition to an amount of nearly two thousand million marks held by the French Government which they similarly exchanged for the benefit of the population of the invaded areas and of Alsace-Lorraine, is a serious aggravation of the exchange position of the mark. It will certainly be desirable for the Belgian and German Governments to come to some arrangement as to its disposal, though this is rendered difficult by the prior lien held by the Reparation Commission over all German assets available for such purposes.

[82]It should be added, in fairness, that the very high claims put forward on behalf of Belgium generally include not only devastation proper, but all kinds of other items, as, for example, the profits and earnings which Belgians might reasonably have expected to earn if there had been no war.

[83]"The Wealth and Income of the Chief Powers," by J.C. Stamp (*Journal of the Royal Statistical Society*, July, 1919).

[84]Other estimates vary from

$12,100,000,000 to $13,400,000,000. See Stamp, *loc. cit.*

[85]This was clearly and courageously pointed out by M. Charles Gide in *L'Emancipation* for February, 1919.

[86]For details of these and other figures, see Stamp, *loc. cit.*

[87]Even when the extent of the material damage has been established, it will be exceedingly difficult to put a price on it, which must largely depend on the period over which restoration is spread, and the methods adopted. It would be impossible to make the damage good in a year or two at any price, and an attempt to do so at a rate which was excessive in relation to the amount of labor and materials at hand might force prices up to almost any level. We must, I think, assume a cost of labor and materials about equal to that current in the world generally. In point of fact, however, we may safely assume that literal restoration will never be attempted. Indeed, it would be very wasteful to do so. Many of the townships were old and unhealthy, and

many of the hamlets miserable. To re-erect the same type of building in the same places would be foolish. As for the land, the wise course may be in some cases to leave long strips of it to Nature for many years to come. An aggregate money sum should be computed as fairly representing the value of the material damage, and France should be left to expend it in the manner she thinks wisest with a view to her economic enrichment as a whole. The first breeze of this controversy has already blown through France. A long and inconclusive debate occupied the Chamber during the spring of 1919, as to whether inhabitants of the devastated area receiving compensation should be compelled to expend it in restoring the identical property, or whether they should be free to use it as they like. There was evidently a great deal to be said on both sides; in the former case there would be much hardship and uncertainty for owners who could not, many of them, expect to recover the effective use of their property perhaps for years to come, and yet would not be free to set themselves up elsewhere; on the other hand, if such persons were allowed to take their compensation and go elsewhere, the countryside of Northern France would never be put right. Nevertheless I believe that the wise course will be to allow great latitude and let economic motives take their own course.

[88]*La Richesse de la France devant la Guerre*, published in 1916.

[89]*Revue Bleue*, February 3, 1919. This is quoted in a very valuable selection of French estimates and expressions of opinion, forming chapter iv. of *La Liquidation financière de la Guerre*, by H. Charriaut and R. Hacault. The general magnitude of my estimate is further confirmed by the extent of the repairs already effected, as set forth in a speech delivered by M. Tardieu on October 10, 1919, in which he said: "On September 16 last, of 2246 kilomètres of railway track destroyed, 2016 had been repaired; of 1075 kilomètres of canal, 700; of 1160 constructions, such as bridges and tunnels,

which had been blown up, 588 had been replaced; of 550,000 houses ruined by bombardment, 60,000 had been rebuilt; and of 1,800,000 hectares of ground rendered useless by battle, 400,000 had been recultivated, 200,000 hectares of which are now ready to be sown. Finally, more than 10,000,000 mètres of barbed wire had been removed."

[90]Some of these estimates include allowance for contingent and immaterial damage as well as for direct material injury.

[91]A substantial part of this was lost in the service of the Allies; this must not be duplicated by inclusion both in their claims and in ours.

[92]The fact that no separate allowance is made in the above for the sinking of 675 fishing vessels of 71,765 tons gross, or for the 1855 vessels of 8,007,967 tons damaged or molested, but not sunk, may be set off against what may be an excessive figure for replacement cost.

[93]The losses of the Greek mercantile

marine were excessively high, as a result of the dangers of the Mediterranean; but they were largely incurred on the service of the other Allies, who paid for them directly or indirectly. The claims of Greece for maritime losses incurred on the service of her own nationals would not be very considerable.

[94]There is a reservation in the Peace Treaty on this question. "The Allied and Associated Powers formally reserve the right of Russia to obtain from Germany restitution and reparation based on the principles of the present Treaty" (Art. 116).

[95]Dr. Diouritch in his "Economic and Statistical Survey of the Southern Slav Nations" (*Journal of Royal Statistical Society*, May, 1919), quotes some extraordinary figures of the loss of life: "According to the official returns, the number of those fallen in battle or died in captivity up to the last Serbian offensive, amounted to 320,000, which means that one half of Serbia's male population, from 18 to 60 years of age,

perished outright in the European War. In addition, the Serbian Medical Authorities estimate that about 300,000 people have died from typhus among the civil population, and the losses among the population interned in enemy camps are estimated at 50,000. During the two Serbian retreats and during the Albanian retreat the losses among children and young people are estimated at 200,000. Lastly, during over three years of enemy occupation, the losses in lives owing to the lack of proper food and medical attention are estimated at 250,000." Altogether, he puts the losses in life at above 1,000,000, or more than one-third of the population of Old Serbia.

[96]*Come si calcola e a quanto ammonta la richezza d'Italia e delle altre principali nazioni*, published in 1919.

[97]Very large claims put forward by the Serbian authorities include many hypothetical items of indirect and non-material damage; but these, however real, are

not admissible under our present formula.

[98]Assuming that in her case $1,250,000,000 are included for the general expenses of the war defrayed out of loans made to Belgium by her allies.

[99]It must be said to Mr. Hughes' honor that he apprehended from the first the bearing of the pre-Armistice negotiations on our right to demand an indemnity covering the full costs of the war, protested against our ever having entered into such engagements, and maintained loudly that he had been no party to them and could not consider himself bound by them. His indignation may have been partly due to the fact that Australia, not having been ravaged, would have no claims at all under the more limited interpretation of our rights.

[100]The whole cost of the war has been estimated at from $120,000,000,000 upwards. This would mean an annual payment for interest (apart from sinking fund) of $6,000,000,000. Could any expert Committee have reported that

Germany can pay this sum?

[101]But unhappily they did not go down with their flags flying very gloriously. For one reason or another their leaders maintained substantial silence. What a different position in the country's estimation they might hold now if they had suffered defeat amidst firm protests against the fraud, chicane, and dishonor of the whole proceedings.

[102]Only after the most painful consideration have I written these words. The almost complete absence of protest from the leading Statesmen of England makes one feel that one must have made some mistake. But I believe that I know all the facts, and I can discover no such mistake. In any case I have set forth all the relevant engagements in Chapter IV. and at the beginning of this chapter, so that the reader can form his own judgment.

[103]In conversation with Frenchmen who were private persons and quite unaffected by political considerations, this aspect became very clear. You might

persuade them that some current estimates as to the amount to be got out of Germany were quite fantastic. Yet at the end they would always come back to where they had started: "But

Germany *must* pay; for, otherwise, what is to happen to France?"

[104]A further paragraph claims the war costs of Belgium "in accordance with Germany's pledges, already given, as to complete restoration for Belgium."

[105]The challenge of the other Allies, as well as the enemy, had to be met; for in view of the limited resources of the latter, the other Allies had perhaps a greater interest than the enemy in seeing that no one of their number established an excessive claim.

[106]M. Klotz has estimated the French claims on this head at $15,000,000,000 (75 milliard francs, made up of 13 milliard for allowances, 60 for pensions, and 2 for widows). If this figure is correct, the others should probably be scaled up also.

[107]That is to say, I claim for the aggregate figure an accuracy within 25 per cent.

[108]In his speech of September 5, 1919, addressed to the French Chamber, M. Klotz estimated the total Allied claims against Germany under the Treaty at $75,000,000,000, which would accumulate at interest until 1921, and be paid off thereafter by 34 annual installments of about $5,000,000,000 each, of which France would receive about $2,750,000,000 annually. "The general effect of the statement (that France would receive from Germany this annual payment) proved," it is reported, "appreciably encouraging to the country as a whole, and was immediately reflected in the improved tone on the Bourse and throughout the business world in France." So long as such statements can be accepted in Paris without protest, there can be no financial or economic future for France, and a catastrophe of disillusion is not far distant.

[109]As a matter of subjective judgment, I estimate for this figure an accuracy of 10 per cent in deficiency and 20 per cent in excess, *i.e.* that the result will lie between $32,000,000,000 and $44,000,000,000.

[110]Germany is also liable under the Treaty, as an addition to her liabilities for Reparation, to pay all the costs of the Armies of Occupation *after* Peace is signed for the fifteen subsequent years of occupation. So far as the text of the Treaty goes, there is nothing to limit the size of these armies, and France could, therefore, by quartering the whole of her normal standing army in the occupied area, shift the charge from her own taxpayers to those of Germany,— though in reality any such policy would be at the expense not of Germany, who by hypothesis is already paying for Reparation up to the full limit of her capacity, but of France's Allies, who would receive so much less in respect of Reparation. A White Paper (Cmd. 240) has, however, been issued, in which is published a

declaration by the Governments of the United States, Great Britain, and France engaging themselves to limit the sum payable annually by Germany to cover the cost of occupation to $60,000,000 "as soon as the Allied and Associated Powers *concerned* are convinced that the conditions of disarmament by Germany are being satisfactorily fulfilled." The word which I have italicized is a little significant. The three Powers reserve to themselves the liberty to modify this arrangement at any time if they agree that it is necessary.

[111]Art. 235. The force of this Article is somewhat strengthened by Article 251, by virtue of which dispensations may also be granted for "other payments" as well as for food and raw material.

[112]This is the effect of Para. 12 (*c*) of Annex II. of the Reparation Chapter, leaving minor complications on one side. The Treaty fixes the payments in terms of *gold marks*, which

are converted in the above rate of 20 to $5.

[113]If, *per impossibile*, Germany discharged $2,500,000,000 in cash or kind by 1921, her annual payments would be at the rate of $312,500,000 from 1921 to 1925 and of $750,000,000 thereafter.

[114]Para. 16 of Annex II. of The Reparation Chapter. There is also an obscure provision by which interest may be charged "on sums arising out of *material damage* as from November 11, 1918, up to May 1, 1921." This seems to differentiate damage to property from damage to the person in favor of the former. It does not affect Pensions and Allowances, the cost of which is capitalized as at the date of the coming into force of the Treaty.

[115]On the assumption which no one supports and even the most optimistic fear to be unplausible, that Germany can pay the full charge for interest and sinking fund *from the outset*, the annual payment would amount to $2,400,000,000.

[116]Under Para. 13 of Annex II. unanimity is

required (i.) for any postponement beyond 1930 of installments due between 1921 and 1926, and (ii.) for any postponement for more than three years of instalments due after 1926. Further, under Art. 234, the Commission may not cancel any part of the indebtedness without the specific authority of *all* the Governments represented on the Commission.

[117]On July 23, 1914, the amount was $339,000,000.

[118]Owing to the very high premium which exists on German silver coin, as the combined result of the depreciation of the mark and the appreciation of silver, it is highly improbable that it will be possible to extract such coin out of the pockets of the people. But it may gradually leak over the frontier by the agency of private speculators, and thus indirectly benefit the German exchange position as a whole.

[119]The Allies made the supply of foodstuffs to Germany during the Armistice, mentioned above, conditional on the provisional transfer

to them of the greater part of the Mercantile Marine, to be operated by them for the purpose of shipping foodstuffs to Europe generally, and to Germany in particular. The reluctance of the Germans to agree to this was productive of long and dangerous delays in the supply of food, but the abortive Conferences of Trèves and Spa (January 16, February 14-16, and March 4-5, 1919) were at last followed by the Agreement of Brussels (March 14, 1919). The unwillingness of the Germans to conclude was mainly due to the lack of any absolute guarantee on the part of the Allies that, if they surrendered the ships, they would get the food. But assuming reasonable good faith on the part of the latter (their behavior in respect of certain other clauses of the Armistice, however, had not been impeccable and gave the enemy some just grounds for suspicion), their demand was not an improper one; for without the German ships the business of transporting the food would have been difficult, if not impossible, and the German ships surrendered or their equivalent were in fact almost wholly employed in transporting food to Germany itself. Up to June 30, 1919, 176 German ships of 1,025,388 gross tonnage had been surrendered, to the Allies in accordance with the Brussels Agreement.

[120]The amount of tonnage transferred may be rather greater and the value per ton rather less. The aggregate value involved is not likely, however, to be less than $500,000,000 or greater than $750,000,000.

[121]This census was carried out by virtue of a Decree of August 23, 1918. On March 22, 1917, the German Government acquired complete control over the utilization of foreign securities in German possession; and in May, 1917, it began to exercise these powers for the mobilization of certain Swedish, Danish, and Swiss securities.

[122]

1892. Schmoller $2,500,000,000
1892. Christians   3,250,000,000
1893- Koch   3,000,000,000

4.

1905.	v. Halle	4,000,000,000	[A]
1913.	Helfferich	5,000,000,000	[B]
1914.	Ballod	6,250,000,000	
1914.	Pistorius	6,250,000,000	
1919.	Hans David	5,250,000,000	[C]

[A]Plus $2,500,000 for investments other than securities.

[B]Net investments, *i.e.* after allowance for property in Germany owned abroad. This may also be the case with some of the other estimates.

[C]This estimate, given in the *Weltwirtschaftszeitung* (June 13, 1919), is an estimate of the value of Germany's foreign investments as at the outbreak of war.

[123]I have made no deduction for securities in the ownership of Alsace-Lorrainers and others who have now ceased to be German nationals.

[124]In all these estimates, I am conscious of being driven by a fear of overstating the case against the Treaty, of giving figures in excess of my own real judgment. There is a great difference between putting down on paper fancy

estimates of Germany's resources and actually extracting contributions in the form of cash. I do not myself believe that the Reparation Commission will secure real resources from the above items by May, 1921, even as great as the *lower* of the two figures given above.

[125]The Treaty (see Art. 114) leaves it very dubious how far the Danish Government is under an obligation to make payments to the Reparation Commission in respect of its acquisition of Schleswig. They might, for instance, arrange for various offsets such as the value of the mark notes held by the inhabitants of ceded areas. In any case the amount of money involved is quite small. The Danish Government is raising a loan for $33,000,000 (kr. 120,000,000) for the joint purposes of "taking over Schleswig's share of the German debt, for buying German public property, for helping the Schleswig population, and for settling the currency question."

[126]Here again my own judgment would carry me much further

and I should doubt the possibility of Germany's exports equaling her imports during this period. But the statement in the text goes far enough for the purpose of my argument.

[127]It has been estimated that the cession of territory to France, apart from the loss of Upper Silesia, may reduce Germany's annual pre-war production of steel ingots from 20,000,000 tons to 14,000,000 tons, and increase France's capacity from 5,000,000 tons to 11,000,000 tons.

[128]Germany's exports of sugar in 1913 amounted to 1,110,073 tons of the value of $65,471,500, of which 838,583 tons were exported to the United Kingdom at a value of $45,254,000. These figures were in excess of the normal, the average total exports for the five years ending 1913 being about $50,000,000.

[129]The necessary price adjustment, which is required, on both sides of this account, will be made *en bloc* later.

[130]If the amount of the sinking fund be

145

reduced, and the annual payment is continued over a greater number of years, the present value—so powerful is the operation of compound interest—cannot be materially increased. A payment of $500,000,000 annually *in perpetuity*, assuming interest, as before, at 5 per cent, would only raise the present value to $10,000,000,000.

[131]As an example of public misapprehension on economic affairs, the following letter from Sir Sidney Low to *The Times* of the 3rd December, 1918, deserves quotation: "I have seen authoritative estimates which place the gross value of Germany's mineral and chemical resources as high as $1,250,000,000,000 or even more; and the Ruhr basin mines alone are said to be worth over $225,000,000,000. It is certain, at any rate, that the capital value of these natural supplies is much greater than the total war debts of all the Allied States. Why should not some portion of this wealth be diverted for a sufficient period from its present owners and assigned to the peoples whom

Germany has assailed, deported, and injured? The Allied Governments might justly require Germany to surrender to them the use of such of her mines, and mineral deposits as would yield, say, from $500,000,000 to $1,000,000,000 annually for the next 30, 40, or 50 years. By this means we could obtain sufficient compensation from Germany without unduly stimulating her manufactures and export trade to our detriment." It is not clear why, if Germany has wealth exceeding $1,250,000,000,000. Sir Sidney Low is content with the trifling sum of $500,000,000 to $1,000,000,000 annually. But his letter is an admirable *reductio ad absurdum* of a certain line of thought. While a mode of calculation, which estimates the value of coal miles deep in the bowels of the earth as high as in a coal scuttle, of an annual lease of $5000 for 999 years at $4,995,000 and of a field (presumably) at the value of all the crops it will grow to the end of recorded time, opens up great possibilities, it is also double-edged. If

Germany's total resources are worth $1,250,000,000,000, those she will part with in the cession of Alsace-Lorraine and Upper Silesia should be more than sufficient to pay the entire costs of the war and reparation together. In point of fact, the *present* market value of all the mines in Germany of every kind has been estimated at $1,500,000,000, or a little more than one-thousandth part of Sir Sidney Low's expectations.

[132]The conversion at par of 5,000 million marks overstates, by reason of the existing depreciation of the mark, the present money burden of the actual pensions payments, but not, in all probability, the real loss of national productivity as a result of the casualties suffered in the war.

[133]It cannot be overlooked, in passing, that in its results on a country's surplus productivity a lowering of the standard of life acts both ways. Moreover, we are without experience of the psychology of a white race under conditions little short of

servitude. It is, however, generally supposed that if the whole of a man's surplus production is taken from him, his efficiency and his industry are diminished, The entrepreneur and the inventor will not contrive, the trader and the shopkeeper will not save, the laborer will not toil, if the fruits of their industry are set aside, not for the benefit of their children, their old age, their pride, or their position, but for the enjoyment of a foreign conqueror.

[134]In the course of the compromises and delays of the Conference, there were many questions on which, in order to reach any conclusion at all, it was necessary to leave a margin of vagueness and uncertainty. The whole method of the Conference tended towards this,—the Council of Four wanted, not so much a settlement, as a treaty. On political and territorial questions the tendency was to leave the final arbitrament to the League of Nations. But on financial and economic questions, the final decision has generally be a left with the Reparation

Commission,—in spite of its being an executive body composed of interested parties.

[135]The sum to be paid by Austria for Reparation is left to the absolute discretion of the Reparation Commission, no determinate figure of any kind being mentioned in the text of the Treaty Austrian questions are to be handled by a special section of the Reparation Commission, but the section will have no powers except such as the main Commission may delegate.

[136]Bulgaria is to pay an indemnity of $450,000,000 by half-yearly instalments, beginning July 1, 1920. These sums will be collected, on behalf of the Reparation Commission, by an Inter-Ally Commission of Control, with its seat at Sofia. In some respects the Bulgarian Inter-Ally Commission appears to have powers and authority independent of the Reparation Commission, but it is to act, nevertheless, as the agent of the latter, and is authorized to tender advice to the Reparation

Commission as to, for example, the reduction of the half-yearly instalments.

[137]Under the Treaty this is the function of any body appointed for the purpose by the principal Allied and Associated Governments, and not necessarily of the Reparation Commission. But it may be presumed that no second body will be established for this special purpose.

[138]At the date of writing no treaties with these countries have been drafted. It is possible that Turkey might be dealt with by a separate Commission.

[139]This appears to me to be in effect the position (if this paragraph means anything at all), in spite of the following disclaimer of such intentions in the Allies' reply:—"Nor does Paragraph 12(b) of Annex II. give the Commission powers to prescribe or enforce taxes or to dictate the character of the German budget."

[140]Whatever that may mean.

[141]Assuming that the capital sum is discharged evenly over a period as short as thirty-three years, this has the effect of *halving* the burden as compared with the payments required on the basis of 5 per cent interest on the outstanding capital.

[142]I forbear to outline the further details of the German offer as the above are the essential points.

[143]For this reason it is not strictly comparable with my estimate of Germany's capacity in an earlier section of this chapter, which estimate is on the basis of Germany's condition as it will be when the rest of the Treaty has come into effect.

[144]Owing to delays on the part of the Allies in ratifying the Treaty, the Reparation Commission had not yet been formally constituted by the end of October, 1919. So far as I am aware, therefore, nothing has been done to make the above offer effective. But, perhaps in view of the circumstances, there has been an extension of the date.

CHAPTER VI

EUROPE AFTER THE TREATY

This chapter must be one of pessimism. The Treaty includes no provisions for the economic rehabilitation of Europe,—nothing to make the defeated Central Empires into good neighbors, nothing to stabilize the new States of Europe, nothing to reclaim Russia; nor does it promote in any way a compact of economic solidarity amongst the Allies themselves; no arrangement was reached at Paris for restoring the disordered finances of France and Italy, or to adjust the systems of the Old World and the New.

The Council of Four paid no attention to these issues, being preoccupied with others,— Clemenceau to crush the economic life of his enemy, Lloyd George to do a deal and bring home something which would pass muster for a week, the President to do nothing that was not just and right. It is an extraordinary fact that the fundamental economic problems of a Europe starving and disintegrating before their eyes, was the one question in which it was impossible to arouse the interest of the Four. Reparation was their main excursion into the economic field, and they settled it as a problem of theology, of polities, of electoral chicane, from every point of view except that of the economic future of the States whose destiny they were handling.

I leave, from this point onwards, Paris, the Conference, and the Treaty, briefly to consider the present situation of Europe, as the War and the Peace have made it; and it will no longer be part of my purpose to distinguish between the inevitable fruits of the War and the avoidable misfortunes of the Peace.

The essential facts of the situation, as I see them, are expressed simply. Europe consists of the densest aggregation of population in the history of the world. This population is accustomed to a relatively high standard of life, in which, even now, some sections of it anticipate improvement rather than deterioration. In relation to other continents Europe is not self-sufficient; in particular it cannot feed Itself. Internally the population is not evenly distributed, but much of it is crowded into a relatively small number of dense industrial centers. This population secured for itself a livelihood before the war, without much margin of surplus, by means of a delicate and immensely complicated organization, of which the foundations were supported by coal, iron, transport, and an unbroken supply of imported food and raw materials from other continents. By the destruction of this organization and the interruption of the stream of supplies, a part of this population is deprived of its means of livelihood. Emigration is not open to the redundant surplus. For it would take years to transport them overseas, even, which is not the case, if countries could be found which were ready to receive them. The danger confronting us, therefore, is the rapid depression of the standard of life of the European populations to a point which will mean actual starvation for some (a point already reached in Russia and approximately reached in Austria). Men will not always die quietly. For starvation, which brings to some lethargy and a helpless despair, drives other temperaments to the nervous instability of hysteria and to a mad despair. And these in their distress may overturn the remnants of organization, and submerge civilization itself in their attempts to satisfy desperately the overwhelming needs of the individual. This is the danger against which all our resources and courage and idealism must now co-operate.

On the 13th May, 1919, Count Brockdorff-Rantzau addressed to the Peace Conference of the Allied and Associated Powers the Report of the German Economic Commission charged with the study of the effect of the conditions of Peace on the situation of the German population. "In the course of the last two generations," they reported, "Germany has become transformed from an agricultural State to an industrial State. So long as she was an agricultural State, Germany could feed forty million inhabitants. As an industrial State she could insure the means of subsistence for a population of sixty-seven millions; and in 1913 the importation of foodstuffs amounted, in round figures, to twelve million tons. Before the war a total of fifteen million persons in Germany provided for their existence by foreign trade, navigation, and the use, directly or indirectly, of foreign raw material." After rehearsing the main relevant provisions of the Peace Treaty the report continues: "After this diminution of her products, after the economic depression resulting from the loss of her colonies, her merchant fleet and her foreign investments, Germany will not be in a position to import from abroad an adequate quantity of raw material. An enormous part of German industry will, therefore, be condemned inevitably to destruction. The need of importing foodstuffs will increase considerably at the same time that the possibility of satisfying this demand is as greatly diminished. In a very short time, therefore, Germany will not be in a position to give bread and work to her numerous millions of inhabitants, who are prevented from earning their livelihood by navigation and trade. These persons should emigrate, but this is a material impossibility, all the more because many countries and the most important ones will oppose any German immigration. To put the Peace conditions into execution would logically involve, therefore, the loss of several millions of persons in Germany. This catastrophe would not be long in coming about, seeing that the health of the population has been broken down during the War by the Blockade, and during the Armistice by the aggravation of the Blockade of famine. No help, however great, or over however long a period it were continued, could prevent those deaths *en masse*." "We do not know, and indeed we doubt," the report concludes, "whether the Delegates of the Allied and Associated Powers realize the inevitable consequences which will take place if Germany, an industrial State, very thickly populated, closely bound up with the economic system of the world, and under the necessity of importing enormous quantities of raw material and foodstuffs, suddenly finds herself pushed back to the phase of her development, which corresponds to her economic condition and the numbers of her population as they were half a century ago. Those who sign this Treaty will sign the death sentence of many millions of German men, women and children."

I know of no adequate answer to these words. The indictment is at least as true of the Austrian, as of the German, settlement. This is the fundamental problem in front of us, before which questions of territorial adjustment and the balance of European power are insignificant. Some of the catastrophes of past history, which have thrown back human progress for centuries, have been due to the reactions following on the sudden termination, whether in the course of nature or by the act of man, of temporarily favorable conditions which have permitted the growth of population beyond what could be provided for when the favorable conditions were at an end.

The significant features of the immediate situation can be grouped under three heads: first, the absolute falling off, for the time being, in Europe's internal productivity; second, the breakdown of transport and exchange by means of which its products could be conveyed where they were most wanted; and third, the inability of Europe to purchase its usual supplies from overseas.

The decrease of productivity cannot be easily estimated, and may be the subject of exaggeration. But the *primâ facie* evidence of it is overwhelming, and this factor has been the main burden of Mr. Hoover's well-considered warnings. A variety of causes have produced it;—violent and prolonged internal disorder as in Russia and Hungary; the creation of new governments and their inexperience in the readjustment of economic relations, as in Poland and Czecho-Slovakia; the loss throughout the Continent of efficient labor, through the casualties of war or the continuance of mobilization; the falling-off in efficiency through continued underfeeding in the Central Empires; the exhaustion of the soil from lack of the usual applications of artificial manures throughout the course of the war; the unsettlement of the minds of the laboring classes on the above all (to quote Mr. Hoover), "there is a great fundamental economic issues of their lives. But relaxation of effort as the reflex of physical exhaustion of large sections of the population from privation and the mental and physical strain of the war." Many persons are for one reason or another out of employment altogether. According to Mr. Hoover, a summary of the unemployment bureaus in Europe in July, 1919, showed that 15,000,000 families were receiving unemployment allowances in one form or another, and were being paid in the main by a constant inflation of currency. In Germany there is the added deterrent to labor and to capital (in so far as the Reparation terms are taken literally), that anything, which they may produce beyond the barest level of subsistence, will for years to come be taken away from them.

Such definite data as we possess do not add much, perhaps, to the general picture of decay. But I will remind the reader of one or two of them. The coal production of Europe as a whole is estimated to have fallen off by 30 per cent; and upon coal the greater part of the industries of Europe and the whole of her transport system depend. Whereas before the war Germany produced 85 per cent of the total food consumed by her inhabitants, the productivity of the soil is now diminished by 40 per cent and the effective quality of the live-stock by 55 per cent.[145] Of the European countries which formerly possessed a large exportable surplus, Russia, as much by reason of deficient transport as of diminished output, may herself starve. Hungary, apart from her other troubles, has been pillaged by the Romanians immediately after harvest. Austria will have consumed the whole of her own harvest for 1919 before the end of the calendar year. The figures are almost too overwhelming to carry conviction to our minds; if they were not quite so bad, our effective belief in them might be stronger.

But even when coal can be got and grain harvested, the breakdown of the European railway system prevents their carriage; and even when goods can be manufactured, the breakdown of the European currency system prevents their sale. I have already described the losses, by war and under the Armistice surrenders, to the transport system of Germany. But even so, Germany's position, taking account of her power of replacement by manufacture, is probably not so serious as that of some of her neighbors. In Russia (about which, however, we have very little exact or accurate information) the condition of the rolling-stock is believed to be altogether desperate,

155

and one of the most fundamental factors in her existing economic disorder. And in Poland, Roumania, and Hungary the position is not much better. Yet modern industrial life essentially depends on efficient transport facilities, and the population which secured its livelihood by these means cannot continue to live without them. The breakdown of currency, and the distrust in its purchasing value, is an aggravation of these evils which must be discussed in a little more detail in connection with foreign trade.

What then is our picture of Europe? A country population able to support life on the fruits of its own agricultural production but without the accustomed surplus for the towns, and also (as a result of the lack of imported materials and so of variety and amount in the saleable manufactures of the towns) without the usual incentives to market food in return for other wares; an industrial population unable to keep its strength for lack of food, unable to earn a livelihood for lack of materials, and so unable to make good by imports from abroad the failure of productivity at home. Yet, according to Mr. Hoover, "a rough estimate would indicate that the population of Europe is at least 100,000,000 greater than can be supported without imports, and must live by the production and distribution of exports."

The problem of the re-inauguration of the perpetual circle of production and exchange in foreign trade leads me to a necessary digression on the currency situation of Europe.

Lenin is said to have declared that the best way to destroy the Capitalist System was to debauch the currency. By a continuing process of inflation, governments can confiscate, secretly and unobserved, an important part of the wealth of their citizens. By this method they not only confiscate, but they confiscate *arbitrarily*; and, while the process impoverishes many, it actually enriches some. The sight of this arbitrary rearrangement of riches strikes not only at security, but at confidence in the equity of the existing distribution of wealth. Those to whom the system brings windfalls, beyond their deserts and even beyond their expectations or desires, become "profiteers,", who are the object of the hatred of the bourgeoisie, whom the inflationism has impoverished, not less than of the proletariat. As the inflation proceeds and the real value of the currency fluctuates wildly from month to month, all permanent relations between debtors and creditors, which form the ultimate foundation of capitalism, become so utterly disordered as to be almost meaningless; and the process of wealth-getting degenerates into a gamble and a lottery.

Lenin was certainly right. There is no subtler, no surer means of overturning the existing basis of society than to debauch the currency. The process engages all the hidden forces of economic law on the side of destruction, and does it in a manner which not one man in a million is able to diagnose.

In the latter stages of the war all the belligerent governments practised, from necessity or incompetence, what a Bolshevist might have done from design. Even now, when the war is over, most of them continue out of weakness the same malpractices. But further, the Governments of Europe, being many of them at this moment reckless in their methods as well as weak, seek to direct on to a class known as "profiteers" the popular indignation against the more obvious consequences of their vicious methods. These "profiteers" are, broadly speaking, the entrepreneur class of capitalists, that is to say, the active and constructive element in the whole capitalist society, who in a period of

156

rapidly rising prices cannot help but get rich quick whether they wish it or desire it or not. If prices are continually rising, every trader who has purchased for stock or owns property and plant inevitably makes profits. By directing hatred against this class, therefore, the European Governments are carrying a step further the fatal process which the subtle mind of Lenin had consciously conceived. The profiteers are a consequence and not a cause of rising prices. By combining a popular hatred of the class of entrepreneurs with the blow already given to social security by the violent and arbitrary disturbance of contract and of the established equilibrium of wealth which is the inevitable result of inflation, these Governments are fast rendering impossible a continuance of the social and economic order of the nineteenth century. But they have no plan for replacing it.

We are thus faced in Europe with the spectacle of an extraordinary weakness on the part of the great capitalist class, which has emerged from the industrial triumphs of the nineteenth century, and seemed a very few years ago our all-powerful master. The terror and personal timidity of the individuals of this class is now so great, their confidence in their place in society and in their necessity to the social organism so diminished, that they are the easy victims of intimidation. This was not so in England twenty-five years ago, any more than it is now in the United States. Then the capitalists believed in themselves, in their value to society, in the propriety of their continued existence in the full enjoyment of their riches and the unlimited exercise of their power. Now they tremble before every insult;—call them pro-Germans, international financiers, or profiteers, and they will give you any ransom you choose to ask not to speak of them so harshly. They allow themselves to be ruined and altogether undone by their own instruments, governments of their own making, and a press of which they are the proprietors. Perhaps it is historically true that no order of society ever perishes save by its own hand. In the complexer world of Western Europe the Immanent Will may achieve its ends more subtly and bring in the revolution no less inevitably through a Klotz or a George than by the intellectualisms, too ruthless and self-conscious for us, of the bloodthirsty philosophers of Russia.

The inflationism of the currency systems of Europe has proceeded to extraordinary lengths. The various belligerent Governments, unable, or too timid or too short-sighted to secure from loans or taxes the resources they required, have printed notes for the balance. In Russia and Austria-Hungary this process has reached a point where for the purposes of foreign trade the currency is practically valueless. The Polish mark can be bought for about three cents and the Austrian crown for less than two cents, but they cannot be sold at all. The German mark is worth less than four cents on the exchanges. In most of the other countries of Eastern and South-Eastern Europe the real position is nearly as bad. The currency of Italy has fallen to little more than a half of its nominal value in spite of its being still subject to some degree of regulation; French currency maintains an uncertain market; and even sterling is seriously diminished in present value and impaired in its future prospects.

But while these currencies enjoy a precarious value abroad, they have never entirely lost, not even in Russia, their purchasing power at home. A sentiment of trust in the legal money of the State is so deeply implanted in the citizens of all countries that they cannot but believe that some day this money must recover a part at least of its former value. To their minds it appears that value is inherent in money as such, and they do not

157

apprehend that the real wealth, which this money might have stood for, has been dissipated once and for all. This sentiment is supported by the various legal regulations with which the Governments endeavor to control internal prices, and so to preserve some purchasing power for their legal tender. Thus the force of law preserves a measure of immediate purchasing power over some commodities and the force of sentiment and custom maintains, especially amongst peasants, a willingness to hoard paper which is really worthless.

The presumption of a spurious value for the currency, by the force of law expressed in the regulation of prices, contains in itself, however, the seeds of final economic decay, and soon dries up the sources of ultimate supply. If a man is compelled to exchange the fruits of his labors for paper which, as experience soon teaches him, he cannot use to purchase what he requires at a price comparable to that which he has received for his own products, he will keep his produce for himself, dispose of it to his friends and neighbors as a favor, or relax his efforts in producing it. A system of compelling the exchange of commodities at what is not their real relative value not only relaxes production, but leads finally to the waste and inefficiency of barter. If, however, a government refrains from regulation and allows matters to take their course, essential commodities soon attain a level of price out of the reach of all but the rich, the worthlessness of the money becomes apparent, and the fraud upon the public can be concealed no longer.

The effect on foreign trade of price-regulation and profiteer-hunting as cures for inflation is even worse. Whatever may be the case at home, the currency must soon reach its real level abroad, with the result that prices inside and outside the country lose their normal adjustment. The price of imported commodities, when converted at the current rate of exchange, is far in excess of the local price, so that many essential goods will not be imported at all by private agency, and must be provided by the government, which, in re-selling the goods below cost price, plunges thereby a little further into insolvency. The bread subsidies, now almost universal throughout Europe, are the leading example of this phenomenon.

The countries of Europe fall into two distinct groups at the present time as regards their manifestations of what is really the same evil throughout, according as they have been cut off from international intercourse by the Blockade, or have had their imports paid for out of the resources of their allies. I take Germany as typical of the first, and France and Italy of the second.

The note circulation of Germany is about ten times[146] what it was before the war. The value of the mark in terms of gold is about one-eighth of its former value. As world-prices in terms of gold are more than double what they were, it follows that mark-prices inside Germany ought to be from sixteen to twenty times their pre-war level if they are to be in adjustment and proper conformity with prices outside Germany.[147] But this is not the case. In spite of a very great rise in German prices, they probably do not yet average much more than five times their former level, so far as staple commodities are concerned; and it is impossible that they should rise further except with a simultaneous and not less violent adjustment of the level of money wages. The existing maladjustment hinders in two ways (apart from other obstacles) that revival of the import trade which is the essential preliminary of the economic reconstruction of the country. In the first place, imported commodities are beyond the purchasing power of the great mass of the population,[148] and the flood of imports which might have been expected to succeed the raising of the blockade was not in fact commercially possible. [149] In the second place, it is a hazardous enterprise for a merchant or a manufacturer to purchase with a foreign credit material for which, when he has imported it or manufactured it, he will receive mark currency of a quite uncertain and possibly unrealizable value. This latter obstacle to the revival of trade is one which easily escapes notice and deserves a little attention. It is impossible at the present time to say what the mark will be worth in terms of foreign currency three or six months or a year hence, and the exchange market can quote no reliable figure. It may be the case, therefore, that a German merchant, careful of his future credit and reputation, who is actually offered a short period credit in terms of sterling or dollars, may be reluctant and doubtful whether to accept it. He will owe sterling or dollars, but he will sell his product for marks, and his power, when the time comes, to turn these marks into the currency in which he has to repay his debt is entirely problematic. Business loses its genuine character and becomes no better than a speculation in the exchanges, the fluctuations in which entirely obliterate the normal profits of commerce.

There are therefore three separate obstacles to the revival of trade: a maladjustment between internal prices and international prices, a lack of individual credit abroad wherewith to buy the raw materials needed to secure the working capital and to re-start the circle of exchange, and a disordered currency system which renders credit operations hazardous or impossible quite apart from the ordinary risks of commerce.

The note circulation of France is more than six times its pre-war level. The exchange value of the franc in terms of gold is a little less than two-thirds its former value; that is to say, the value of the franc has not fallen in proportion to the increased volume of the currency.[150] This apparently superior situation of France is due to the fact that until recently a very great part of her imports have not been paid for, but have been covered by loans from the Governments of Great Britain and the United States. This has allowed a want of equilibrium between exports and imports to be established, which is becoming a very serious factor, now that the outside assistance is being gradually discontinued. The internal economy of France and its price level in relation to the note circulation and the foreign exchanges is at present based on an excess of imports over exports which cannot possibly continue. Yet it is difficult to see how the position can be readjusted except by a lowering of the standard of consumption in France, which, even if it is only temporary, will provoke a great deal of discontent.[151]

The situation of Italy is not very different. There the note circulation is five or six times its pre-war level, and the exchange value of the lira in terms of gold about half its former value. Thus the adjustment of the exchange to the volume of the note circulation has proceeded further in Italy than in France. On the other hand, Italy's "invisible" receipts, from emigrant remittances and the expenditure of tourists, have been very injuriously affected; the disruption of Austria has deprived her of an important market; and her peculiar dependence on foreign shipping and on imported raw materials of every kind has laid her open to special injury from the increase of world prices. For all these reasons her position is grave, and her excess of imports as serious a symptom as in the case of France.[152]

The existing inflation and the maladjustment of international trade are aggravated, both in France and in Italy, by the unfortunate budgetary position of the Governments of these countries.

In France the failure to impose taxation is notorious. Before the war the aggregate French and British budgets, and also the average taxation per head, were about equal; but in France no substantial effort has been made to cover the increased expenditure. "Taxes increased in Great Britain during the war," it has been estimated, "from 95 francs per head to 265 francs, whereas the increase in France was only from 90 to 103 francs." The taxation voted in France for the financial year ending June 30, 1919, was less than half the estimated normal *post-bellum* expenditure. The normal budget for the future cannot be put below $4,400,000,000 (22 milliard francs), and may exceed this figure; but even for the fiscal year 1919-20 the estimated receipts from taxation do not cover much more than half this amount. The French Ministry of Finance have no plan or policy whatever for meeting this prodigious deficit, except the expectation of receipts from Germany on a scale which the French officials themselves know to be baseless. In the meantime they are helped by sales of war material and surplus American stocks and do not scruple, even in the latter half of 1919, to meet the deficit by the yet further expansion of the note issue of the Bank of France.[153]

The budgetary position of Italy is perhaps a little superior to that of France. Italian finance throughout the war was more enterprising than the French, and far greater efforts were made to impose taxation and pay for the war. Nevertheless Signor Nitti, the Prime Minister, in a letter addressed to the electorate on the eve of the General Election (Oct., 1919), thought it necessary to make public the following desperate analysis of the situation:—(1) The State expenditure amounts to about three times the revenue. (2) All the industrial undertakings of the State, including the railways, telegraphs, and telephones, are being run at a loss. Although the public is buying bread at a high price, that price represents a loss to the Government of about a milliard a year. (3) Exports now leaving the country are valued at only one-quarter or one-fifth of the imports from abroad. (4) The National Debt is increasing by about a milliard lire per month. (5) The military expenditure for one month is still larger than that for the first year of the war.

But if this is the budgetary position of France and Italy, that of the rest of belligerent Europe is yet more desperate. In Germany the total expenditure of the Empire, the Federal States, and the Communes in 1919-20 is estimated at 25 milliards of marks, of which not above 10 milliards are covered by previously existing taxation. This is without allowing anything for the payment of the indemnity. In Russia, Poland, Hungary, or Austria such a thing as a budget cannot be seriously considered to exist at all.[154]

Thus the menace of inflationism described above is not merely a product of the war, of which peace begins the cure. It is a continuing phenomenon of which the end is not yet in sight.

All these influences combine not merely to prevent Europe from supplying immediately a sufficient stream of exports to pay for the goods she needs to import, but they impair her credit for securing the working capital required to re-start the circle of exchange and also, by swinging the forces of economic law yet further from equilibrium rather than towards it, they favor a continuance of the present conditions instead of a recovery from them. An inefficient, unemployed, disorganized Europe faces us, torn by internal strife and international hate, fighting, starving, pillaging, and lying. What warrant is there for a picture of less somber colors?

I have paid little heed in this book to Russia, Hungary, or Austria.[155] There the miseries of life and the disintegration of society are too notorious to require analysis; and these countries are already experiencing the actuality of what for the rest of Europe is still in the realm of prediction. Yet they comprehend a vast territory and a great population, and are an extant example of how much man can suffer and how far society can decay. Above all, they are the signal to us of how in the final catastrophe the malady of the body passes over into malady of the mind. Economic privation proceeds by easy stages, and so long as men suffer it patiently the outside world cares little. Physical efficiency and resistance to disease slowly diminish,[156] but life proceeds somehow, until the limit of human endurance is reached at last and counsels of despair and madness stir the sufferers from the lethargy which precedes the crisis. Then man shakes himself, and the bonds of custom are loosed. The power of ideas is sovereign, and he listens to whatever instruction of hope, illusion, or revenge is carried to him on the air. As I write, the flames of Russian Bolshevism seem, for the moment at least, to have burnt themselves out, and the peoples of Central and Eastern Europe are held in a dreadful torpor. The lately gathered harvest keeps off the worst privations, and Peace has been declared at Paris. But winter approaches. Men will have nothing to look forward to or to nourish hopes on. There will be little fuel to moderate the rigors of the season or to comfort the starved bodies of the town-dwellers.

But who can say how much is endurable, or in what direction men will seek at last to escape from their misfortunes?

FOOTNOTES:

[145]Professor Starling's *Report on Food Conditions in Germany*. (Cmd. 280.)

[146]Including the *Darlehenskassensch eine* somewhat more.

[147]Similarly in Austria prices ought to be between twenty and thirty times their former level.

[148]One of the moat striking and symptomatic difficulties which faced the Allied authorities in their

administration of the occupied areas of Germany during the Armistice arose out of the fact that even when they brought food into the country the inhabitants could not afford to pay its cost price.

[149]Theoretically an unduly low level of home prices should stimulate exports and so cure itself. But in Germany, and still more in Poland and Austria, there is little or nothing to export. There must be imports *before* there can be exports.

[150]Allowing for the diminished value of gold, the exchange value of the franc should be less than 40 per cent of its previous value, instead of the actual figure of about 60 per cent, if the fall were proportional to the increase in the volume of the currency.

[151]How very far from equilibrium France's international exchange now is can be seen from the following table:

Monthly Average	Imports $1,000	Exports $1,000	Excess of Imports $1,000
1913	140,355	114,670	25,685
1914	106,705	81,145	25,560
1918	331,915	69,055	262,860

	Imports	Exports	Excess of Imports
Jan.-Mar. 1919	387,140	66,670	320,470
Apr.-June 1919	421,410	83,895	337,515
July 1919	467,565	123,675	343,890

These figures have been converted, at approximately par rates, but this is roughly compensated by the fact that the trade of 1918 and 1919 has been valued at 1917 official rates. French imports cannot possibly continue at anything approaching these figures, and the semblance of prosperity based on such a state of affairs is spurious.

[152]The figures for Italy are as follows:

Monthly Average	Imports $1,000	Exports $1,000	Excess of Imports $1,000
1913	60,760	41,860	18,900
1914	48,720	36,840	11,880
1918	235,025	41,390	193,635
Jan.-Mar. 1919	229,240	38,685	191,155
Apr.-June 1919	331,035	69,250	261,785
July-Aug. 1919	223,535	84,515	139,020

[153]In the last two returns of the Bank of France available as I write (Oct. 2 and 9, 1919) the increases in the note issue on the week amounted to $93,750,000 and $94,125,000 respectively.

[154]On October 3, 1919, M. Bilinski made his financial statement to the Polish Diet. He estimated his expenditure for the next nine months at rather more than double his expenditure for the past nine months, and while during the first period his revenue had amounted to one-fifth of his expenditure, for the coming months he was budgeting for receipts equal to one-eighth of his outgoings. The *Times* correspondent at Warsaw reported that "in general M. Bilinski's tone was optimistic and appeared to satisfy his audience."

[155]The terms of the Peace Treaty imposed on the Austrian Republic bear no relation to the real facts of that State's desperate situation. The *Arbeiter Zeitung* of Vienna on June 4, 1919, commented on them as follows: "Never has the substance of a treaty of peace so grossly betrayed the intentions which were said to have guided its construction as is the case with this Treaty . . . in which every provision is permeated with ruthlessness and pitilessness, in which no breath of human

sympathy can be detected, which flies in the face of everything which binds man to man, which is a crime against humanity itself, against a suffering and tortured people." I am acquainted in detail with the Austrian Treaty and I was present when some of its terms were being drafted, but I do not find it easy to rebut the justice of this outburst.

[156]For months past the reports of the health conditions in the Central Empires have been of such a character that the imagination is dulled, and one almost seems guilty of sentimentality in quoting them. But their general veracity is not disputed, and I quote the three following, that the reader may not be unmindful of them: "In the last years of the war, in Austria alone at least 35,000 people died of tuberculosis, in Vienna alone 12,000. Today we have to reckon with a number of at least 350,000 to 400,000 people who require treatment for tuberculosis.... As the result of malnutrition a bloodless generation is growing up with undeveloped muscles, undeveloped joints, and

undeveloped brain" (*Neue Freie Presse,* May 31, 1919). The Commission of Doctors appointed by the Medical Faculties of Holland, Sweden, and Norway to examine the conditions in Germany reported as follows in the Swedish Press in April, 1919: "Tuberculosis, especially in children, is increasing in an appalling way, and, generally speaking, is malignant. In the same way rickets is more serious and more widely prevalent. It is impossible to do anything for these diseases; there is no milk for the tuberculous, and no cod-liver oil for those suffering from rickets.... Tuberculosis is assuming almost unprecedented aspects, such as have hitherto only been known in exceptional cases. The whole body is attacked simultaneously, and the illness in this form is practically incurable.... Tuberculosis is nearly always fatal now among adults. It is the cause of 90 per cent of the hospital cases. Nothing can be done against it owing to lack of food-stuffs.... It appears in the most terrible forms, such as glandular

166

tuberculosis, which turns into purulent dissolution." The following is by a writer in the *Vossische Zeitung*, June 5, 1919, who accompanied the Hoover Mission to the Erzgebirge: "I visited large country districts where 90 per cent of all the children were ricketty and where children of three years are only beginning to walk.... Accompany me to a school in the Erzgebirge. You think it is a kindergarten for the little ones. No, these are children of seven and eight years. Tiny faces, with large dull eyes, overshadowed by huge puffed, ricketty foreheads, their small arms just skin and bone, and above the crooked legs with their dislocated joints the swollen, pointed stomachs of the hunger oedema.... 'You see this child here,' the physician in charge explained; 'it consumed an incredible amount of bread, and yet did not get any stronger. I found out that it hid all the bread it received underneath its straw mattress. The fear of hunger was so deeply rooted in the child that it collected stores instead of eating the food: a misguided animal instinct made the dread of hunger worse than the actual pangs.'" Yet there are many persons apparently in whose opinion justice requires that such beings should pay tribute until they are forty or fifty years of age in relief of the British taxpayer.

CHAPTER VII

REMEDIES

It is difficult to maintain true perspective in large affairs. I have criticized the work of Paris, and have depicted in somber colors the condition and the prospects of Europe. This is one aspect of the position and, I believe, a true one. But in so complex a phenomenon the prognostics do not all point one way; and we may make the error of expecting consequences to follow too swiftly and too inevitably from what perhaps are not *all* the relevant causes. The blackness of the prospect itself leads us to doubt its accuracy; our imagination is dulled rather than stimulated by too woeful a narration, and our minds rebound from what is felt "too bad to be true." But before the reader allows himself to be too much swayed by these natural reflections, and before I lead him, as is the intention of this chapter, towards remedies and ameliorations and the discovery of happier tendencies, let him redress the balance of his thought by recalling two contrasts—England and Russia, of which the one may encourage his optimism too much, but the other should remind him that catastrophes can still happen, and that modern society is not immune from the very greatest evils.

In the chapters of this book I have not generally had in mind the situation or the problems of England. "Europe" in my narration must generally be interpreted to exclude the British Isles. England is in a state of transition, and her economic problems are serious. We may be on the eve of great changes in her social and industrial structure. Some of us may welcome such prospects and some of us deplore them. But they are of a different kind altogether from those impending on Europe. I do not perceive in England the slightest possibility of catastrophe or any serious likelihood of a general upheaval of society. The war has impoverished us, but not seriously;—I should judge that the real wealth of the country in 1919 is at least equal to what it was in 1900. Our balance of trade is adverse, but not so much so that the readjustment of it need disorder our economic life.[157] The deficit in our Budget is large, but not beyond what firm and prudent statesmanship could bridge. The shortening of the hours of labor may have somewhat diminished our productivity. But it should not be too much to hope that this is a feature of transition, and no one who is acquainted with the British workingman can doubt that, if it suits him, and if he is in sympathy and reasonable contentment with the conditions of his life, he can produce at least as much in a shorter working day as he did in the longer hours which prevailed formerly. The most serious problems for England have been brought to a head by the war, but are in their origins more fundamental. The forces of the nineteenth century have run their course and are exhausted. The economic motives and ideals of that generation no longer satisfy us: we must find a new way and must suffer again the *malaise*, and finally the pangs, of a new industrial birth. This is one element. The other is that on which I have enlarged in Chapter II.;—the increase in the real cost of food and the diminishing response of nature to any further increase in the population of the world, a tendency which must be especially injurious to the greatest of all industrial countries and the most dependent on imported supplies of food.

But these secular problems are such as no age is free from. They are of an altogether different order from those which may afflict the peoples of Central Europe. Those readers who, chiefly mindful of the British conditions with which they are familiar, are apt to indulge their optimism, and still more those whose immediate environment is American, must cast their minds to Russia, Turkey, Hungary, or Austria, where the most dreadful material evils which men can suffer—famine, cold, disease, war, murder, and anarchy—are an actual present experience, if they are to apprehend the character of the misfortunes against the further extension of which it must surely be our duty to seek the remedy, if there is one.

What then is to be done? The tentative suggestions of this chapter may appear to the reader inadequate. But the opportunity was missed at Paris during the six months which followed the Armistice, and nothing we can do now can repair the mischief wrought at that time. Great privation and great risks to society have become unavoidable. All that is now open to us is to redirect, so far as lies in our power, the fundamental economic tendencies which underlie the events of the hour, so that they promote the re-establishment of prosperity and order, instead of leading us deeper into misfortune.

We must first escape from the atmosphere and the methods of Paris. Those who controlled the Conference may bow before the gusts of popular opinion, but they will never lead us out of our troubles. It is hardly to be supposed that the Council of Four can retrace their steps, even if they wished to do so. The replacement of the existing Governments of Europe is, therefore, an almost indispensable preliminary.

I propose then to discuss a program, for those who believe that the Peace of Versailles cannot stand, under the following heads:

> 1.The Revision of the Treaty.
> 2.The settlement of inter-Ally indebtedness.
> 3.An international loan and the reform of the currency.
> 4.The relations of Central Europe to Russia.

1. *The Revision of the Treaty*

Are any constitutional means open to us for altering the Treaty? President Wilson and General Smuts, who believe that to have secured the Covenant of the League of Nations outweighs much evil in the rest of the Treaty, have indicated that we must look to the League for the gradual evolution of a more tolerable life for Europe. "There are territorial settlements," General Smuts wrote in his statement on signing the Peace Treaty, "which will need revision. There are guarantees laid down which we all hope will soon be found out of harmony with the new peaceful temper and unarmed state of our former enemies. There are punishments foreshadowed over most of which a calmer mood may yet prefer to pass the sponge of oblivion. There are indemnities stipulated which cannot be enacted without grave injury to the industrial revival of Europe, and which it will be in the interests of all to render more tolerable and moderate.... I am confident that the League of Nations will yet prove the path of escape for Europe out of the ruin brought about by this war." Without the League, President Wilson informed the Senate when he presented the Treaty to them early in July, 1919, "...long-continued supervision of the task of reparation which Germany was to undertake to complete within the next generation might entirely break down;[158] the reconsideration and revision of administrative arrangements and restrictions which the Treaty prescribed, but which it recognized might not provide lasting advantage or be entirely fair if too long enforced, would be impracticable."

Can we look forward with fair hopes to securing from the operation of the League those benefits which two of its principal begetters thus encourage us to expect from it? The relevant passage is to be found in Article XIX. of the Covenant, which runs as follows:

"The Assembly may from time to time advise the reconsideration by Members of the League of treaties which have become inapplicable and the consideration of international conditions whose continuance might endanger the peace of the world."

But alas! Article V. provides that "Except where otherwise expressly provided in this Covenant or by the terms of the present Treaty, decisions at any meeting of the Assembly or of the Council shall require the agreement of all the Members of the League represented at the meeting." Does not this provision reduce the League, so far as concerns an early reconsideration of any of the terms of the Peace Treaty, into a body merely for wasting time? If all the parties to the Treaty are unanimously of opinion that it requires alteration in a particular sense, it does not need a League and a Covenant to put the business through. Even when the Assembly of the League is unanimous it can only "advise" reconsideration by the members specially affected.

But the League will operate, say its supporters, by its influence on the public opinion of the world, and the view of the majority will carry decisive weight in practice, even though constitutionally it is of no effect. Let us pray that this be so. Yet the League in the hands of the trained European diplomatist may become an unequaled instrument for obstruction and delay. The revision of Treaties is entrusted primarily, not to the Council,

170

which meets frequently, but to the Assembly, which will meet more rarely and must become, as any one with an experience of large Inter-Ally Conferences must know, an unwieldy polyglot debating society in which the greatest resolution and the best management may fail altogether to bring issues to a head against an opposition in favor of the *status quo*. There are indeed two disastrous blots on the Covenant,—Article V., which prescribes unanimity, and the much-criticized Article X., by which "The Members of the League undertake to respect and preserve as against external aggression the territorial integrity and existing political independence of all Members of the League." These two Articles together go some way to destroy the conception of the League as an instrument of progress, and to equip it from the outset with an almost fatal bias towards the *status quo*. It is these Articles which have reconciled to the League some of its original opponents, who now hope to make of it another Holy Alliance for the perpetuation of the economic ruin of their enemies and the Balance of Power in their own interests which they believe themselves to have established by the Peace.

But while it would be wrong and foolish to conceal from ourselves in the interests of "idealism" the real difficulties of the position in the special matter of revising treaties, that is no reason for any of us to decry the League, which the wisdom of the world may yet transform into a powerful instrument of peace, and which in Articles XI.-XVII. [159] has already accomplished a great and beneficent achievement. I agree, therefore, that our first efforts for the Revision of the Treaty must be made through the League rather than in any other way, in the hope that the force of general opinion and, if necessary, the use of financial pressure and financial inducements, may be enough to prevent a recalcitrant minority from exercising their right of veto. We must trust the new Governments, whose existence I premise in the principal Allied countries, to show a profounder wisdom and a greater magnanimity than their predecessors.

We have seen in Chapters IV. and V. that there are numerous particulars in which the Treaty is objectionable. I do not intend to enter here into details, or to attempt a revision of the Treaty clause by clause. I limit myself to three great changes which are necessary for the economic life of Europe, relating to Reparation, to Coal and Iron, and to Tariffs.

Reparation.—If the sum demanded for Reparation is less than what the Allies are entitled to on a strict interpretation of their engagements, it is unnecessary to particularize the items it represents or to hear arguments about its compilation. I suggest, therefore, the following settlement:—

(1) The amount of the payment to be made by Germany in respect of Reparation and the costs of the Armies of Occupation might be fixed at $10,000,000,000.

(2) The surrender of merchant ships and submarine cables under the Treaty, of war material under the Armistice, of State property in ceded territory, of claims against such territory in respect of public debt, and of Germany's claims against her former Allies, should be reckoned as worth the lump sum of $2,500,000,000, without any attempt being made to evaluate them item by item.

(3) The balance of $7,500,000,000 should not carry interest pending its repayment, and should be paid by Germany in thirty annual instalments of $250,000,000, beginning in 1923.

(4) The Reparation Commission should be dissolved, or, if any duties remain for it to perform, it should become an appanage of the League of Nations and should include representatives of Germany and of the neutral States.

(5) Germany would be left to meet the annual instalments in such manner as she might see fit, any complaint against her for non-fulfilment of her obligations being lodged with the League of Nations. That is to say, there would be no further expropriation of German private property abroad, except so far as is required to meet private German obligations out of the proceeds of such property already liquidated or in the hands of Public Trustees and Enemy Property Custodians in the Allied countries and in the United States; and, in particular, Article 260 (which provides for the expropriation of German interests in public utility enterprises) would be abrogated.

(6) No attempt should be made to extract Reparation payments from Austria.

Coal and Iron.—(1) The Allies' options on coal under Annex V. should be abandoned, but Germany's obligation to make good France's loss of coal through the destruction of her mines should remain. That is to say, Germany should undertake "to deliver to France annually for a period not exceeding ten years an amount of coal equal to the difference between the annual production before the war of the coal mines of the Nord and Pas de Calais, destroyed as a result of the war, and the production of the mines of the same area during the years in question; such delivery not to exceed twenty million tons in any one year of the first five years, and eight million tons in any one year of the succeeding five years." This obligation should lapse, nevertheless, in the event of the coal districts of Upper Silesia being taken from Germany in the final settlement consequent on the plebiscite.

(2) The arrangement as to the Saar should hold good, except that, on the one hand, Germany should receive no credit for the mines, and, on the other, should receive back both the mines and the territory without payment and unconditionally after ten years. But this should be conditional on France's entering into an agreement for the same period to supply Germany from Lorraine with at least 50 per cent of the iron-ore which was carried from Lorraine into Germany proper before the war, in return for an undertaking from Germany to supply Lorraine with an amount of coal equal to the whole amount formerly sent to Lorraine from Germany proper, after allowing for the output of the Saar.

(3) The arrangement as to Upper Silesia should hold good. That is to say, a plebiscite should be held, and in coming to a final decision "regard will be paid (by the principal Allied and Associated Powers) to the wishes of the inhabitants as shown by the vote, and to the geographical and economic conditions of the locality." But the Allies should declare that in their judgment "economic conditions" require the inclusion of the coal districts in Germany unless the wishes of the inhabitants are decidedly to the contrary.

(4) The Coal Commission already established by the Allies should become an appanage of the League of Nations, and should be enlarged to include representatives of Germany and the other States of Central and Eastern Europe, of the Northern Neutrals, and of Switzerland. Its authority should be advisory only, but should extend over the distribution of the coal supplies of Germany, Poland, and the constituent parts of the former Austro-Hungarian Empire, and of the exportable surplus of the United Kingdom.

All the States represented on the Commission should undertake to furnish it with the fullest information, and to be guided by its advice so far as their sovereignty and their vital interests permit.

Tariffs.—A Free Trade Union should be established under the auspices of the League of Nations of countries undertaking to impose no protectionist tariffs[160] whatever against the produce of other members of the Union, Germany, Poland, the new States which formerly composed the Austro-Hungarian and Turkish Empires, and the Mandated States should be compelled to adhere to this Union for ten years, after which time adherence would be voluntary. The adherence of other States would be voluntary from the outset. But it is to be hoped that the United Kingdom, at any rate, would become an original member.

By fixing the Reparation payments well within Germany's capacity to pay, we make possible the renewal of hope and enterprise within her territory, we avoid the perpetual friction and opportunity of improper pressure arising out of Treaty clauses which are impossible of fulfilment, and we render unnecessary the intolerable powers of the Reparation Commission.

By a moderation of the clauses relating directly or indirectly to coal, and by the exchange of iron-ore, we permit the continuance of Germany's industrial life, and put limits on the loss of productivity which would be brought about otherwise by the interference of political frontiers with the natural localization of the iron and steel industry.

By the proposed Free Trade Union some part of the loss of organization and economic efficiency may be retrieved, which must otherwise result from the innumerable new political frontiers now created between greedy, jealous, immature, and economically incomplete nationalist States. Economic frontiers were tolerable so long as an immense territory was included in a few great Empires; but they will not be tolerable when the Empires of Germany, Austria-Hungary, Russia, and Turkey have been partitioned between some twenty independent authorities. A Free Trade Union, comprising the whole of Central, Eastern, and South-Eastern Europe, Siberia, Turkey, and (I should hope) the United Kingdom, Egypt, and India, might do as much for the peace and prosperity of the world as the League of Nations itself. Belgium, Holland, Scandinavia, and Switzerland might be expected to adhere to it shortly. And it would be greatly to be desired by their friends that France and Italy also should see their way to adhesion.

It would be objected, I suppose, by some critics that such an arrangement might go some way in effect towards realizing the former German dream of Mittel-Europa. If other countries were so foolish as to remain outside the Union and to leave to Germany all its advantages, there might be some truth in this. But an economic system, to which every one had the opportunity of belonging and which gave special privilege to none, is surely absolutely free from the objections of a privileged and avowedly imperialistic scheme of exclusion and discrimination. Our attitude to these criticisms must be determined by our whole moral and emotional reaction to the future of international relations and the Peace of the World. If we take the view that for at least a generation to come Germany cannot be trusted with even a modicum of prosperity, that while all our recent Allies are angels of light, all our recent enemies, Germans, Austrians, Hungarians, and the rest, are children of the devil, that year by year Germany must be kept impoverished and her children starved and crippled, and that she must be ringed round by enemies; then we shall reject all the proposals of this chapter, and particularly those which may assist Germany to regain a part of her former material prosperity and find a means of livelihood for the industrial population of her towns. But if this view of nations and of their relation to one another is adopted by the democracies of Western Europe, and is financed by the United States, heaven help us all. If we aim deliberately at the impoverishment of Central Europe, vengeance, I dare predict, will not limp. Nothing can then delay for very long that final civil war between the forces of Reaction and the despairing convulsions of Revolution, before which the horrors of the late German war will fade into nothing, and which will destroy, whoever is victor, the civilization and the progress of our generation. Even though the result disappoint us, must we not base our actions on better expectations, and believe that the prosperity and happiness of one country promotes that of others, that the solidarity of man is not a fiction, and that nations can still afford to treat other nations as fellow-creatures?

Such changes as I have proposed above might do something appreciable to enable the industrial populations of Europe to continue to earn a livelihood. But they would not be enough by themselves. In particular, France would be a loser on paper (on paper only, for she will never secure the actual fulfilment of her present claims), and an escape from her embarrassments must be shown her in some other direction. I proceed, therefore, to proposals, first, for the adjustment of the claims of America and the Allies amongst themselves; and second, for the provision of sufficient credit to enable Europe to re-create her stock of circulating capital.

2. *The Settlement of Inter-Ally Indebtedness*

In proposing a modification of the Reparation terms, I have considered them so far only in relation to Germany. But fairness requires that so great a reduction in the amount should be accompanied by a readjustment of its apportionment between the Allies themselves. The professions which our statesmen made on every platform during the war, as well as other considerations, surely require that the areas damaged by the enemy's invasion should receive a priority of compensation. While this was one of the ultimate objects for which we said we were fighting, we never included the recovery of separation allowances amongst our war aims. I suggest, therefore, that we should by our acts prove ourselves sincere and trustworthy, and that accordingly Great Britain should waive altogether her claims for cash payment in favor of Belgium, Serbia, and France. The whole of the payments made by Germany would then be subject to the prior charge of repairing the material injury done to those countries and provinces which suffered actual invasion by the enemy; and I believe that the sum of $7,500,000,000 thus available would be adequate to cover entirely the actual costs of restoration. Further, it is only by a complete subordination of her own claims for cash compensation that Great Britain can ask with clean hands for a revision of the Treaty and clear her honor from the breach of faith for which she bears the main responsibility, as a result of the policy to which the General Election of 1918 pledged her representatives.

174

With the Reparation problem thus cleared up it would be possible to bring forward with a better grace and more hope of success two other financial proposals, each of which involves an appeal to the generosity of the United States.

The first is for the entire cancellation of Inter-Ally indebtedness (that is to say, indebtedness between the Governments of the Allied and Associated countries) incurred for the purposes of the war. This proposal, which has been put forward already in certain quarters, is one which I believe to be absolutely essential to the future prosperity of the world. It would be an act of far-seeing statesmanship for the United Kingdom and the United States, the two Powers chiefly concerned, to adopt it. The sums of money which are involved are shown approximately in the following table:—[161]

Loans to	By United States	By United Kingdom	By France	Total
	Million Dollars	Million Dollars	Million Dollars	Million Dollars
United Kingdom	4,210	....	....	4,210
France	2,750	2,540	....	5,290
Italy	1,625	2,335	175	4,135
Russia	190	2,840 [162]	800	3,830
Belgium	400	490 [163]	450	1,340
Serbia and Jugo-Slavia	100	100 [163]	100	300
Other Allies	175	395	250	820
Total	9,450 [164]	8,700	1,775	19,925

Thus the total volume of Inter-Ally indebtedness, assuming that loans from one Ally are not set off against loans to another, is nearly $20,000,000,000. The United States is a lender only. The United Kingdom has lent about twice as much as she has borrowed. France has borrowed about three times as much as she has lent. The other Allies have been borrowers only.

If all the above Inter-Ally indebtedness were mutually forgiven, the net result on paper (*i.e.* assuming all the loans to be good) would be a surrender by the United States of about $10,000,000,000 and by the United Kingdom of about $4,500,000,000. France would gain about $3,500,000,000 and Italy about $4,000,000,000. But these figures overstate the loss to the United Kingdom and understate the gain to France; for a large part of the loans made by both these countries has been to Russia and cannot, by any stretch of imagination, be considered good. If the loans which the United Kingdom has made to her Allies are reckoned to be worth 50 per cent of their full value (an arbitrary but convenient assumption which the Chancellor of the Exchequer has adopted on more than one occasion as being as good as any other for the purposes of an approximate national balance sheet), the operation would involve her neither in loss nor in gain. But in whatever way the net result is calculated on paper, the relief in anxiety which such a

175

liquidation of the position would carry with it would be very great. It is from the United States, therefore, that the proposal asks generosity.

Speaking with a very intimate knowledge of the relations throughout the war between the British, the American, and the other Allied Treasuries, I believe this to be an act of generosity for which Europe can fairly ask, provided Europe is making an honorable attempt in other directions, not to continue war, economic or otherwise, but to achieve the economic reconstitution of the whole Continent, The financial sacrifices of the United States have been, in proportion to her wealth, immensely less than those of the European States. This could hardly have been otherwise. It was a European quarrel, in which the United States Government could not have justified itself before its citizens in expending the whole national strength, as did the Europeans. After the United States came into the war her financial assistance was lavish and unstinted, and without this assistance the Allies could never have won the war,[165] quite apart from the decisive influence of the arrival of the American troops. Europe, too, should never forget the extraordinary assistance afforded her during the first six months of 1919 through the agency of Mr. Hoover and the American Commission of Relief. Never was a nobler work of disinterested goodwill carried through with more tenacity and sincerity and skill, and with less thanks either asked or given. The ungrateful Governments of Europe owe much more to the statesmanship and insight of Mr. Hoover and his band of American workers than they have yet appreciated or will ever acknowledge. The American Relief Commission, and they only, saw the European position during those months in its true perspective and felt towards it as men should. It was their efforts, their energy, and the American resources placed by the President at their disposal, often acting in the teeth of European obstruction, which not only saved an immense amount of human suffering, but averted a widespread breakdown of the European system.[166]

But in speaking thus as we do of American financial assistance, we tacitly assume, and America, I believe, assumed it too when she gave the money, that it was not in the nature of an investment. If Europe is going to repay the $10,000,000,000 worth of financial assistance which she has had from the United States with compound interest at 5 per cent, the matter takes on quite a different complexion. If America's advances are to be regarded in this light, her relative financial sacrifice has been very slight indeed.

Controversies as to relative sacrifice are very barren and very foolish also; for there is no reason in the world why relative sacrifice should necessarily be equal,—so many other very relevant considerations being quite different in the two cases. The two or three facts following are put forward, therefore, not to suggest that they provide any compelling argument for Americans, but only to show that from his own selfish point of view an Englishman is not seeking to avoid due sacrifice on his country's part in making the present suggestion. (1) The sums which the British Treasury borrowed from the American Treasury, after the latter came into the war, were approximately offset by the sums which England lent to her other Allies *during the same period* (i.e. excluding sums lent before the United States came into the war); so that almost the whole of England's indebtedness to the United States was incurred, not on her own account, but to enable her to assist the rest of her Allies, who were for various reasons not in a position to draw their assistance from the United States direct.[167] (2) The United Kingdom has disposed of about $5,000,000,000 worth of her foreign securities, and in addition has incurred foreign debt to the amount of about $6,000,000,000. The United

176

States, so far from selling, has bought back upwards of $5,000,000,000, and has incurred practically no foreign debt. (3) The population of the United Kingdom is about one-half that of the United States, the income about one-third, and the accumulated wealth between one-half and one-third. The financial capacity of the United Kingdom may therefore be put at about two-fifths that of the United States. This figure enables us to make the following comparison:—Excluding loans to Allies in each case (as is right on the assumption that these loans are to be repaid), the war expenditure of the United Kingdom has been about three times that of the United Sates, or in proportion to capacity between seven and eight times.

Having cleared this issue out of the way as briefly as possible, I turn to the broader issues of the future relations between the parties to the late war, by which the present proposal must primarily be judged.

Failing such a settlement as is now proposed, the war will have ended with a network of heavy tribute payable from one Ally to another. The total amount of this tribute is even likely to exceed the amount obtainable from the enemy; and the war will have ended with the intolerable result of the Allies paying indemnities to one another instead of receiving them from the enemy.

For this reason the question of Inter-Allied indebtedness is closely bound up with the intense popular feeling amongst the European Allies on the question of indemnities,—a feeling which is based, not on any reasonable calculation of what Germany can, in fact, pay, but on a well-founded appreciation of the unbearable financial situation in which these countries will find themselves unless she pays. Take Italy as an extreme example. If Italy can reasonably be expected to pay $4,000,000,000, surely Germany can and ought to pay an immeasurably higher figure. Or if it is decided (as it must be) that Austria can pay next to nothing, is it not an intolerable conclusion that Italy should be loaded with a crushing tribute, while Austria escapes? Or, to put it slightly differently, how can Italy be expected to submit to payment of this great sum and see Czecho-Slovakia pay little or nothing? At the other end of the scale there is the United Kingdom. Here the financial position is different, since to ask us to pay $4,000,000,000 is a very different proposition from asking Italy to pay it. But the sentiment is much the same. If we have to be satisfied without full compensation from Germany, how bitter will be the protests against paying it to the United States. We, it will be said, have to be content with a claim against the bankrupt estates of Germany, France, Italy, and Russia, whereas the United States has secured a first mortgage upon us. The case of France is at least as overwhelming. She can barely secure from Germany the full measure of the destruction of her countryside. Yet victorious France must pay her friends and Allies more than four times the indemnity which in the defeat of 1870 she paid Germany. The hand of Bismarck was light compared with that of an Ally or of an Associate. A settlement of Inter-Ally indebtedness is, therefore, an indispensable preliminary to the peoples of the Allied countries facing, with other than a maddened and exasperated heart, the inevitable truth about the prospects of an indemnity from the enemy.

It might be an exaggeration to say that it is impossible for the European Allies to pay the capital and interest due from them on these debts, but to make them do so would certainly be to impose a crushing burden. They may be expected, therefore, to make constant attempts to evade or escape payment, and these attempts will be a constant

177

source of international friction and ill-will for many years to come. A debtor nation does not love its creditor, and it is fruitless to expect feelings of goodwill from France, Italy, and Russia towards this country or towards America, if their future development is stifled for many years to come by the annual tribute which they must pay us. There will be a great incentive to them to seek their friends in other directions, and any future rupture of peaceable relations will always carry with it the enormous advantage of escaping the payment of external debts, if, on the other hand, these great debts are forgiven, a stimulus will be given to the solidarity and true friendliness of the nations lately associated.

The existence of the great war debts is a menace to financial stability everywhere. There is no European country in which repudiation may not soon become an important political issue. In the case of internal debt, however, there are interested parties on both sides, and the question is one of the internal distribution of wealth. With external debts this is not so, and the creditor nations may soon find their interest inconveniently bound up with the maintenance of a particular type of government or economic organization in the debtor countries. Entangling alliances or entangling leagues are nothing to the entanglements of cash owing.

The final consideration influencing the reader's attitude to this proposal must, however, depend on his view as to the future place in the world's progress of the vast paper entanglements which are our legacy from war finance both at home and abroad. The war has ended with every one owing every one else immense sums of money. Germany owes a large sum to the Allies, the Allies owe a large sum to Great Britain, and Great Britain owes a large sum to the United States. The holders of war loan in every country are owed a large sum by the State, and the State in its turn is owed a large sum by these and other taxpayers. The whole position is in the highest degree artificial, misleading, and vexatious. We shall never be able to move again, unless we can free our limbs from these paper shackles. A general bonfire is so great a necessity that unless we can make of it an orderly and good-tempered affair in which no serious injustice is done to any one, it will, when it comes at last, grow into a conflagration that may destroy much else as well. As regards internal debt, I am one of those who believe that a capital levy for the extinction of debt is an absolute prerequisite of sound finance in everyone of the European belligerent countries. But the continuance on a huge scale of indebtedness between Governments has special dangers of its own.

Before the middle of the nineteenth century no nation owed payments to a foreign nation on any considerable scale, except such tributes as were exacted under the compulsion of actual occupation in force and, at one time, by absentee princes under the sanctions of feudalism. It is true that the need for European capitalism to find an outlet in the New World has led during the past fifty years, though even now on a relatively modest scale, to such countries as Argentine owing an annual sum to such countries as England. But the system is fragile; and it has only survived because its burden on the paying countries has not so far been oppressive, because this burden is represented by real assets and is bound up with the property system generally, and because the sums already lent are not unduly large in relation to those which it is still hoped to borrow. Bankers are used to this system, and believe it to be a necessary part of the permanent order of society. They are disposed to believe, therefore, by analogy with it, that a comparable system between Governments, on a far vaster and definitely oppressive

178

scale, represented by no real assets, and less closely associated with the property system, is natural and reasonable and in conformity with human nature.

I doubt this view of the world. Even capitalism at home, which engages many local sympathies, which plays a real part in the daily process of production, and upon the security of which the present organization of society largely depends, is not very safe. But however this may be, will the discontented peoples of Europe be willing for a generation to come so to order their lives that an appreciable part of their daily produce may be available to meet a foreign payment, the reason of which, whether as between Europe and America, or as between Germany and the rest of Europe, does not spring compellingly from their sense of justice or duty?

On the one hand, Europe must depend in the long run on her own daily labor and not on the largesse of America; but, on the other hand, she will not pinch herself in order that the fruit of her daily labor may go elsewhere. In short, I do not believe that any of these tributes will continue to be paid, at the best, for more than a very few years. They do not square with human nature or agree with the spirit of the age.

If there is any force in this mode of thought, expediency and generosity agree together, and the policy which will best promote immediate friendship between nations will not conflict with the permanent interests of the benefactor.[168]

3. *An International Loan*

I pass to a second financial proposal. The requirements of Europe are *immediate*. The prospect of being relieved of oppressive interest payments to England and America over the whole life of the next two generations (and of receiving from Germany some assistance year by year to the costs of restoration) would free the future from excessive anxiety. But it would not meet the ills of the immediate present,—the excess of Europe's imports over her exports, the adverse exchange, and the disorder of the currency. It will be very difficult for European production to get started again without a temporary measure of external assistance. I am therefore a supporter of an international loan in some shape or form, such as has been advocated in many quarters in France, Germany, and England, and also in the United States. In whatever way the ultimate responsibility for repayment is distributed, the burden of finding the immediate resources must inevitably fall in major part upon the United States.

The chief objections to all the varieties of this species of project are, I suppose, the following. The United States is disinclined to entangle herself further (after recent experiences) in the affairs of Europe, and, anyhow, has for the time being no more capital to spare for export on a large scale. There is no guarantee that Europe will put financial assistance to proper use, or that she will not squander it and be in just as bad case two or three years hence as she is in now;—M. Klotz will use the money to put off the day of taxation a little longer, Italy and Jugo-Slavia will fight one another on the proceeds, Poland will devote it to fulfilling towards all her neighbors the military rôle which France has designed for her, the governing classes of Roumania will divide up the booty amongst themselves. In short, America would have postponed her own capital developments and raised her own cost of living in order that Europe might continue for

179

another year or two the practices, the policy, and the men of the past nine months. And as for assistance to Germany, is it reasonable or at all tolerable that the European Allies, having stripped Germany of her last vestige of working capital, in opposition to the arguments and appeals of the American financial representatives at Paris, should then turn to the United States for funds to rehabilitate the victim in sufficient measure to allow the spoliation to recommence in a year or two?

There is no answer to these objections as matters are now. If I had influence at the United States Treasury, I would not lend a penny to a single one of the present Governments of Europe. They are not to be trusted with resources which they would devote to the furtherance of policies in repugnance to which, in spite of the President's failure to assert either the might or the ideals of the people of the United States, the Republican and the Democratic parties are probably united. But if, as we must pray they will, the souls of the European peoples turn away this winter from the false idols which have survived the war that created them, and substitute in their hearts for the hatred and the nationalism, which now possess them, thoughts and hopes of the happiness and solidarity of the European family,—then should natural piety and filial love impel the American people to put on one side all the smaller objections of private advantage and to complete the work, that they began in saving Europe from the tyranny of organized force, by saving her from herself. And even if the conversion is not fully accomplished, and some parties only in each of the European countries have espoused a policy of reconciliation, America can still point the way and hold up the hands of the party of peace by having a plan and a condition on which she will give her aid to the work of renewing life.

The impulse which, we are told, is now strong in the mind of the United States to be quit of the turmoil, the complication, the violence, the expense, and, above all, the unintelligibility of the European problems, is easily understood. No one can feel more intensely than the writer how natural it is to retort to the folly and impracticability of the European statesmen,—Rot, then, in your own malice, and we will go our way—

> Remote from Europe; from her blasted hopes;
> Her fields of carnage, and polluted air.

But if America recalls for a moment what Europe has meant to her and still means to her, what Europe, the mother of art and of knowledge, in spite of everything, still is and still will be, will she not reject these counsels of indifference and isolation, and interest herself in what may prove decisive issues for the progress and civilization of all mankind?

Assuming then, if only to keep our hopes up, that America will be prepared to contribute to the process of building up the good forces of Europe, and will not, having completed the destruction of an enemy, leave us to our misfortunes,—what form should her aid take?

I do not propose to enter on details. But the main outlines of all schemes for an international loan are much the same, The countries in a position to lend assistance, the neutrals, the United Kingdom, and, for the greater portion of the sum required, the United States, must provide foreign purchasing credits for all the belligerent countries of continental Europe, allied and ex-enemy alike. The aggregate sum required might not be so large as is sometimes supposed. Much might be done, perhaps, with a fund of $1,000,000,000 in the first instance. This sum, even if a precedent of a different kind had been established by the cancellation of Inter-Ally War Debt, should be lent and should be borrowed with the unequivocal intention of its being repaid in full. With this object in view, the security for the loan should be the best obtainable, and the arrangements for its ultimate repayment as complete as possible. In particular, it should rank, both for payment of interest and discharge of capital, in front of all Reparation claims, all Inter-Ally War Debt, all internal war loans, and all other Government indebtedness of any other kind. Those borrowing countries who will be entitled to Reparation payments should be required to pledge all such receipts to repayment of the new loan. And all the borrowing countries should be required to place their customs duties on a gold basis and to pledge such receipts to its service.

Expenditure out of the loan should be subject to general, but not detailed, supervision by the lending countries.

If, in addition to this loan for the purchase of food and materials, a guarantee fund were established up to an equal amount, namely $1,000,000,000 (of which it would probably prove necessary to find only a part in cash), to which all members of the League of Nations would contribute according to their means, it might be practicable to base upon it a general reorganization of the currency.

In this manner Europe might be equipped with the minimum amount of liquid resources necessary to revive her hopes, to renew her economic organization, and to enable her great intrinsic wealth to function for the benefit of her workers. It is useless at the present time to elaborate such schemes in further detail. A great change is necessary in public opinion before the proposals of this chapter can enter the region of practical politics, and we must await the progress of events as patiently as we can.

4. *The Relations of Central Europe to Russia*

I have said very little of Russia in this book. The broad character of the situation there needs no emphasis, and of the details we know almost nothing authentic. But in a discussion as to how the economic situation of Europe can be restored there are one or two aspects of the Russian question which are vitally important.

From the military point of view an ultimate union of forces between Russia and Germany is greatly feared in some quarters. This would be much more likely to take place in the event of reactionary movements being successful in each of the two countries, whereas an effective unity of purpose between Lenin and the present essentially middle-class Government of Germany is unthinkable. On the other hand, the same people who fear such a union are even more afraid of the success of Bolshevism; and yet they have to recognize that the only efficient forces for fighting it are, inside Russia, the reactionaries, and, outside Russia, the established forces of order and authority in Germany. Thus the advocates of intervention in Russia, whether direct or indirect, are at perpetual cross-purposes with themselves. They do not know what they want; or, rather, they want what they cannot help seeing to be incompatibles. This is one of the reasons why their policy is so inconstant and so exceedingly futile.

The same conflict of purpose is apparent in the attitude of the Council of the Allies at Paris towards the present Government of Germany. A victory of Spartacism in Germany might well be the prelude to Revolution everywhere: it would renew the forces of Bolshevism in Russia, and precipitate the dreaded union of Germany and Russia; it would certainly put an end to any expectations which have been built on the financial and economic clauses of the Treaty of Peace. Therefore Paris does not love Spartacus. But, on the other hand, a victory of reaction in Germany would be regarded by every one as a threat to the security of Europe, and as endangering the fruits of victory and the basis of the Peace. Besides, a new military power establishing itself in the East, with its spiritual home in Brandenburg, drawing to itself all the military talent and all the military adventurers, all those who regret emperors and hate democracy, in the whole of Eastern and Central and South-Eastern Europe, a power which would be geographically inaccessible to the military forces of the Allies, might well found, at least in the anticipations of the timid, a new Napoleonic domination, rising, as a phoenix, from the ashes of cosmopolitan militarism. So Paris dare not love Brandenburg. The argument points, then, to the sustentation of those moderate forces of order, which, somewhat to the world's surprise, still manage to maintain themselves on the rock of the German character. But the present Government of Germany stands for German unity more perhaps than for anything else; the signature of the Peace was, above all, the price which some Germans thought it worth while to pay for the unity which was all that was left them of 1870. Therefore Paris, with some hopes of disintegration across the Rhine not yet extinguished, can resist no opportunity of insult or indignity, no occasion of lowering the prestige or weakening the influence of a Government, with the continued stability of which all the conservative interests of Europe are nevertheless bound up.

The same dilemma affects the future of Poland in the rôle which France has cast for her. She is to be strong, Catholic, militarist, and faithful, the consort, or at least the favorite, of victorious France, prosperous and magnificent between the ashes of Russia and the ruin of Germany. Roumania, if only she could be persuaded to keep up appearances a little more, is a part of the same scatter-brained conception. Yet, unless her great neighbors are prosperous and orderly, Poland is an economic impossibility with no industry but Jew-baiting. And when Poland finds that the seductive policy of France is pure rhodomontade and that there is no money in it whatever, nor glory either, she will fall, as promptly as possible, into the arms of somebody else.

The calculations of "diplomacy" lead us, therefore, nowhere. Crazy dreams and childish intrigue in Russia and Poland and thereabouts are the favorite indulgence at present of those Englishmen and Frenchmen who seek excitement in its least innocent form, and believe, or at least behave as if foreign policy was of the same *genre* as a cheap melodrama.

Let us turn, therefore, to something more solid. The German Government has announced (October 30, 1919) its continued adhesion to a policy of non-intervention in the internal affairs of Russia, "not only on principle, but because it believes that this policy is also justified from a practical point of view." Let us assume that at last we also adopt the same standpoint, if not on principle, at least from a practical point of view. What are then the fundamental economic factors in the future relations of Central to Eastern Europe?

Before the war Western and Central Europe drew from Russia a substantial part of their imported cereals. Without Russia the importing countries would have had to go short. Since 1914 the loss of the Russian supplies has been made good, partly by drawing on reserves, partly from the bumper harvests of North America called forth by Mr. Hoover's guaranteed price, but largely by economies of consumption and by privation. After 1920 the need of Russian supplies will be even greater than it was before the war; for the guaranteed price in North America will have been discontinued, the normal increase of population there will, as compared with 1914, have swollen the home demand appreciably, and the soil of Europe will not yet have recovered its former productivity. If trade is not resumed with Russia, wheat in 1920-21 (unless the seasons are specially bountiful) must be scarce and very dear. The blockade of Russia, lately proclaimed by the Allies, is therefore a foolish and short-sighted proceeding; we are blockading not so much Russia as ourselves.

The process of reviving the Russian export trade is bound in any case to be a slow one. The present productivity of the Russian peasant is not believed to be sufficient to yield an exportable surplus on the pre-war scale. The reasons for this are obviously many, but amongst them are included the insufficiency of agricultural implements and accessories and the absence of incentive to production caused by the lack of commodities in the towns which the peasants can purchase in exchange for their produce. Finally, there is the decay of the transport system, which hinders or renders impossible the collection of local surpluses in the big centers of distribution.

I see no possible means of repairing this loss of productivity within any reasonable period of time except through the agency of German enterprise and organization. It is impossible geographically and for many other reasons for Englishmen, Frenchmen, or Americans to undertake it;—we have neither the incentive nor the means for doing the work on a sufficient scale. Germany, on the other hand, has the experience, the incentive, and to a large extent the materials for furnishing the Russian peasant with the goods of which he has been starved for the past five years, for reorganizing the business of transport and collection, and so for bringing into the world's pool, for the common advantage, the supplies from which we are now so disastrously cut off. It is in our interest to hasten the day when German agents and organizers will be in a position to set in train in every Russian village the impulses of ordinary economic motive. This is a process quite independent of the governing authority in Russia; but we may surely predict with some certainty that, whether or not the form of communism represented by Soviet government proves permanently suited to the Russian temperament, the revival of trade, of the comforts of life and of ordinary economic motive are not likely to promote the extreme forms of those doctrines of violence and tyranny which are the children of war and of despair.

Let us then in our Russian policy not only applaud and imitate the policy of non-intervention which the Government of Germany has announced, but, desisting from a blockade which is injurious to our own permanent interests, as well as illegal, let us encourage and assist Germany to take up again her place in Europe as a creator and organizer of wealth for her Eastern and Southern neighbors.

There are many persons in whom such proposals will raise strong prejudices. I ask them to follow out in thought the result of yielding to these prejudices. If we oppose in detail every means by which Germany or Russia can recover their material well-being, because we feel a national, racial, or political hatred for their populations or their Governments, we must be prepared to face the consequences of such feelings. Even if there is no moral solidarity between the nearly-related races of Europe, there is an economic solidarity which we cannot disregard. Even now, the world markets are one. If we do not allow Germany to exchange products with Russia and so feed herself, she must inevitably compete with us for the produce of the New World. The more successful we are in snapping economic relations between Germany and Russia, the more we shall depress the level of our own economic standards and increase the gravity of our own domestic problems. This is to put the issue on its lowest grounds. There are other arguments, which the most obtuse cannot ignore, against a policy of spreading and encouraging further the economic ruin of great countries.

I see few signs of sudden or dramatic developments anywhere. Riots and revolutions there may be, but not such, at present, as to have fundamental significance. Against political tyranny and injustice Revolution is a weapon. But what counsels of hope can Revolution offer to sufferers from economic privation, which does not arise out of the injustices of distribution but is general? The only safeguard against Revolution in Central Europe is indeed the fact that, even to the minds of men who are desperate, Revolution offers no prospect of improvement whatever. There may, therefore, be ahead of us a long, silent process of semi-starvation, and of a gradual, steady lowering of the standards of life and comfort. The bankruptcy and decay of Europe, if we allow it to proceed, will affect every one in the long-run, but perhaps not in a way that is striking or immediate.

This has one fortunate side. We may still have time to reconsider our courses and to view the world with new eyes. For the immediate future events are taking charge, and the near destiny of Europe is no longer in the hands of any man. The events of the coming year will not be shaped by the deliberate acts of statesmen, but by the hidden currents, flowing continually beneath the surface of political history, of which no one can predict the outcome. In one way only can we influence these hidden currents,—by setting in motion those forces of instruction and imagination which change *opinion*. The assertion of truth, the unveiling of illusion, the dissipation of hate, the enlargement and instruction of men's hearts and minds, must be the means.

In this autumn of 1919, in which I write, we are at the dead season of our fortunes. The reaction from the exertions, the fears, and the sufferings of the past five years is at its height. Our power of feeling or caring beyond the immediate questions of our own material well-being is temporarily eclipsed. The greatest events outside our own direct experience and the most dreadful anticipations cannot move us.

> In each human heart terror survives
> The ruin it has gorged: the loftiest fear
> All that they would disdain to think were true:
> Hypocrisy and custom make their minds
> The fanes of many a worship, now outworn.
> They dare not devise good for man's estate,

And yet they know not that they do not dare.
The good want power but to weep barren tears.
The powerful goodness want: worse need for them.
The wise want love; and those who love want wisdom;
And all best things are thus confused to ill.
Many are strong and rich, and would be just,
But live among their suffering fellow-men
As if none felt: they know not what they do.

We have been moved already beyond endurance, and need rest. Never in the lifetime of men now living has the universal element in the soul of man burnt so dimly.

For these reasons the true voice of the new generation has not yet spoken, and silent opinion is not yet formed. To the formation of the general opinion of the future I dedicate this book.

THE END

FOOTNOTES:

[157]The figures for the United Kingdom are as follows:

Monthly Average	Net Imports $1,000	Exports $1,000	Excess of Imports $1,000
1913	274,650	218,850	55,800
1914	250,485	179,465	71,020
Jan.-Mar. 1919	547,890	245,610	302,280
April-June 1919	557,015	312,315	244,700
July-Sept. 1919	679,635	344,315	335,320

But this excess is by no means so serious as it looks; for with the present high freight earnings of the mercantile marine the various "invisible" exports of the United Kingdom are probably even higher than they were before the war, and may average at least $225,000,000 monthly.

[158]President Wilson was mistaken in suggesting that the supervision of Reparation payments has been entrusted to the League of Nations. As I pointed out in Chapter V., whereas the League is invoked in regard to most of the continuing economic and territorial provisions of the Treaty, this is not the case as regards Reparation, over the problems and modifications of which the Reparation Commission is supreme without appeal of any kind to the League of Nations.

[159]These Articles, which provide safeguards against the outbreak of war between members of the League and also between members and non-members, are the solid achievement of the Covenant. These Articles make substantially less probable a war between organized Great Powers such as that of 1914. This alone should commend the League to all men.

[160]It would be expedient so to define a "protectionist tariff" as

to permit (*a*) the total prohibition of certain imports; (*b*) the imposition of sumptuary or revenue customs duties on commodities not produced at home; (*c*) the imposition of customs duties which did not exceed by more than five per cent a countervailing excise on similar commodities produced at home; (*d*) export duties. Further, special exceptions might be permitted by a majority vote of the countries entering the Union. Duties which had existed for five years prior to a country's entering the Union might be allowed to disappear gradually by equal instalments spread over the five years subsequent to joining the Union.

[161]The figures in this table are partly estimated, and are probably not completely accurate in detail; but they show the approximate figures with sufficient accuracy for the purposes of the present argument. The British figures are taken from the White Paper of October 23, 1919 (Cmd. 377). In any actual settlement, adjustments would be required in connection with certain

187

loans of gold and also in other respects, and I am concerned in what follows with the broad principle only. The total excludes loans raised by the United Kingdom on the market in the United States, and loans raised by France on the market in the United Kingdom or the United States, or from the Bank of England.

[162]This allows nothing for interest on the debt since the Bolshevik Revolution.

[163]No interest has been charged on the advances made to these countries.

[164]The actual total of loans by the United States up to date is very nearly $10,000,000,000, but I have not got the latest details.

[165]The financial history of the six months from the end of the summer of 1916 up to the entry of the United States into the war in April, 1917, remains to be written. Very few persons, outside the half-dozen officials of the British Treasury who lived in daily contact with the immense anxieties and impossible financial requirements of those days, can fully realize

what steadfastness and courage were needed, and how entirely hopeless the task would soon have become without the assistance of the United States Treasury. The financial problems from April, 1917, onwards were of an entirely different order from those of the preceding months.

[166]Mr. Hoover was the only man who emerged from the ordeal of Paris with an enhanced reputation. This complex personality, with his habitual air of weary Titan (or, as others might put it, of exhausted prize-fighter), his eyes steadily fixed on the true and essential facts of the European situation, imported into the Councils of Paris, when he took part in them, precisely that atmosphere of reality, knowledge, magnanimity, and disinterestedness which, if they had been found in other quarters also, would have given us the Good Peace.

[167]Even after the United States came into the war the bulk of Russian expenditure in the United States, as well as the whole of

that Government's other foreign expenditure, had to be paid for by the British Treasury.

[168]It is reported that the United States Treasury has agreed to fund (*i.e.* to add to the principal sum) the interest owing them on their loans to the Allied Governments during the next three years. I presume that the British Treasury is likely to follow suit. If the debts are to be paid ultimately, this piling up of the obligations at compound interest makes the position progressively worse. But the arrangement wisely offered by the United States Treasury provides a due interval for the calm consideration of the whole problem in the light of the after-war position as it will soon disclose itself.

www.ingramcontent.com/pod-product-compliance
Lightning Source LLC
Chambersburg PA
CBHW031957190326
41520CB00007B/284